DANCE OF WAR

THE STORY OF THE BATTLE OF EGYPT

PETER BATES

DANCE OF WAR

THE STORY OF THE BATTLE OF EGYPT

PETER BATES

LEO COOPER
Pen & Sword Books Ltd
London

In association with
Peter Bates

First published in Great Britain 1992 by
Leo Cooper, 190 Shaftesbury Avenue,
London WC2H 8 JL.
An imprint of Pen & Sword Books Ltd.,
47 Church Street, Barnsley, S. Yorks S70 2AS
Copyright © Peter Bates 1992
A CIP catalogue record for this book is available
from the British Library.
ISBN: O 85052 453 9
Simultaneously published in New Zealand by
Peter Bates, 43 Raukawa Street, Stokes Valley,
Lower Hutt.

0850524539

Printed in Hong Kong

To facilitate clarity, the German spelling has
been retained for Afrika Korps; Italian corps are
identified by Roman numerals; and British corps
by Arabic numerals. For the same reason,
German armoured units are referred to as
panzers. Except for occasional references to
Italian armoured units, an armoured division or
brigade, so referred to, is British.

Pictures marked ATL are from the Alexander
Turnbull Library, Wellington. Those marked
IWM are from the Imperial War Museum,
London.

Design, production and typesetting by
ART *services*
Typeset in 9.5pt New Baskerville on 13pt body

CONTENTS

In memory of Joan, who waited patiently
but did not see the end.

I am deeply grateful to the many people who
have assisted me in the research for this book.
In particular I should like to mention General
Sir Leonard Thornton, Field Marshal Lord
Carver, Brian Stone, George Kaye, and the
staffs of: the Lower Hutt Public Library, the
National Library of New Zealand, the
Alexander Turnbull Library, the Defence
Library (NZ), the National Archives (NZ), the
Imperial War Museum, the Public Record
Office (Kew), the Liddell Hart Centre for
Military Archives (Kings College, London),
the John Rylands University Library of
Manchester, the Australian War Memorial
(Canberra), the Australian High Commission,
Wellington, the South African Embassy,
London, and the South African Defence
Forces Archives, Pretoria.

PROLOGUE
THE MEN OF JULY

As light begins to filter through the desert dark, officers of the 6th New Zealand Infantry Brigade prepare to establish defence positions against the inevitable German counter-attack. The survivors of one depleted battalion, who have fought their way with bayonet and bomb to this depression a few kilometres from El Alamein dignified on the map with the name El Mreir, hold themselves ready to move to where daylight will show to be the best place to site their machine-guns, mortars and anti-tank guns. A second battalion, almost complete, is tramping over the rim from the rock-hard plain into the soft sand drifts that wind has swept into this inviting place of concealment. These men will fill a gap left by a missing third battalion so that when the enemy strikes, this captured location within his lines can be held. It is a perilous situation, fraught with uncertainty, but British tanks will arrive soon-indeed, are due at any moment. It has all been planned with meticulous care, and armoured corps liaison officers who have moved up with the attack have alerted their commanders to the infantry's vulnerability. Panzers are known to be somewhere near, ready to strike, and until the New Zealanders can range themselves with their weapons in tactical array, changing from night attack mode to daytime defence, they are a soft target, a naked pupa inviting the attention of predators.

And under cover of darkness the predators have been gathering. German and Italian tanks and infantry have closed in and now form almost a circle, weapons trained inwards towards the men and vehicles crowding into the depression. A single stream of tracer arcs across, bright in the still muted light, and in an instant shells, mortar bombs and bullets turn the morning calm into a thunderous fire storm. Men dig frantically or find shelter where they can. Vehicles erupt in fire. The tanks of the liaison officers blow themselves apart. Within the hour those who still live and are

1

able to walk are marched into captivity. No British tanks have come to their aid, and they are now tramping west, disarmed and powerless, towards the objective they planned, eventually, to take by force - Benghasi. The Eighth Army attack launched the previous night as a master-stroke to end Rommel's desert adventures has become a disastrous fiasco, just one of a series that has characterised British attempts to destroy the Axis forces while, battle weary and few in number, they struggle to attain the gleaming goals of Cairo and Alexandria.

This is July 1942. One war is ending, another will soon begin.

The dividing line between the time of losing and the time of winning in the war Britain and her Commonwealth Allies fought against the Germans between 1939 and 1945 is so clearly defined that it is truly two wars, fought back to back, as current television jargon has it. That line is July 1942. Everything before that time belongs to a different war from everything else that follows.

Not that the time before July was without its victories, but the military operations of that period were characterised by failure. Always, it seemed, the Germans could do things so much better than we could. Always, it seemed, we comforted ourselves with the assurance that we had somehow snatched victory of a kind out of defeat - by rescuing the BEF from France in 1940, by slaughtering German paratroopers on Crete in 1941, finally by stopping Rommel at the gates of Cairo and Alexandria in 1942. After that time the victories kept coming, not without their setbacks but certainly with the promise of an inevitable victory. The men who fought in that earlier war laid the foundation for those victories in the second. Though they suffered defeats they were not defeated, and in the circumstances in which they fought, this was an achievement. They made it possible for a renewed army with better weapons and a more enlightened command to attack and pursue and at last to overcome.

In a way, the men who fought at Alamein during July 1942, the last of the old army, epitomize all those who fought during the first three years - in France, in Crete, in the Western Desert. No medals were struck for them. They were lauded at the time, but then forgotten. The drudgery of their task could not compare with the excitement of the chase when the Germans began falling back, or even, for that matter, with the glamour of 'the few' who defended Britain's skies during the Blitz of that 'first' war. And yet that closing month of the old war has a story that compares with any of the new. The men who fought there, 'the few' of the Desert, stood between the Germans and a campaign victory that would have plunged the Allies more deeply into defeat than even Dunkirk had done. Egypt was the last bastion against the loss of the Middle East oil fields and a fast track through to Russia and India; and the psychological impact of defeat here, particularly after so many defeats over the previous three years, would have been devastating.

In fighting this battle, the men of July had to contend not just with the enemy, but also the inadequacies of their own army. Attacks collapsed and literally thousands became casualties - killed, wounded or prisoner of war - either because troops unskilled in desert ways had to be thrown into battle or because army command failed to come to terms with the desperation of the moment and directed affairs as though they were an exercise on Salisbury Plain. I feel free to elect myself to write this story because I was there and because, my own contribution to the struggle being so modest, I am able to speak freely without appearing to boast about the deeds of men whom history has largely ignored. My own involvement was a 12-hour engagement with the enemy that ended in capture, and like many who served at Alamein, for all I accomplished I might as well have stayed at home. At the time it was a cause for a grudge, shared with many others who resentfully submitted to barbed wire confinement in and around Benghasi. As we chased lice and waited for empty days to pass we vented our anger against the army in general and the British armour in particular, because it seemed to us that the failure of our tanks was the fundamental cause of our plight. This book has not been written to work off that grudge. On the contrary, it searches for the true reasons why the Eighth Army failed to overcome an enemy that was not only numerically inferior but also at the extremity of physical endurance and his lines of communication. The conclusion can only be that we were the last of the old army fighting the old war in the old ways.

By way of a pre-emptive strike against critics of inaccuracy, I will concede in advance that I have no doubt there are errors of detail in this story. Searching for the truth of such an event is like groping through mist, and in the end there is much that can never be known; I can say only that I have checked and cross-checked with diligence, and sought confirmation and correction wherever I could. And my truth is as good as anyone else's. In any case, as important as accuracy is, it is equally important to convey the feeling of the time and to give recognition to the men of July. It is to them that this book is dedicated.

PART ONE

THE BACKGROUND

CHAPTER ONE

BATTLE WITHOUT A NAME

N o moment in the Second World War was more critical than July 1942. Yet the men of July have been given only a small part in history. The world hardly knows them. Their battle, fought in the dusty heat of North Africa, bears no official title, no medal marks their success, they are denied, even, the Eighth Army clasp on the ribbon of their Africa Star. Historians have suggested their own name, First Alamein, but who has heard of it or could place it in time? Yet this was the point at which the war turned in favour of the Western Allies; it was ebb tide, the absolute nadir of our fortunes, the beginning of the upward climb.

In popular thought, and indeed in history books, *the* Battle of Alamein, which opened on 23 October 1942, under Bernard Montgomery, is accorded that distinction and is so honoured, its near thousand guns remembered with the small boats of Dunkirk, the Spitfires of the Battle of Britain and the landing craft of Normandy. The so-called First Battle of Alamein, which was fought through July 1942 under Claude Auchinleck, has no such place. At the time the news bulletins were non-committal, concealing more than they disclosed, quietly brushing under the carpet things neither friend nor foe should know, and even when peace returned and secrecy was irrelevant, Churchill gave it bare nodding recognition. In his history of the Second World War he devoted only three vague paragraphs to the battle towards the end of a chapter, concluding, 'The Eighth Army under Auchinleck had weathered the storm, and in its stubborn stand had taken several thousand prisoners. Egypt was safe.'[1] Such faint praise!

To Churchill, First Alamein was just a holding action, the curtain-raiser for the main event in October, and one of the band of Auchinleck admirers who set out in the post-war years to rehabilitate the general's name remarks that Churchill's gross undervaluation of Auchinleck's achievements in July was symbolised by the fact that he never graced the battle with a name.[2]

Yet far from being a mere road block, this was a pivotal point of the war, the time and place where Panzerarmee Afrika was brought to a halt and the initiative firmly wrested from the Germans.

Warren Tute in his *The North African War* concedes cautiously that 'to-day most military historians and analysts would probably agree that an important turning point, perhaps often overlooked, is that of First Alamein'.[3]

John Connell in his massive work *Auchinleck* says more emphatically, 'July 1942 ... was strategically the real turning point of World War II'.[4]

The official Australian historian concludes his account of the month's battles by saying, 'If the Eighth Army was uneasy in the last days of July and the first days of August, its confidence was not undermined. It had stopped the enemy. It had thrown him on the defensive ...The long ebb of British military fortune had ceased. The tide had turned, though the set the other way was not yet discernable.'[5]

The official New Zealand historian, looking at it from the other end of the battle, is in agreement. 'The battle about to be joined,' he wrote, 'was the real turning point of Allied fortunes in the Middle East, more so than the Alamein of the following October ... Contemporary accounts and records of the period pass quickly over the plans and actions of July with such expressions as "successful stabilisation" and "recovery of morale". This was in fact a month of almost continuous fighting in which the Eighth Army lost some 750 officers and 12,500 men, took 7,000 prisoners, and stopped the enemy advance.'[6]

Various members of the Auchinleck club have done something to lift First Alamein in the eyes of history, yet their accounts tend to be fogged over by the wider theme of their biographies, and the sceptical reader might feel their admiration of the general could inflate their assessment of that July stand. What is needed is an objective appraisal, as true an account as is possible of the battle that stopped the renowned Rommel in his tracks. It was the battle in which he was trapped, glued to the Alamein positions like a fly to flypaper by the lure of Cairo and Alexandria, just a few hours' tank ride away. We know now that with the resources available to him he had no way of reaching these alluring destinations, unless self-delusion and fear were to bring down the Eighth Army defences, and he remained a captive first of the all-consuming drive that had led him here against the judgement of more cautious advisers, and later, when he considered withdrawal, by the orders of higher authority. He became the prisoner of Alamein, where his army was to suffer execution.

At the time, the Desert war was generally viewed as a side-show to the titanic struggle then taking place in Russia, a mere inconsequential series of battles between forces of insignificant size; and that view prevails even today. Yet failure here would certainly have changed the course of the war, probably lengthened it and possibly led to defeat. The size of the forces engaged is irrelevant. What are important are the consequences.

The first and most obvious is that the Axis would have assumed total control of the Mediterranean, and any Allied operations there would have become difficult, probably impossible. We could not have invaded Italy or southern France.

Without question, the Axis would have seized the Middle East oilfields, greatly enhancing their ability to wage war and greatly diminishing ours. As they moved into this area, the unstable Middle East governments would have swung towards what they perceived as the winning side, and even Turkey might have declared its hand in their favour. How all this might have impacted on India and Russia is a matter for conjecture, but at the very least it would have created grave difficulties.

Far away in Washington, President Roosevelt observed North African events with alarm, because, besides these perilous possibilities, he feared Axis expansion into Tunis, Algeria, Morocco and Dakar, and even as far as Freetown and Liberia. From here shipping in the South Atlantic would be threatened, and he saw also a serious danger to Brazil and the whole eastern coast line of South America. And with the Axis thus established in Africa, Spain and Portugal would begin to feel the squeeze.

A meeting of the Japanese and Germans across India was another possibility that haunted the president, and he saw the Indian Ocean becoming secure for Japanese naval forces, which were already active there on a limited scale.

Possibilities are, of course, just that, and no one can say with certainty just what would have happened had the Eighth Army given way in July, but so long as it held, the Axis could not even contemplate such encouraging expansion.

What is certain is that the arrival of the Germans in Palestine would have had consequences that don't bear thinking about, and if Judaism had saints, Auchinleck should be one.

All these dire consequences and possibilities were averted by a tiny army, some of whose men were unseasoned and even strangers to the Desert. Some sideshow!

What must also be said, however, is that the Eighth Army's success in holding Rommel was a failure as well. The Eighth Army was within an ace, not once but several times, of destroying Rommel's army or throwing it back, but with remarkable ineptitude succeeded only in snatching defeat out of victory. Why this was so is an important part of this story. Whether Auchinleck was to blame for these Eighth Army failures is a question for nice judgement, and all this will be explored.

His task as army commander called for the qualities of master tactician, supreme organiser and skilful diplomat. At a time when every ounce of effort was needed to hold back the foe, he had to contend with self-willed generals whose loyalties and authority lay in diverse political backgrounds and who all had reservations about the way the army was being run. At particular points both the Australian and New Zealand divisional commanders, Morshead and Inglis, flatly refused to obey direct orders, and on the eve of a critical battle Morshead confronted Auchinleck with scathing criticism of the plan. The South African divisional commander, Pienaar, pursued by the ghost of Tobruk, openly questioned the wisdom of trying to stand at Alamein, and in a showdown with Auchinleck on the second day of battle threatened to ask to be relieved of his command if one of his brigades was refused permission to move to a less lethal part of the desert. On top of all this, the armour commanders followed a policy of independence to the point where their tanks were late on the battlefield on three important occasions, with resultant disastrous infantry losses.

Fifty years after the event is an appropriate time to bring the memory of this battle into the present and bestow on it the place it deserves. And this half century later we can consider what happened with due regard too for the enemy who, though he was fighting for a detestable regime, which as Churchill rightly remarked threatened to engulf the world in a new dark age, was caught up in the patriotic fervor that led whole nations to close ranks to oppose each other.

Beyond this, July 1942 is a good story. If the Battle of Alamein in October was an extravaganza, a great orchestrated production, a set piece battle with all the trimmings, July was high drama, with a touch of tragicomedy, an affair of improvisation as the enemy hammered at the door of Egypt slammed shut by a lean and hungry army.

And what happened in July really matters. It matters because truth matters. It matters because the propaganda of war lives on into the peace as myth, warping our understanding of the past; and while total truth is unknowable, we have a debt to those men whose actions in the past helped form our present to seek out as much of the truth as can be found.

We owe it to ourselves as well. In a very real way we are part of a flow of humanity that moves from the past through the present and into the future. As we understand the past we understand ourselves. And especially if we see the past in terms of real people, feeling them to be *of* us rather than detached stereotyped figures who are *other* than us, we find our lives illuminated and enriched. If we can achieve that, we might have a greater care for the present and the values we pass on to those who follow us.

At the very least First Alamein should be given a name. Once it has a name it is a recognisable entity; it has a place in history.

First Alamein won't do because it implies a second and even third Alamein if the Battle of Alam Halfa, which was fought on the same battlefield in September 1942, is taken into account. Besides, what is now simply called the Battle of Alamein is embedded in 50 years of literature and engraved on memorials around the world. The name that Auchinleck used in his Order of the Day for 30 June, perhaps not intending it as an official title, seems eminently suitable.

'We are fighting the Battle of Egypt,' he said, 'a battle in which the enemy must be destroyed.'

The Battle of Egypt was a human tragedy ... Well, all war is tragedy, but this was one of those particular tragedies that occur within war, when success slips away as brave men grasp for it. Memories of war are, alas, so overlaid with sentimentality, ridicule or apathy that the true feeling of the times is elusive and probably beyond recall. It isn't so much a matter of heroism, which is sometimes dubious, or sacrifice, which is a cliche, or even death, which is a commonplace not unfamiliar in peace, as of men whose daily work was hardship and danger, who killed because killing was necessary and who accepted death with sad stoicism, however much they might fear it, because it was simply a way of life that held a promise of great benefits to come, if not for them, then for others after them.

And this battle promised so much yet gave so little. The Germans and Italians saw their goal so tantalisingly close. The long road and hard desert were behind them, and they brushed with their fingertips the anticipation of journey's end among the palms and pleasures of the Delta. The British Commonwealth forces turned retreat and impending disaster into a prospect of victory that fell from their hands each time they reached for it.

The Battle of Egypt was a microcosm of war in general, in which everything went wrong, and which yielded casualty lists and bitter memories ... but also hope for the future.

It was more than just another battle; it was also a state of mind, a mood almost of despair, in the outside world if not on the battlefield itself. If we had not yet lost the war, neither could we see how we were going to win it. True, we now had the Americans on our side, but we also had the Japanese against us, and they had swept back our forces with the same effortless ease with which the Germans had overwhelmed Poland and France. Indeed, the first six months of 1942 were the worst of the war for the Allies, and the stand at Alamein the traumatic climax, the last heart-stopping crisis when disaster was a way of life.

Fending off a motion of no confidence Winston Churchill told the House of Commons in July: 'We are at this moment in the presence of a recession of our hopes and prospects in the Middle East and the Mediterranean unequalled since the fall of France.'

Disaster, indeed, had etched its mark on the history of the war since September 1939 in Poland, in France, in Greece, on Crete, in Russia and finally in the Pacific. Prisoners in their tens of thousands went into Axis and Japanese prisoner-of-war cages, and vast quantities of stores and equipment fell into enemy hands. Almost everything the Allies touched went wrong - almost, because in North and North-East Africa we had shown that against the Italians at least we could win victories.

1941 closed with a series of appalling naval disasters in the Mediterranean and the Far East, and in 1942 it began all over again. Rommel started it with a modest attack that pushed the Eighth Army back into Cyrenaica from the El Agheila position in the Gulf of Sirte that it had reached after its successful if bloody Crusader campaign in November-December 1941. In Russia the German armies surged forward with 300 divisions in the Volga region, driving the defenders back more than 600 kilometres to a place called Stalingrad. Britain's convoys to Russia were being savaged by the Arctic weather and German submarines and aircraft, and in July, a month in which crisis piled on top of crisis, two thirds of Convoy PQ17 was sent to the bottom when it was dispersed by an ill-judged order from the Admiralty. In the Far East the Japanese swept down through Malaya, gathering in Britain's sources of rubber and tin, and seized the 'bastion' of Singapore, threatened Burma and island-hopped towards Australia, which they dealt a relatively slight but morally devasting blow with air raids on the Far North. Suddenly even the remote outposts of civilisation were under threat. Burma fell to them, and India was endangered.

In the Desert, Rommel attacked again in May, and the world gasped as Tobruk, the fortress that had previously withstood siege for 242 days, fell in a day, with the loss of 33,000 troops, and stores and equipment enough to keep the Axis forces rolling forward. Nothing, it seemed, could go right for the Eighth Army as it fell back, leaving thousands more prisoners and vast dumps of supplies in enemy hands.

This was the atmosphere of catastrophe when at last the Eighth Army turned for its last ditch stand at Alamein. One step back and all would be lost, however resolved Auchinleck might be to fight back through the Delta and beyond.

Of course, reality often has little to do with immediate perception. We know now that this was the trough. Rommel had gone as far as he could go. So had the Germans in Russia, and by July even the Japanese had reached the outer limit of their expansion. With the wisdom of hindsight, we know now that Pearl Harbour decided the war in favour of the Western Allies by mobilising the vast resources of the United States. While winning was to be no easy ride, there was now an inevitability about the end.

From the beginning the Desert has had a special place in the war history of Britain and the Commonwealth. After the fall of France and the loss of Greece and Crete it was the only point of contact between Allied armies and those of the Axis.

At the start, the Desert was the Italian theatre of war and one in which the Germans had no desire to become involved. They had all they could handle in the occupied countries and, later, Russia, and Africa was no more than a diversion, somewhere for the Italians to play. They came to Africa when Wavell's small but better-equipped army, not yet the Eighth Army, chased the Italians out of Egypt and Cyrenaica. With never more than three German divisions, the newcomer Rommel kept the British busy for the next 18 months, pushing them back into Egypt, thrashing them when, still under Wavell, they attempted a come back in the ill-fated *Battleaxe* campaign, and submitting at last to Auchinleck's newly-named Eighth Army in *Crusader*, in November and December 1941. The whole business of the see saw became known to the troops as the El Agheila Derby, El Agheila being each time the furthest point reached by the British, the point where diminishing British strength matched Axis resistance, and stalemate resulted.

The Desert fighting came to life again on 21 January 1942, when Rommel bounced back into Cyrenaica, catching the British offguard and mauling the recently arrived 1st Armoured Division in the process. A shortage of petrol halted Rommel where the Eighth Army established a line running south from Gazala, just west of Tobruk. And here for the next four months the Axis and Eighth Army faced each other while they made their plans for the future.

Rommel struck yet again on 26 May, issuing a ringing call to arms that resounded with hyperbole. 'The high quality and warlike ardour of the Italian and German soldiers combined with the superiority of our arms guarantee victory,' he proclaimed in the version issued to the Italians. 'I expect every man at his post will remain faithful to the high traditions of his own country and his own army, will do his duty and will give himself wholly to the inviolable alliance of our arms. Long live his Majesty, the King of Italy and Emperor of Ethiopia! Long live the Duce of the Roman Empire! Long live the Fuhrer of Great Germany!' Heady stuff. The Gazala battle that followed was a classic in the failure of British command, and its one redeeming feature is that it ground down the enemy forces as well as our own. In the 25 days that it took Rommel to achieve his victory, his own strength became so diminished that only capture of British supplies enable him to pursue his quarry.

As the Gazala Line collapsed, Tobruk fell, and the 2nd South African Division thereby suffered much unmerited opprobrium. Tobruk was a fiasco of word play and misunderstanding and its fall a catastrophe compounded. A withdrawal from Tobruk, with all material destroyed, would not have been welcomed in London, but no doubt Churchill would have been amenable to appeasement. But this telling blow by Rommel against all expectations was beyond bearing at a time when everything was going wrong.

Despite demolitions, Rommel charged across the Egyptian border, on British wheels, eating British food and firing British guns, in 'relentless pursuit', brushing aside rearguards as, at last, 18 months after his arrival in North Africa with the assignment of preventing the British from taking Tripoli, he had turned the tables and was now almost within sight of Cairo and Alexandria. His primary target was Cairo, which was the capital and the only place where he could cross the Nile. Cairo offered bridges, if only he could capture them intact. In his plan of action after his hoped-for break-through, his main force, consisting of 15th Panzer and 90th Light, with some Italians units, would have driven to Cairo, thence Suez and Ismailia, and a lighter force based on 21st Panzer would have taken Alexandria.

The intriguing thing about all this is that is was not supposed to happen this way at all, and indeed the prophets of doom on the Axis side warned of likely dire consequences - consequences that in fact came about. The trouble is that influential people got carried away. When Rommel was given permission to attack in May he was given only the limited objective of clearing Cyrenaica. The intention then was to halt while the Germans and Italians turned their attention to invading Malta.

But when Rommel saw the Eighth Army in full retreat and his own forces re-equipped with captured booty, his instinct for the chase was aroused, and he saw victory in Egypt within his grasp without the need to invade Malta. His military superiors were against it, so he appealed over their heads to Hitler and Mussolini. Hitler agreed he could go. 'Destiny,' he told Mussolini, 'has offered us a chance that will never occur twice in the same theatre of war.' Anyway, he had his private doubts about the Malta enterprise. Mussolini, also scenting victory in Africa, gladly gave his approval, and shortly afterwards flew to Derna, piloting his own aircraft, followed by another aircraft carrying the white charger on which he was to make his triumphal entry into Alexandria. The aircraft carrying his chef and barber was shot down but another with flags and bands got through.

And so the great venture approached its climax. On 28 June, as the Eighth Army defences around Mersa Matruh were giving way, Bastico, the Supreme Commander in Africa, despatched detailed instructions for what would follow the final break-through.

The message ends: 'The Duce wishes both German and Italian troops to take part in the advance to the canal. Relations between the Army and the Government and people of Egypt will be reported as soon as possible.'

The last hopeful message came on 1 July from the Italian Supreme Command: 'The Duce has ordered the following relations with the State of Egypt: "Our relations with the population will be friendly, and also our relations with the Egyptian Government if it deserves it. These instructions apply specially to the air force, which is to avoid attacking any target on Egyptian soil that is not of purely miliary importance."'

Within days, Rommel was pleading for supplies to avoid 'a serious crisis'.

Mussolini, meanwhile, dallied in North Africa, though with what hope of riding into Alexandria is unclear. He was still at Derna in mid-July when a group of New Zealand prisoners of war were paraded for his edification, and he was photographed for publicity purposes inspecting them while holding a sub-machine gun. One prisoner reports that he quickly handed it back afterwards. According to the official New Zealand war history, he looked 'insignificant and dispirited'[7]. Perhaps at last the true situation was making itself evident even to those normally protected from harsh reality, and he went home on 20 July without even meeting Rommel.

Mussolini was not the only one to anticipate the imminent arrival of the Axis forces in the Delta. As Rommel's army approached, a panic of monstrous proportions developed in Cairo and Alexandria, known ever after as *The Flap*. For so long the Delta had been a peaceful haven. Now it was transformed into a scene of manic activity. Civilians who had cause to fear the enemy sought ways of escape, packing trains beyond their capacity; others with an interest in an Axis victory fuelled the flames of disorder by circulating misleading stories. The army contributed its share by clogging the roads with retreating motor transport that in places jammed itself into an immovable mass. Members of women's auxiliary units were despatched up the Nile by rail in conditions of extreme discomfort, presumably to protect their virtue, and at Middle East Headquarters at Cairo as well as at the British Embassy secret papers were turned into a funeral pyre of British hopes, and as the smoke rose, a gentle shower of ash floated down on to the streets. As the day on which this event took place was Wednesday 1 July it became known as Ash Wednesday.

The Royal Navy, concerned now at the close proximity of Axis airfields, moved its ships out of Alexandria, not bothering to take the time to tell the army. Even the patched up Queen Elizabeth, damaged by Italian frog-men, was taken away for repairs elsewhere.

The residents of Alexandria retreated behind closed doors, and as early as 27 June a British officer came in from the Desert to find this bustling city of several millions seemingly deserted.

'In the centre of the city I stopped to survey this quite unreal scene when suddenly a little Greek popped out of a shop like a rabbit out of its hole,' he records. 'Rushing across the road, he seized my arm, and, quite terrified, asked if it was true that Rommel was about to enter the city.'

Having just seen the New Zealand Division, fresh and fully equipped, moving up into the Desert, the officer gave an assurance that Rommel was 'not entering the city today' and would never enter it[8].

The air force suddenly had a space crisis on its hands. Airfields that had served bombers were now needed for the short range fighters and medium bombers supporting the army, and a fair amount of activity was created as heavier bombers were flown off to more distant airfields in Palestine and other aircraft moved in.

The Egyptian Government had a diplomatic problem because it was not at war with the Axis powers though its country was being used by the enemies of the Axis, and nice questions of relationships with Germany and Italy would arise if the British were driven out. The Egyptian Cabinet withdrew into more or less permanent session.

For the men at the front, unaware of events behind them, the only question was how Rommel was to be stopped.

As it fell back into Egypt, the Eighth Army under Ritchie had taken up a defensive position at Mersa Matruh, 105 kilometres west of El Alamein. Here a defensive box had been built on the coast and minefields laid inland. It was, though, scarcely a defensible position with the forces available as it was very run down and could be easily outflanked. In any case, Ritchie had his forces there split into two, with a gap between them covered only by two weak battle groups, making Eighth Army ripe for the plucking. It was at this climactic moment that Auchinleck resolved that it was time for him to act, and on 25 June he came forward from Cairo and took over direct command of the army.

Now the opponents were Auchinleck and Rommel.

The Battle of Egypt brought face to face as army commanders for the first and only time these two renowned generals of conflicting tempera-ment-Claude John Eyre Auchinleck and Johannes Erwin Eugen Rommel. For just over a month they confronted each other: Rommel the audacious, the charismatic, driving a flagging force to the limits of human endurance; Auchinleck the calm, the analytical, trying to lead an army whose inner strengths eluded him.

But there is a third element in this equation of generals, a man largely ignored except as an incidental figure of ignominy. He is Major-General Eric Dorman Smith, acting Deputy Chief of General Staff during the July battles and Auchinleck's one-man think-tank and *alter ego*. It was Dorman Smith who conceived the broad strategy as well as some of the detailed tactics that governed the events of July, and it is now hard to distinguish where Auchinleck finishes and Dorman Smith begins. Auchinleck's story is inseparable from Dorman Smith's. As the army commander, Auchinleck carries all responsibility, but it was the fertile mind of Dorman Smith that created his impact on the battlefield. Indeed, Dorman Smith himself was later to view the experience in an almost mystical light. An Irish Roman Catholic, as he was himself to stress when in his years in the wilderness he blamed Ulster Unionist bigots for his downfall, he was to write: 'God did not intend humanity should be handed over to Hitler, Mussolini and Hirohito. Under God the development of that purpose was left to three men, Auchinleck, Corbett* and myself. Foolish things chosen to confound the wise ... It was for us to act while the world waited and held its breath[(9)].'

At the end, when all the battles had been fought - actually, as the last battle was being fought - it was Dorman Smith who wrote a detailed appreciation of what was wrong with the army and how it could be corrected. Alas, it was too late. As Churchill ousted the old guard and installed the new, a shocked Dorman Smith was sent home to England and demoted to his substantive rank of colonel, and learned that he was being described as Auchinleck's 'evil genius'. He was subsequently given brigade commands, and served in Italy until he was dismissed again without explanation except that he was unfit for brigade command. He retired in 1944, embittered and with a burning anger against the England he had served so faithfully throughout his life. He returned to Ireland, discarding the English 'Smith' and taking the old family name of O'Gowan. Thereafter, as Dorman O'Gowan, he fought for recognition of the critical place of the July Battle of Egypt in the war's outcome.

He told the *Liverpool Daily Post* in the early 1950's: 'What is not generally understood even now is that the Eisenhower "walk-in" invasion of French North Africa was possible only because in July 1942 Rommel failed to capture Egypt ... That the Allies did not lose the war between 30 June and 4 July 1942 is due, as Rommel chivalrously records, to Auchinleck's handling of his own forces "with very considerable skill, with decided coolness".'

---

* Lieutenant-General T.W. Corbett, Auchinleck's Chief of Staff

CHAPTER TWO

THE ARMIES OF JULY

W as there another battlefield in modern times when the armies were so diverse yet so small? El Alamein brought together men from around the world in a profusion of cultures, each secure in their own sense of identity and ready to assert a particular point of view as the occasion arose.

There were, in fact, not two armies, but two groupings of armies.

In theory North Africa was the Italian theatre, and the Germans came reluctantly and then sent no more than three divisions as a 'blocking force' except near the end, when it was too late. The Italians had most of their front-line forces there, and the Commander-in-Chief was an Italian, though once the Germans arrived, Rommel in effect ran the Desert war . for the Axis.

On the British side it was very much a Commonwealth and 'Empire' war, with Australians, New Zealanders, South Africans and Indians joined with United Kingdom formations, supplemented by Free French and Poles, though none of the latter two fought at Alamein in July. Army and corps commanders were from the British and Indian Armies.

Looking at the many nationalities involved, the obvious curiosity is that the North African campaign became essentially a struggle between the Germans on the one side and the British and the Commonwealth forces on the other. The Germans were always the shock troops and it was the Germans who at times of crisis rushed hither and thither to plug holes and fling in counter-attacks.

At best the Italians were regarded by friend and foe with wry amusement, at worst with contempt. While this must be accepted as wartime stereotyping, it is true that Rommel had to interlace Italian troops at Alamein with Germans to prevent the line from giving way. It is also true that Italian units quickly collapsed before determined attack, and that they were sometimes absent when their German allies needed them. It may even be true, as Desmond Young reports, that in the face of an Australian attack outside Tobruk in 1941, the Italian troops fell on their knees with cries of 'Sancta Maria'. Rommel, so the story goes, crisply told the Italian commander to 'stop them praying and persuade them to shoot'[1].

Even to say there were times when the Italians did fight with ferocity is to sound patronising, and does not alter the fact that in 1940 a massive Italian army advanced only hesitantly into Egypt and was then over-whelmed by an opportunist British force a fraction of its size.

The truth of that, though, is that the Italians had no tanks or anti-tank weapons that could touch the British infantry tank, the Matilda, and even the British cruisers ran rings around them. Ill-armed, poorly equipped with transport and badly led, the Italian forces could neither stand and fight nor flee, and had no choice but to throw up their hands - gratefully, perhaps, because there was no enthusiasm among them for fighting. These days that might be seen as a virtue rather than a vice, but in the 1940s such liberality was not highly regarded. The stakes were too high. Yet it was more complicated than that.

The Italians were truly not interested in war, and their militaristic image of pre-war years was no more than a Fascist charade. So far as the alliance with Germany is concerned, not even the Fascists were wedded to the idea of a neighbour dominated by a Teutonic version of their own totalitarian creed. Liaison between Italians and Germans was poor, sometimes non-existent, and the Pact of Steel that created the Rome-Berlin Axis was as phoncy as Mussolini's bluster. This antipathy penetrated to the lowest levels.

The adjutant of the 1st Battalion, 5th Panzer Regiment, noted in his diary after visiting an Italian shop in North Africa on 2 September 1941, '... any nationality is served more cheerfully than a German'. His own view of the Italians is reflected in an entry for 30 August when he recorded: 'An English U boat damaged an Italian vessel. The Italians took revenge - excelled themselves by shooting down a plane - unfortunately a German Ju85.'

All this was read with pleasure after the diary's capture, and related in British intelligence summaries.

The plain fact is that the Italians were unprepared in mind and equipment for war and, thanks to Fascism, which perpetuated privilege, a strong caste system dominated the army command structure. Many

Italians had an affinity with the English that leached away enthusiasm for a war with Britain, and considering that Mussolini was once highly regarded in England, the alliance might well have gone the other way.

Even Rommel, who was caustic in his criticism of the Italians, offered a plea in mitigation for the Italian soldier. He was, he said, poorly equipped* and poorly led by a privileged officer class who did not always consider it necessary to make an appearance in battle, and who enjoyed the luxury of having meals of several courses while the troops did not even have field kitchens. He might also have added that the officers' life-style included flamboyant wardrobes and travelling brothels.

There is very likely a cultural component in this, too. Italians are people who express their every emotion, often with no restraint. By contrast, the Germans, British and Commonwealth troops came from more phlegmatic traditions, and this is a distinct advantage when death or mutilation threatens. To release emotion is to invite panic, and when everyone around about is doing the same, only disaster can result.

Moreover, the making of a soldier demands more than putting a man into uniform, giving him a gun, filling him with propaganda and pointing him towards the enemy. There's a necessary conditioning, a delving into the psyche for primitive drives that enable a man to thrust a bayonet into another human being and put his foot on the corpse while he pulls out a blade dripping red. Soldiering is not about brass bands and heroics, or even impersonal killing at a distance. It's a bloody business that requires a man to be prepared to kill or be killed, and in the process put aside all other considerations, including thought for the future. The British, too, had no great heart for the war, at least until it started, and they did not properly prepare for it. Their forces were to some extent blighted by the class system, and great losses were suffered in consequence. Auchinleck was hard put to find a good army commander, and at Alamein, where he himself commanded, his subordinates failed him.

In the House of Commons, during the debate on a motion of censure during July 1942, while the battle raged at Alamein, one speaker scathingly suggested that there were generals in the Czech, Polish and French forces in Britain who could do better than the British generals then engaged in Egypt. If Rommel had been in the British Army, he said, he would be no more than a sergeant, and there was in fact a sergeant in a

---

* Italian equipment included weapons recovered as booty after the collapse of the Austro-Hungarian Empire in 1918.

British armoured brigade who had been chief of staff in the Spanish Civil War and had won the Battle of Ebro.

'The fact of the matter is,' he said, 'that the British Army is ridden with class prejudice.'[2]

The British, though, had a commitment to the war the Italians lacked, and they were not shackled to a partner who despised them. And for the British, winning was a matter of survival. It's doubtful if the Italians could see any good for themselves whichever way the war went. They were in a no-win situation, and once the sense of adventure was gone they lacked motivation.

In short, a significant factor in Rommel's failure in North Africa was not simple Italian unwillingness to fight but a tangled complex of political and sociological factors that hobbled the will of the men with the weapons.

Of course the Italians suffered by comparison with their German allies, who must be considered the best soldiers in the world. Though they may not have been the supermen we sometimes thought, they were remarkable in both attack and defence, and no less than astonishing in their ability to fight much stronger forces on so many fronts, and in their tenacity in the face of their country's ruin. In the Desert, Rommel was able time and again, in a manner that seemed almost miraculous, to pull together scratch German forces to repair holes punched in his line by the Eighth Army.

'The German soldier always seemed capable of making one more supreme effort,' says the official British history.[3]

An American writer, Colonel T.N. Dupuy, who has done some scientific modelling on this subject, reckons that in 1943 German soldiers had a 20 per cent superiority over American and British fighting men. In other words, 100 Germans roughly equalled 120 American or British soldiers. He attributes this superiority not to any innate propensity for fighting, but to the effectiveness of the German General Staff.[4] It is difficult not to feel, however, that this superiority does not also relate to the Germans' strong sense of national identity, of being *Germans*, to their tradition of obedience to authority, and the powerful military ethos established by that General Staff - not something for which they were admired but it served them well when they were beset by enemies.

The Germans had never before fought a desert war, though they had campaigned elsewhere in Africa. Officers sent to Russia viewed the African adventure with a jaundiced eye and accused those who went there of 'unauthorised absence' from the Eastern front, but in their isolated world, and commanded as they were by a general who was a national hero, the 'Africans' wrapped themselves in their own sense of elitism. In Africa they were cut off from their familiar world, with no nearby compensations of civilisation available on leave, such as the Eighth Army had in Cairo, and no comfortable alternative theatre to which they could be posted, such as the British had in Syria and other Middle Eastern countries.

Once in North Africa they were trapped in the heat and sand, fighting often without reserves and existing on rations that did little to preserve good health.

But lest he seem larger than life, it should be said that the German soldier could find the prospect of fighting for victory daunting. On 21 August 1941, our panzer regiment diarist wrote: 'I often wonder how this war, which must be victorious, is to be carried on. Such vast spaces to be conquered against that huge power, England, with her inexhaustible resources. We can only match her with our very best soldiers. But there is a shortage of everything - of material; of reserve manpower; our very vehicles are on their bare rims. Poor rations have made more than 80 per cent of the regiment unfit to be sent forward.'

The German soldier shared, too, the irreverence men of all armies have for the army in general and their superiors in particular. Our diarist perhaps had a stomach ulcer as he recorded breakfast as being 'carbolic flavoured coffee and mouldy bacon with dauerbrot, the very thing for my stomach!' and this may explain his description of general staff officers·as 'old bald-headed bureaucrats and conceited young whippersnappers'.

The Germans' sense of isolation is reflected in a satirical story found sewn into the lining of a coat worn by a prisoner of war describing the return of the Afrika Korps to Berlin 'long after the war', when Hitler and Goering are enjoying the quiet of a Europe at peace. The leaders spare the time for an occasional glance out of the window, and then suddenly 'a caravan of wild-looking creatures comes around the corner driving along crowds of donkeys, laden mainly with stones and sand, others rusty tins which on closer inspection, are found to be Italian AM meat'.

These 'wild looking creatures', though German, speak only Arabic, and Goering wonders who they can be. Then a light glows in his memory. Of course, Germany fought a war in North Africa. But what to do with these long forgotten men? Because they could not be integrated into a normal life, they are put on Huneberg Heath, where 'owing to the absence of sand storms and AM tinned meat, it was not long before their miserable existence terminated'.

The prize for sardonic humour, though, must go to *The Desert Song*, a poem that was apparently the cause of a German court of inquiry. It bewails the fate of the'compulsory volunteers' of the Desert, badly fed, without pay and deprived of the company of women, and with victory columns 'just another tale'. One verse portrays Rommel as a hard task master in these terms:

Came dear old Papa Rommel to see this front one day.
He said, No more I'll permit that, here my army stay.
Advance, those armoured cars and roll on this wheeled host,
I'll see you devils sweat and toil, I'll make you devils roast.

Which is pretty much a picture of the man as history portrays him.

A more prosaic but equally telling view of German feelings was given by a German captured during the July fighting. This talkative prisoner told his captors that before the fighting began at Gazala in May 1942, German soldiers could be divided into three categories - the 'old Africans', proud of their self-invented title but 'browned off' with the climate and lack of leave; recent reinforcements combed out from desk jobs, young and confidently ignorant; and those who had come from Russia, believing, to the annoyance of the 'old Africans', that their new theatre was a rest cure. Since then, the 'old Africans' had found this the most arduous campaign yet experienced, the young and confident had had 'the surprise of their young lives', and, to the unrepressed delight of the 'old Africans', the others had realised their mistake and were yearning for the 'joys of Russia'.

Yet in the face of hardship, German discipline held.

The oddity of the Eighth Army was that though this was essentially Britain's war, at Alamein in July the infantry almost all came from the Dominions, with divisions present from Australia, New Zealand, South Africa and India. Small in population and remote from the centre of conflict, these countries had sent their men from the security of distance to fight what truly in those days was seen as a crusade. Even with all the disillusionment of 1914-18 behind them, there was a sense of urgency and necessity that drove these countries to commit themselves to a war that did not directly threaten them, in the beginning at least, and if there was a degree of self-interest centering on trade in this willing support, there was also an element of idealism, naive though it might seem in our more cynical times. However brutal and unnecessary the Kaiser's war may have seemed, Hitler's was inescapable. The Nazis truly were bent on world domination, bolstered by an evil theory of racial superiority, and nothing that has come to light since the war has changed that. Without this understanding the commitment of men to a battle in a North African desert against an enemy they grudgingly respected cannot be appreciated.

Until the disasters of the Battle of Egypt, when an intense bitterness was generated, there was a degree of benevolent tension between Commonwealth troops and those from Britain. Though they respected veterans like the Desert Rats (the 7th Armoured Division, which was created in the Desert), they affected a mild arrogance towards 'the Poms', born partly, perhaps, from their sense of national identity, and partly from the fact that, being men accustomed to the open spaces of their own countries, they saw United Kingdom troops as being more at home in big cities and out of place in the wilderness. Moreover, UK troops, for their part, tended to regard those from the Commonwealth as 'colonials' and in their vast ignorance of places on the other side of the world were apt to ask galling questions. Commonwealth nations were self-governing democracies, and though they might have lacked some of Europe's sophistication, they were civilised countries with all the amenities this implies, and Commonwealth troops were scathingly amused to receive inquiries suggesting that their homelands resembled darkest Africa.

The fact that the Eighth Army was run by the British probably didn't help, either, especially when things went wrong and it was clear that army command was at fault. This is not to suggest that Commonwealth and British troops were at daggers drawn, but there was tension.

For whatever reason, Rommel appears to have regarded the New Zealanders as the elite of the Eighth Army. Certainly they were different, and in some ways more like a tribe or a family, with the huge Bernard Freyberg VC, affectionately known as Tiny, as a father figure at their head. Freyberg, who began life as a dentist, had been a strong swimmer in his youth and gained some fame during the Gallipoli campaign, where he served with the Hood Battalion, when he swam ashore on a mission. He gained a VC in France, and after the war stayed on in the British Army. Though Surrey born, and truly a British Army officer, he grew up in New Zealand, and soon after the outbreak of the Second World War was appointed to command the New Zealand Division.

Wounded during the abortive defence of the Mersa Matruh positions in June 1942 he handed over to the pipe-smoking Inglis, a barrister by profession, promoted to major-general for the occasion.

The New Zealanders came from one of the most geographically

isolated countries on earth, just a few blobs of land in the South Pacific, almost on the International Date Line and nearly 2,000 kilometres from the nearest neighbour, Australia. In this fastness, an ambivalent culture was suspended half way between the nostalgia of those who still called England Home, with a capital H, and the realism of an enforced growing South Pacific identity. Though there were some regional rivalries among the New Zealanders - those from the sparsely populated South Island liked to say theirs was the mainland - they hung together as a *de facto* national army of a country of only 1.6 million people, no more than a medium-sized European city, and while there were also many New Zealanders serving in the air force and navy, the army was the centre of attention at home, and this enhanced their self-awareness. It was a larger division than the normal British formation, as it came with supplementary fighting units and all its own back-up services, its own 'cavalry' - a reconnaissance unit in light tanks - and even a spare battalion - the 28th (Maori) Battalion, established especially for the country's ethnic minority. The Maoris at one time or another were posted to different brigades and were in the thick of the fighting.

So pervasive is wartime propaganda (and what country will denigrate its soldiers either during a war or afterwards?) it is hard even now to say how good the New Zealanders really were. Tuker* thought the division was 'a very ponderous affair ... like dear old Freyberg', and Dorman Smith considered it had not responded easily to the 'scrambling, impromptu' sort of fighting of July. Auchinleck, if he did not regard the New Zealanders as the best, at least used them as a criterion by which others could be judged. Writing in 1942 to Sir Walter Monkton, Minister of State in Cairo, he said 'The Indian Army, as you know, has gained a name for itself which is second to none, not even the New Zealanders.'

Like the Australians and South Africans, the New Zealand Division enjoyed a degree of independence and could refuse an order or ask for Government approval, though this was not something done lightly. The primary political concern was that so small an army should not be annihilated in a single action, and the New Zealanders had vivid memories of a sequence of disasters that had accumulated enormous casualties in dead, wounded and prisoners of war.

The Australians, coming from a larger, more self-confident country, were more flamboyant, and they had a reputation for indiscipline. But

* Major General Tuker, at this time a divisional commander

according to the wartime writer Chester Wilmot their commander at Alamein, Morshead, was 'something of a martinet', and the troops, he said, responded to discipline.

Known to his troops as Ming the Merciless, Morshead was certainly the antithesis of the Australian stereotype. In the words of Australia's military historian, Dr C.E.W. Bean, he was a 'dapper little schoolmaster', a dumpy man with a toothbrush moustache and a quick temper. Originally the Australians had three divisions in the Middle East, and when two were taken home after Japan entered the war, Morshead became, like Freyberg, the protector of his nation's one division in this theatre.

The Australians liked to rough up the Italians, who greatly feared them, though according to Desmond Young, Rommel was amused by this and felt that it did not show a 'bad heart'.[5] When the Italians discovered on 10 July that they had been attacked by Australians, their incredulity, according to the commander of 2/24th Battalion, Lieutenant-Colonel Hammer, 'was almost pathetic'. The Germans were surprised, too, thinking all the Australians had gone home, and a message from the commander of the 86th Infantry Regiment to a battalion commander on 20 July, warned, 'Div has just rung up at this very moment to say that units in front of you are Australians - notable patrollers. Keep your eyes open. Don't withdraw your patrols further than 100 metres from the strong-point or you will find yourself left high and dry and with only an alarm bell for protection.'

The Australians were no lesser soldiers than the New Zealanders, and their part in the 242-day seige of Tobruk fully established their credentials. Indeed, at Tobruk they bested Rommel by having the troops lie low while the panzers went by, to emerge to fight off the surprised following infantry. The tanks, meanwhile, charged on into a trap of guns from which the survivors escaped only by retreat.

Barrie Pitt says they lacked the hard professionalism of regular soldiers but made up for it in sheer size and physical strength, and he describes them as being of immense physique, with rifles in their hands looking 'like boys' air guns'.[6] Of course, many Englishmen could not tell Australians and New Zealanders apart - they still can't - just as many of us can't distinguish Canadians from Americans, but the story of Australians using captured enemy guns in Tobruk is unadultered Okker. As the guns lacked sights, the procedure for changing elevation was 'Cock the bastard up a bit', and when the gun appeared to be on target, 'Let her go, mate.'

The South Africans *were* Africans, and they were committed only to the defence of the African continent, a condition imposed so literally that when Auchinleck made plans to withdraw from the Delta should the Axis break through at Alamein, part of his army would have had to withdraw south up the Nile. To have taken the South Africans east across the Suez Canal would have required them to enter Asia.

The South Africans were commanded at Alamein by the prickly Dan Pienaar, who had been appointed as recently as March. He was a student of the Bible and a fatalist, but in his approach to the enemy he exercised a Gilbertian sense of humour. He had German mines sewn in front of Italian troops and Italian mines sewn in front of Germans, and when he learned that the Germans listened to Lili Marlene singing love songs on their forces radio at midnight, he instituted a shelling programme at 11.57 pm.

The South Africans were a people apart among the Commonwealth troops, and their distinctive culture came through in their long 'a' and rolled 'r', the pace and music of their speech, their exotic songs, and their frequent use of the Afrikaans language, through which they wove army colloquialisms in English. They were, incidentally, the natural rugby rivals of the New Zealanders. They, too, had their sense of identity, and they came to the Western Desert with a successful campaign in East Africa behind them.

After the fall of Tobruk in June 1942 a fairly savage antipathy developed between the South Africans and Australians, who felt their own record entitled them to pass judgement, and the story is told of an Australian who offered a South African a seat in a Cairo bar because, he said, 'you must be tired after running all the way from Tobruk'. A monstrous brawl ensued.

The Indians were Empire rather than Commonwealth, the last vestiges of the greatest empire the world has known. They were professionals under British command, and in this they contrasted with the more relaxed attitude of the so-called colonials, who were in the army for the duration only.

The Indians had served in East Africa, too, and at Keren had won a battle not many people know about, even today. Here, in rugged terrain, they had battled against tenacious Italians to fight their way up through the Dongolass Gorge to achieve one of the memorable victories of the war. Not all the Indians who came to Alamein were veterans, and some who had never previously heard a shot fired in anger were to stake their own claim to fame by stopping the panzers.

The Indian Army was not entirely made up of Indians, and included British regiments.

It is difficult to generalise about the troops from the UK in the Middle East because they were less homogeneous, a mixture of crack professional regiments and run-of-the-mill support units whose manpower ingredients were English, Irish, Scottish and Welsh, each with their individual regional origins, a combination of dialects and identities that invited rivalries and even a degree of antipathy. Rommel dismissed them as promising amateurs.[7] To the Commonwealth troops, the British, with their 'funny' way of talking, were quite strange beings, and as the British ran the army and as it was the British Red Caps and British punishment centres that imposed general discipline on free ranging 'colonials', they commonly appeared as authority figures to be resented. It has to be remembered that in pre-war days, tourism was a pastime mainly for the rich, and there was no television to provide us with daily images and sounds from around the globe. For New Zealanders and Australians living at the far end of the Earth, Britain was at least a month's steaming away, and there was a rich folklore from earlier times of 'new chums' from 'Home' trying awkwardly to cope with what we now recognise as a culture shock, and the 'Empire' was sometimes used as a refuge by misfit Englishmen who hadn't been able to cope with life in their own country. British kinsfolk in general were almost foreigners, regarded rather patronisingly by New Zealanders and Australians. After the disasters of July, they came to be regarded rather more angrily as 'Pommie bastards'.

The United Kingdom forces contained a rift of another kind: the perpetual division between infantry and armour - the cavalry, who saw themselves as a kind of military aristocracy. It was all a curious extension of the English class system based on the cult of the horse.

Not that there were many United Kingdom infantry there in July. Those that were came in the form of a rebuilt brigade and various mobile columns from 50th Division, which had suffered severely in the Gazala fighting and lost one entire brigade. But infantry officers held sway in army command, and the rift between infantry and armour can be inferred from Dorman Smith's caustic reference, following an unpleasant scene on 4 July, to 'temperamental cavalry generals', his allusion to 'gross snobbery' in cavalry regiments and his belief that those in armoured regiments regarded infantry battles as 'vulgar brawls'.

And he quotes with implied approval a statement attributed to Wavell in 1932: 'I was once attached to a cavalry regiment. I only heard one order given at any time. It was, "Trot on, Algie".'

For its part, the cavalry made its own implied reference to this rift in a memorandum by Lieutenant-Colonel E. O. Burne of 12th Lancers, who presumably wished his views to be known to posterity. He appears to have been in a state of explosive anger when he tore off his protest against army reforms that curbed the cavalry practice of seeking out and recruiting the brightest young officers, a custom he justified with the argument that the Englishman was the inventor of the club, the club system was in his blood, 'and not unnaturally he likes to belong to the best club. A good regiment is regarded as a good club by both officers and men, and round it are built up innumerable welfare associations and social societies'.

'The argument that popular regiments get a monopoly of the best class of officer is but a point in favour of the old system,' he wrote. 'Under the new system the RAC will not get the good officers at all. The powerful trade unions of the Guards Brigades and Rifle Regiments will see to that.' Trade unions, indeed!

Such were the divisions on both sides. Dorman Smith blamed many of the July failures on the pig-headed independence of the Dominion formations, and in particular accused the Australians of causing the final catastrophe on 27 July. He mourned the absence of 'docile, obedient, bull-headed British divisions instead of these brave but temperamental Dominion troops, each totally different from every other contingent'. 'Eighth Army,' he was to write, 'was very distinctly labelled, "Handle with care".'

Auchinleck, too, had his reservations about his Dominion troops. In a letter to Brooke on 25 July, reviewing the recent disastrous events and the absence of trained mobile troops, he complained that despite their 'magnificent material' they were 'very hard to teach'.

'They are apt to think that once they have been in battle they have little to learn and are on the whole suspicious of any attempts to teach them. Some of them say quite openly that we are incompetent ourselves and so unfit to teach them or anyone else. They are not alone in this, of course.

'... there is no doubt that their intensely democratic feelings make it most difficult for their officers to insist on real hard work being done when they are out of the battle zone. They simply do not understand the meaning of continuous and intensive training. Freyberg is an exception, of course, and does insist on hard training, but he has very few trained or experienced officers to back him up and he has to send the best of his leaders back to New Zealand.'*

Rommel, for his part, intoned his own lamentation over the Italians, who undeniably were resistant not just to work but also to accepting the dangers of battle. Whatever Auchinleck may have thought of his Dominion troops, they faced up to shot and shell and could be relied on to fight with spirit.

This mix of nationalities imposed its own pattern on the battles of July.

The initial Axis attacks fell on the South Africans and Indians. By the second day of battle the British were in the field with their tanks and some battle groups, while the South Africans held on in and around Alamein. As the Eighth Army turned to counter-attack, the Australians, New Zealanders and more Indian units took up the fight, with the British tanks more or less nibbling at the edges, at least until the arrival of a brand new armoured brigade that threw itself into the fray with such abandon that it disintegrated on impact. Remembering that Germany's foe was, as the German song had it, England, Rommel might reasonably have wondered where his true enemy was.

But then he really had little time to ponder such niceties of identification. The British shrewdly hacked away at the Italians, whom Rommel ruefully confessed were 'easy meat', with the intention of so isolating the Germans that they could be more easily overcome. To strengthen his positions, Rommel was compelled to take away formations from his already weak German units and scatter them among the Italians. The pattern for Rommel became one of frenetic mobility as crisis followed crisis and the collapse of the Axis positions seemed imminent.

Looking at the relative strengths of the two armies, we might wonder why there was so much panic at the time. But of course those in Egypt did not have our perspective, and Pienaar, the South African commander, and Gott, the 13th Corps commander, both feared the worst, while in Cairo there was a distinct impression that the gothic hordes would soon be tramping down the coast road to Cairo. Around the world people held their breath.

Yet Rommel reached the Alamein defences with minuscule German forces, to be opposed by an army superior in numbers and fire power, and

*This is apparently a reference to officers being sent home to prepare troops for home defence after the entry of Japan into the war.

in much better physical shape. The German forces consisted, supposedly, of three divisions - 15th and 21st Panzer Divisions, which made up the Afrika Korps, and the 90th Light Division, normally under direct Army control. Between them they could not muster the strength of one division. At full strength they would have fielded 37,000 men, 371 tanks and 466 anti-tank guns, plus artillery, and in addition there would have been the army artillery with another 3,000 men. The head count on 1 July would be no more than a tenth of that number.

90th Light, which should have had 12,000 men, attacked on 1 July with 76 officers and 1,600 other ranks, of which just over 1,000 were infantry. They had a mixed bag of British, Russian and German artillery pieces, and only 32 anti-tank guns, of which two were British six-pounders and 12 were Russian guns, booty from the Russian front.

The two panzer divisions had between them only 55 tanks, all that was left of the 332 tanks with which they had begun the offensive at Gazala on 26 May, and 15 armoured cars.

On 8 July, when there had been a long enough pause to take stock, the Germans found they had 50 tanks between the two divisions, with each division having a rifle regiment of 300 men and ten anti-tank guns, and two batteries of artillery. 90th Light had an overall strength of 1,500 men, 12 per cent of establishment, 30 anti-tank guns, two batteries and three reconnaissance battalions with 15 armoured cars between them. Then there was the army artillery, which had 11 heavy and 4 light batteries, and the army anti-aircraft artillery with 26, 88 mm and 25, 20 mm guns.

The Italian XX Motorised Corps, which should have had 430 tanks among 3 divisions, Ariete, Littorio and Trieste, could field only 54 tanks and 8 motor battalions with an overall strength of 1,600 men. Also present were 'elements' of X and XXI Corps consisting of 11 infantry battalions, each of about 200 men.

In the course of July reinforcements did come forward, though casualties largely offset these and Rommel's forces did not gain in strength either in men or tanks. By 15 July more than 2,000 Germans had flown in from Crete and a start made with bringing in the 164th Light African Division. Towards the end of July the Ramcke Parachute Brigade arrived, an event that led Auchinleck to warn his army of a possible airborne attack.

The Italians were making arrangements to bring in substantial forces that included tanks, armoured cars and self-propelled guns. Seven infantry regiments and 4 artillery regiments were flown in. The Folgore

Parachute Division was to come at once, to be followed by Pistoia and Friuli Divisions. But all this would take time, and throughout July Rommel watched his Italian forces diminish and his German forces barely hold their own.

But if the British overestimated their enemy, so also did the Germans, though Rommel believed - or perhaps hoped - that he could drive right through to Cairo. Rommel saw a continuous defence line across his path, yet the number of British and Commonwealth troops who stood to at first light on 1 July would probably total no more than 25,000. This was few enough, but there was a good concentration in the north at least, and to a greater or lesser degree all units were dug in.

The only complete division, less a small number of companies that had been sent to the rear, was the 2nd New Zealand, which had reassembled after a wild break out by two of its brigades from Minqar Qaim, south of Mersa Matruh, a few days earlier. The 1st South African was a coherent division, but two of its brigades had been converted to battle groups. There were two Indian brigades, the 18th and 6th, in different areas, and 7th Motor Brigade, a remnant of the veteran 7th Armoured Division, able to field only light tanks and armoured cars. The only armoured forces available on that first morning were 18 tanks of 1st Armoured Division. The rest of the division's forces, which were, in any case, in a more or less dazed state after a fighting withdrawal, were either trapped in soft sand or awaiting repair. The 1st Armoured Division was really a division in name only, as its two brigades were a make-and-mend job from the fragments left over from the Gazala battle. It was not a force with the coherence that comes from long training together.

There were therefore strengths and weaknesses in the Eighth Army of which Rommel was unaware. Auchinleck had reinforcements close at hand in Syria, Iraq and Persia (now Iran) in the shape of formations stationed there to ward off any German incursion from the north, and through force of circumstances he was compelled, with reluctance, to call them down. While the outside world worried about what might happen at El Alamein, the strategists were also concerned about what would happen should the Russians give way, and Auchinleck was in effect fighting with the occasional glance over his shoulder. His hope was to achieve a quick decision in the Desert and return the borrowed units to the north, and this was an unseen factor in what happened during July.

The New Zealanders had come from Syria, and the Indians from Persia. Back at the Delta and soon to come forward was the 9th Australian

Division, fully manned but short of equipment, which had also come from Syria. Further Indian brigades were brought down from the north during the month.

Eighth Army's ace card should have been its tank reserves. 1st Armoured quickly built up its numbers to easily outnumber Rommel's few panzers, and another armoured division, the 8th, was already on its way from Britain. Part of this new division was sunk, part sent to India by mistake, and part delayed at Durban for ship repairs, but by some miracle of efficiency one brigade, the 23rd, arrived early in July and was flung into the fray on 22 July. At that time, its arrival brought Auchinleck's tank numbers up to 450 compared with Rommel's 33 on that day. A cynic might argue, however, that the enemy profited most from this disproportionate number of British tanks; they provided him with excellent target practice for his anti-tank guns.

In looking at the armies of July, an obvious question that comes to mind is why was Rommel left to languish with so slender resources when victory in Africa would have yielded such rich prizes. In a sense, Alamein was to become a German Gallipoli, an alternative front where opportunities were lost for lack of military commitment and political will.

The reason for this neglect, according to a German admiral, was that the German Army was obsessed by a Continental attitude. Germany was a Continental power experienced in Continental wars, and engaged in a Continental struggle with Russia. Vice-Admiral Weichold, Chief German Liaison Officer in Rome and Flag Officer, German Naval Command, 1940-43, asserted in a post-war essay that Germany's failure to understand the importance of sea power deprived her of the will to seize control of the Mediterranean, which would have enabled more ready supply and rein-forcement of Rommel, and blinded her to what could be achieved in North Africa. The Italians, who had a fleet in the Mediterranean, might have pulled it off, but, as with their army, the fleet's technology and command structure were both outdated, and there was a 'silent admis-sion' of British naval superiority in experience and achievement in battle. We might feel that the Italians saw the Royal Navy as we, in our more pessimistic moments, saw the German Army.

Rommel complained constantly and bitterly about his army's ne-glected supply position, blaming those in Rome who did not recognise that the North African war had reached its climax, and the ineffectual Italian navy, a great many of whose officers, he believed, 'like many other

Italians', were not supporters of Mussolini and preferred German defeat to victory. Even Fascist authorities, he asserted, were too pompous and corrupt to help. For whatever reason, Rommel never had enough of anything, and at Alamein he wrote despairingly of how the British were sparing no effort to master the situation.

'The peril of the hour moved the British to tremendous exertions,' he wrote. And he viewed with despair his 'Africans', as he called them, moving up time and again to fight yet another engagement, while the British, as he saw it, were able to bring up fresh units and withdraw others for rest.

This view of the British situation was a rosy one, but certainly things were in better shape on the Delta side of the line. Rather than a few brave survivors standing with Alexandria at their backs, the Eighth Army was still full of fight, though anyone seeing the helter-skelter flight of broken remnants down the coast road as the enemy drew near might reasonably have assumed that the end was near. Of course, the end *was* near, but it was not what anyone was expecting.

CHAPTER THREE

THE WEAPONS OF JULY

When war broke out in 1939 no one was ready - not the British, not the French, not eventhe Germans. The Nazis, indeed, were still trying audaciously to build a continental empire on which to base an industrial and military structure that would ensure their world dominance. It was an exercise in deadly brinkmanship they hoped would carry them through at least to the mid-1940s before they would have to meet enemies of substance. But like a piece of scorched paper on a smouldering fire, the world was suddenly ablaze.

The guns of France had been silent for only 21 years when the fighting began. Quartermasters' stores throughout the world had the left-overs prudently stacked away in grease and naptha, and many of those who fought in 1914-18 were on hand to provide the leadership and tactical thinking for the new generation of soldiers, most of whom had been born either during or after the last struggle. It wasn't quite just a matter of unpacking, reissuing and starting all over again, but Britain and Germany entered the new war with predominantly infantry armies whose pudding basin helmets on the one side and coal scuttle helmets on the other created a sense of *déjà vu*.

Surface appearances, however, were illusory. The harvest of the machine-gun, scything stumbling infantry in Flanders, had led to a resolve to combine fire power with mobility, and the new armies used wheels, tracks and wings. The Germans had the lead, at least until July1942. Their panzer divisions gave a cutting edge to attack, and their dive bombers, vaulting over land barriers, were overhead artillery, combining pinpoint accuracy with intimidating sound. For their part the British fumbled with innovation, at least until El Alamein in July 1942, after which American tanks and bigger and better anti-tank guns began to swing the balance.

The base line for these novelties remained the infantryman, the soldier with a rifle. And despite all the technological innovations that, in the Desert especially, changed the face of warfare, the primitive gleaming steel of the bayonet retained its place, a symbol, in a way, of the dehumanizing brutality of war. Though the shell and bomb might wreak greater havoc and inflict more horrendous injuries, the bayonet required one man to confront another, face to face, and thrust a blade into his body, and to prepare him for this the army indulged in bayonet practice in which inoffensive straw dummies were attacked with great ferocity and manic shouts.

The whole range of infantry equipment, with rifles, machine-guns, mortars and artillery, tended to perpetuate an infantry structure similar to that of the First World War, despite a number of changes, and it was this rigidity that both sides sought to reshape in the Desert, where marching columns of old fashioned infantry were as anachronistic as the Mary Rose would have been at the Coral Sea. Of course motor transport for troops was now supplied in greater numbers, and in the Desert the effectiveness of the infantry depended on there being capacity for everyone to be carried on wheels, and when motor trucks were lacking, commanders sought to trim down their infantry forces to the number that *could* be carried. This was yet another factor to impact on what happened at Alamein in July. Essentially, on a battlefield where mobility was critical, the soldier on foot was a helpless pedestrian in a stampede of bulls.

Barbed wire was of little consequence in the Desert, but the minefields it surrounded were. Mines became significant from Gazala on, and at El Alamein in particular were a factor in determining success or failure in attack. As the main emphasis in sewing minefields was to put up a barrier to vehicles, infantry could usually pass through on foot like fluid through a membrane, but tanks, guns and lorry-borne support weapons were filtered out unless a way through could be made for them. A critical element in attack therefore became the ability to clear and mark adequate lanes, and for follow-up forces to be shown where they were. And simple as this operation might sound, it was the inability of Eighth Army formations to accomplish this that led to disaster. At Alamein, this passive device, lying dormant in the sand, affected the course of history and played its part in the destruction of military careers.

The aircraft and the tank brought new, or rather more efficient, weapons on to the scene to counter them. Both sides had their light, medium and heavy anti-aircraft guns. The tank also brought forth a family of infantry and artillery weapons to oppose it, and it was here that the Germans were dominant, at least until mid-1942.

The Germans had two anti-tank guns that slaughtered British tanks - the 50mm PAK (PAK is an abbreviation for the German word for anti-tank gun, as FLAK is for anti-aircraft gun, and distinguishes it from the KWK gun fitted to tanks), and the monstrous 88mm dual-purpose gun, sometimes referred to as triple purpose. The 88 is almost a beast of mythology. It was designed as an anti-aircraft gun, and proved itself to be a fearsome weapon also against tanks and infantry. It had tremendous range, something like 15 kilometres, and it has been said could kill whatever it could see. Even the Matilda, the most heavily armoured British tank, was vulnerable as far away as 3,000 metres. And because its effective range was so enormous, one or two 88s could wipe out a tank attack before the unfortunate British could bring them to within range of their puny two-pounders.

There was a British gun available that could have transformed the Desert scene and put the panzers to flight. The British had at their disposal a 3.7 inch anti-aircraft gun that could have done the same job as the German 88. It was a better gun than the 88, and it was on hand in good numbers, spending most of its time in Egypt searching an empty sky.

One embittered officer of the 57th Light Anti-Aircraft Battery, Major D.F. Parry, in an unpublished book written after the war called *Eighth Army - Defeat and Disgrace*, claimed that more than a thousand 3.7's 'stood silent' in the Middle East, many never firing a shot in anger, when they could have reversed the fortunes of our armies in the field.[1] In fact the 3.7 was used at least twice but only temporarily. In the first few days of July 1942 a battery of 3.7s, intercepted on their way to Persia, wiped off the map everything they could find, and showed how they could have redressed the balance in tank warfare. Alas, they were never used on a permanent basis, and British armoured forces suffered as a result.

The tank was the queen of the Desert battlefield. In the wide-open space of North Africa, armoured formations, with their triple qualities of mobility, protection and fire power, could overwhelm unprotected infantry, and the foot soldier could survive only if he was in partnership with his own tanks or anti-tank guns, and preferably with access to his own wheels. Rommel's view was that North Africa 'was the only theatre where the principles of motorised and tank warfare as they were taught theoretically before the war could be applied to the full and developed further.

It was the only theatre where the pure tank battle between formations was fought ... based on the principles of complete mobility.'

In the battle of the tanks the Germans were clearly the masters, at least until American Shermans were delivered as Montgomery assumed command of the Eighth Army in August 1942.

Despite his references to tank battles, Rommel saw the destruction of enemy armour primarily as a task for the anti-tank guns. His panzers were a mailed first directed at the enemy army. In full desert formation a panzer division formed a mobile box, with tanks around the outside and support and command vehicles inside. As enemy were encountered, the whole formation could deploy for instant action, with panzers, artillery and anti-tank guns working in unison. A favourite device against British armour was the 'sword and shield' tactic in which the panzers flaunted themselves before the British attackers - the sword - and then retired behind a shield of anti-tank guns. They re-emerged later to clean up what was left after the anti-tank guns had done their work.

All this imposed immense strains on the command structure, and, making a virtue out of necessity, the Germans evolved a tight organisation that permitted an agile response to the changing demands of battle. And after the Gazala battles, the British press was to remark on the speed with which the Germans could make decisions, contrasting this with the sluggish reactions of British command.

The German objective was speed - to strike quickly before the enemy could gather his wits - and to this end they would sometimes ignore radio codes, permit bunching of troops and even drive at night with lights. They were not incautious, but they responded to circumstances with what seemed appropriate action rather than be bound by the book. Of course, this sometimes led to mistakes, and eventually to the stand-off at Alamein.

The British never matched the German sophistication of command, and worked, moreover, to a totally different philosophy. The primary aim of the British armour was to seek out the enemy armour and destroy it. They saw armoured warfare in terms of cavalry clashes, even knightly encounter.

This led to the development of two types of tank with different roles. The cavalry units, formed into armoured brigades, were equipped with fast cruiser tanks, and infantry fighting was foreign to them. Working with infantry was the task of the infantry tank, slow and heavily armoured, which was organised into army tank brigades. Thus, while the Germans fielded cohesive units in which panzers and other arms worked together, the

British divided up tank tasks, leaving a yawning gap between the two roles.

The final impediment was the dispersed nature of British command, whose elements were scattered across the landscape, requiring hours of travel by commanders from the various levels to achieve consultation and receive orders. And as the role of British armour was to seek out the panzers, it was necessary first to find out where the enemy was on any particular day by sending out armoured cars on reconnaissance before decisions could be made. Carver writes what sounds almost like parody as he describes the comings and goings of officers between headquarters in different parts of the Desert as conferences are held and orders passed down. By the time the attack is launched it is almost last light[2].

And then there is the much debated question of the quality of those earlier British tanks. Throughout the war and long afterwards an all-pervasive song of sorrow was sung over them, and it's true that German tanks were more mechanically reliable, had better optics for their gun sights, and had better ammunition, but the true reason for the superiority of the panzers lay in their command structure and support weapons.

In July 1942 the main British battle tank - the tank to fight other tanks - was the Crusader.

It was fast, agile and elegant but, alas, heir to mechanical problems, and many fell by the wayside while moving into battle. The main weapon was the standard 40 mm two-pounder, which was generally accepted as a 'pop gun'.

Then there were two types of infantry tank - the tank designed to fight with infantry. They were the Matilda and the Valentine.

The Matilda, the most heavily armoured, was almost impervious to everything thrown at it until the arrival of the Germans. It suffered from mechanical unreliability, but the Germans were not averse to painting black crosses on captured models and facing them the other way. After all, British anti-tank guns couldn't penetrate them, either. Its great weakness was that it had the same two-pounder as the Crusader rather than a larger gun firing high explosive (HE) with which to sweep enemy infantry. For that task it had only a machine-gun.

The Valentine was a dainty little tank whose size belied its toughness. The product of Vickers, it was ten tonnes lighter than the Matilda, but it was still heavily armoured, and mechanically it was as reliable as anything else on the battlefield. It remained in service when others had gone or been demoted from the ranks of battle tanks. It, too, had the universal two-pounder, but it was upgunned to a six-pounder for the advance into

Tunisia in 1943. It had an excellent profile, and despite its slow speed was used also as a cruiser. Had it been built with a cruiser's speed it would have sorely troubled the panzers.

The Germans fielded two types of battle tank in July 1942 - the Mark III and the Mark IV, both roughly the same size as the Matilda but more lightly armoured and rather faster. The leader of the pack was the Mark III, though even in mid-1942 it was becoming obsolescent as new heavier tanks with bigger guns to match the Russian armour were coming into production.

The IV was not a later model but a complementary tank to the III. It was roughly the same size and weight, and shared a common mechanical parentage, an advantage the diverse British types did not enjoy. The IV's main armament was a low velocity 75mm gun, equipped, as was the III's 50mm, with various types of shells.

Both German tanks were upgunned in 1942 with weapons of the same calibre as before but with longer barrels and higher muzzle velocity. The 50mm KWK now corresponded to the 50mm PAK. These new tanks, distinguished by the suffix 'Special', definitely outclassed British tanks, but fortunately there were not many of them in North Africa up to July 1942, and ammunition for them was often scarce or non-existent.

There were also some light obsolescent Mark IIs in the Desert. The Mark II had been the mainstay of the invasion of Poland in 1939, but was now useful only for reconnaissance.

The tank controversy is a complex story, and from it emerged that sense of inferiority that affected British morale, among both infantry and armoured personnel. The atmosphere changed when American tanks arrived. The first was the Honey. Strictly it was the Stuart, but after a test drive someone pronounced it a 'honey' and the name stuck. But this was still only a light tank, and the weight of armour did not begin to swing in British favour until the arrival of the Grant (and a few Lees, the same tank with an additional machine-gun cupola on top). Even then British armour fought at some disadvantage. Though the Grant had a punchy 75mm gun that dismayed the Germans, this was mounted in a sponson in the hull, and could be traversed only slightly. Thus, to shoot at the enemy the Grant had to present its whole towering height (and it was a tall tank) to the enemy, front on, to the full view of its opponent. This defect was remedied in the Sherman, which had its gun in a revolving turret, but these did not make their appearance until after July 1942.

Both the Honey and the Grant were fast and reliable, and at last British tank crews felt they could meet the panzers on even ground. Certainly at Alamein in July it was the Grants that underpinned our armoured defence.

While German tanks ruled the battlefield for the first three years of the war, German aircraft claimed the skies.

On the battlefield the Germans were disciples of the dive bomber. The dive bomber par excellence was, of course, the Stuka, the Ju87, a slow, vulnerable machine but one that, in the absence earlier in the war of strong air opposition, established itself as a precision bomber and terror weapon. A distinctly-shaped single-engined monoplane with inverted gull wing, it was instantly recognisable, and the howl of its siren as it plunged into its dive reinforced the fear induced by its mere appearance.

The Luftwaffe continued its winning way in North Africa. With the Stuka, the Me109 single seat fighter, the Me110 twin-engined fighter, and the Ju88 medium twin-engined bomber, the Luftwaffe gave effective support to Rommel's panzers.

But if the British were slow to adapt to better army weapons, their response in the air was much sharper. The answer to the dive-bomber was the fighter bomber - not quite the same thing, but as a fighter modified to bomb and strafe from low altitudes it was much faster and better able to look after itself. And in the Desert, the RAF unveiled its tank destroyer - tank buster, the army called it, though the RAF thought this vulgar - which was a Hurricane IID armed with two 40mm Vickers, guns of the same calibre as the army's primary anti-tank gun of the time. They were flown with great audacity, and during the Gazala battles, one aircraft swooped so low that it clipped an enemy tank and flew home minus the tail wheel and bottom half of its rudder.

In Africa, the British reinforced their own aircraft with American types, both bombers and fighters, and during Gazala and again at El Alamein - and especially at El Alamein - the British air arm assumed critical importance in the outcome. From the beginning of Rommel's attack at Gazala in May 1942, the Desert Air Force (a branch of the RAF) ran a shuttle service over the battle areas, with its Bostons and Baltimore bombers and Hurricane and Kittyhawk fighters, bombing and straffing. They would fly back to the shimmering Desert landing strips, re-fuel and re-arm, and roar away again, dust billowing back as they rose into the air. Ground crews abandoned their tents and dug themselves holes beside the aircraft dispersal points. They worked through the heat and far into the night, often through bombing raids, pulling blankets over their heads in the night hours so that they could work by torchlight. As opportunity offered they would roll into their slit trenches to catch some sleep. As the army turned to fight at El Alamein, Air Marshall Tedder, commanding the RAF in the Middle East, threw in everything he could lay his hands on. Hurricane IIs came from training units, Spitfires from Malta, Beaufighters from naval co-operation. Spitfires and Hurricanes consigned to India were diverted to Egypt, and Halifax and Liberator bombers were ordered to fly in. The sight of the silver-bellied bombers floating in over the battlefield became reassuringly familiar to the troops on the ground. Hurricanes, Kittyhawks and a few newly-arrived Spitfires pounded the enemy lines, and Beaufighters reached to enemy airfields and transport services further back. By night the faithful old Wellingtons, now based in Palestine, bombed by the light of flares dropped by obsolescent Albacore biplanes, including the port of Tobruk in their itinerary, and Liberators went as far as Benghasi to beat up this port, so critical to the enemy's supply line.

Rommel, meanwhile, had exhausted the Luftwaffe, or very nearly so, and when the pursuit to Egypt began he suffered the consequences, less from combat loss than from exhaustion among crews and mechanical failure in over-stressed aircraft, in addition, of course, to the attentions of the DAF. And there was the perpetual fuel shortage. Intercepts showed that by mid-July German air transports were grounded and operational aircraft could be used only sparingly. Not until the arrival of a tanker on 25 July did things improve, and by then the July battle was nearly over.

In his subsequent despatch, Auchinleck said: 'Our air forces could not have done more than they did to help sustain the Eighth Army in its struggle. Their effort was continuous by day and night, and the effect on the enemy tremendous. I am certain that had it not been for their devoted and exceptional efforts we should not have been able to stop the enemy at the Alamein position ....'

Though it sounds like the proper sort of thing a general should say, it is all true.

So at Alamein the Desert Air Force and the Royal Air Force reclaimed the sky, and just as this was the turning point for ground operations, so it was in the air. The day of the Luftwaffe as an unchallenged terror weapon was over and henceforth it would be Germans who looked up with fear.

There was one trump card in the British armoury, the absolute ace. It might not be thought to be strictly a weapon, but it was, in the sense that any device that supports attack on the enemy can be so considered. This was Ultra, the system for intercepting and decoding high level messages that disclosed the Germans' every move. Based at Bletchley Park in England, Ultra stripped away all secrecy from the enemy, and while it could not always work fast enough to be a deciding factor in a rapidly-moving battle, it enabled the British to anticipate the next move, and it kept our Malta base informed of movements of convoys to Africa.

By 3 July more than 100 deciphered messages a day were reaching the Eighth Army through Ultra, providing detail of enemy ground positions, his supply movements and intentions, as well as the state of the Luftwaffe. It even reported a state of tension between Rommel and Kesselring.

Ultra was supplemented by our Y service, which listened to enemy tactical radio messages in the field. Ultra gave the broad picture, Y the battlefield situation. The army, navy and air force each had its own Y service, as did the German services. But the Germans had nothing like Ultra and never suspected that we had. The secret was kept until many years after the war.

'During the July fighting,' says *British Intelligence in the Second World War*[3] 'Eighth Army was well supplied with operational intelligence as with the essential facts about the state of the enemy's forces and his plans for improving it. Once again Enigma* was the chief source, but army Y was scarcely less important.'

The tragedy is that with such powerful technological forces working for us we often failed where it mattered - in direct confrontation on the battlefield ... at the point of the bayonet.

*Enigma was the name of the machine used by the Germans to encipher their messages. Ultra was the system used by the British to break the codes and read the messages.

CHAPTER FOUR

THE BATTLEFIELD

The Desert was like no other battlefield on Earth. Extremes of heat and cold gripped a land stripped almost bare of vegetation, and the winds that came daily lifted soft, silt-like ochre sand in clouds that clogged pores, choked lungs and shrouded equipment. A single shell-burst could stir up a puffball, and a bombing raid or a battle sent a great curtain towering to the sky. In some places low shrubs dotted the landscape; in others, stones littered the surface; in others, again, where the wind had stripped the ground clean, heat shimmered off naked rock.

Because space was almost limitless, armies met not in orderly lines but in swirling confusion, and the general planning a battle could truly almost take a clean sheet of paper and sketch arrows at will, relating them more to the known positions of the enemy than to terrain. Even at Alamein, where there was the constriction between the sea and the Qattara Depression, the battlefield was 60 kilometres wide, and neither side had the troops to cover the whole distance. Where they did confront each other they allowed themselves space, and men in observation posts peered through binoculars into haze or dust that veiled the enemy, and it was possible for battle groups to venture out in daylight in search of a fight. Unlike the soldier of 1914-18, who spent long months eyeball to eyeball with the opposing army, the Desert soldier, with no more than a slit trench for home, stood at a distance from his foe and rarely saw him. In quiet times, the only assurance that an enemy existed was occasional random shelling, a sneak run by a reconnaissance aircraft or a sudden bombing raid. Of course the patrols knew he was there - the patrols that shuffled softly through the night to find out where he was and what he was up to, to kill a few and bring back some alive for questioning. But to front line soldier the war for much of the time might almost have been a mirage. Even the daytime sky was concealed by haze, and gazing up at the sound of machine-gun fire, the infantryman might glimpse no more than the flash of sun on wings as opposing fighters tangled.

Shade was unknown, except for whatever cover might be improvised, mainly at headquarters, and in June 1941 Rommel wrote to his wife, Lu, that the temperature the previous day had been 42°C and in that heat tanks rose to 61°C, 'which is too hot to touch.'[1]

And there were the flies. Flies were the vermin of the Desert. As rats and lice had possessed the soldiers of the Western Front, a black legion of flies engulfed the men of the Western Desert, spawned in the richly nutritious breeding grounds of body wastes and wasting bodies. They swarmed in crawling clusters, sucking sweat from clinging shirts, competing with humans for food at meal times, rising when disturbed and resettling to delve and discomfort, as indifferent to human suffering as they were to their own demise when struck down by tormented soldiers.

'As one fly, one dark horrible force guided by one mind, ubiquitous and immensely powerful, they addressed themselves to one task, which was to destroy us body and soul,' wrote one New Zealand historian. 'It was useless to kill them for they despised death and made no effort to avoid it. They existed only in the common will, and to weaken that we would have to destroy countless millions of them. None the less, we killed them unceasingly.'[2]

More prosaically, the war diary of the South African Assistant Director of Medical Services noted on 4 July 1942, giving a clue to their origin: 'Flies present in myriads and more of a plague than had been for some time. The whole area had been contaminated by Egyptian labourers, and there is a real danger of the development of dysentery, especially as under Div instructions to retain only the most essential fighting services, many unit commanders had sent away hygiene personnel.' Italian troops were also noted for their fouling of the battlefield, and Eighth Army men were rarely able to use their slit trenches when ground was captured.

There were lice, too, but British troops did not encounter these until enclosed within the indifferent hygiene of Italian prisoner-of-war cages.

The men enjoyed - if that's the word for it - a love-hate relationship with the Desert. It was an awful place to be, and it imposed enormous strains on strength and endurance. Yet it was a wilderness, an empty place with the sense of freedom that comes from the absence of civilisation. And it was a place where armies could grapple without hurting anyone else. The major operations of the war all took place along a broad shelf between the Mediterranean and the inland sand sea. Only the Long Range Desert

Group made regular use of the inland dunes to outflank the enemy and attack him by charging out of this southern wilderness in swift surprise raids. Near the coast the going was mainly firm, allowing easy movement of vehicles, although sand tyres were necessary on wheeled vehicles to negotiate soft drifts. Apart from the Delta, the only part mellowed by green was an area of Cyrenaica between the Atlas Mountains and the sea in the general area of Derna. Regular rainfall made possible farming and afforestation, and it was here that Mussolini's immigrant farmers established themselves before the war, living in homes flamboyantly embellished with Fascist slogans on the exterior walls, notably 'Viva Duce', and admonitions to believe, obey and work.

Though there were the occasional palms, some scrubby shrubs and even wells (bir), water was fouled by passing armies and everything needed to support lift had to be brought in. In popular parlance, the Desert was the tactician's paradise and the quartermaster's nightmare. There was literally nothing available. Feeding hundreds of thousands of men in the field, besides providing the transport, petrol, oil, spare parts and replacement vehicles to move them around, and the weapons and ammunition to fight the war, all called for an immense quartermastering effort, which the British certainly mastered, though for the Axis it was a constant struggle against the odds.

On the British side there was a long haul around the Cape of Good Hope from home bases in Britain and the United States but once the supplies were in Egypt there was a good road as far as the border of Tripolitania, and a good railway as far as Tobruk, and there was also coastal shipping protected by the Royal Navy. The railway, built and operated by the New Zealanders, was a trump card. It meant that troops and all the impedimenta of war could be moved up to the Desert without the expenditure of so much as a litre of petrol, except to transfer everything from the railhead to camps and dumps.

The Axis problem was first to get men and supplies across the Mediterranean under the harrassing attentions of the torpedo bombers from Malta, which, thanks to Ultra, always knew when the convoys were sailing, and then carry them all by motor trucks using either petrol or diesel from Tripoli or at times more convenient ports further east, depending on the current state of battle. Travelling at a steady 65 k.p.h, the round trip from El Alamein to Benghazi and back took a lorry seven days.

Aircraft were also used to ferry troops in limited numbers across the

Mediterranean, and at times of crisis warships brought supplies, but they were poor load carriers. The railway was rarely available to the Axis as naturally the British withdrew locomotives whenever they retreated.

Except for the escarpment, an old sea coast that ran the length of the embattled area, the ground is generally gently undulating or quite flat, punctuated by wadis (dry water courses), escarpments and occasional hills. In some areas maps tend to be almost blank sheets of paper, criss crossed with grid lines, showing little more than a few vague contour lines and, with luck, a bir (well), an alam (cairn), a tell (hill), or a sidi (saint's tomb), the latter normally on rising ground. Wherever battles were fought, deirs (depressions) were avidly sought as they provided some protection and could be used as defence bases and supply dumps, but for those whose task it was to act as guides across a landscape devoid of rivers, roads, towns or other accepted signs of civilisation, the features that stood above ground were straws to be grasped.

There were deserted settlements along the coast (deserted, of course, because of the war), and that black ribbon of the coast road, but movement across the desert required navigation by dead reckoning, and the prismatic compass or Bagnold sun compass were indispensable instruments of survival, and knowledge of the intricacies of true north, magnetic north and the angle of declination a necessary part of arriving at the correct destination. The instruments at hand and their method of use were fairly primitive, and the prismatic compass suffered the handicap of being   sensitive to the changing magnetic fields set up by the motorvehicle in which it was being carried, but the navigator who paid attention to detail couldnormally arrive where he expected.

During the day, periodic checks were carried out en route, with the vehicle's odometer providing the information of distance travelled. But on foot at night - and this applied especially to troops attacking - everything depended on a man carrying a compass and another two (one to check the other) counting paces, an exercise made difficult when troops had to diverge from their chosen course to deal with enemy at one side or the other. It was in this way, in the heat of an engagement, that they became lost in the dark, and commanders not infrequently found on arrival at their objective that some, even a substantial part, of their force was missing.

The Alamein position was a little different in that, being closer to the Delta, it had identifiable tracks and telegraph lines that criss-crossed the area, and these features provided good navigational checks and could be used to define objectives. All the same, the terminal point of an attack could well be a piece of unidentifiable desert, and getting lost was one of the ever-present hazards of Desert warfare.

If the Desert offered the tactician almost limitless scope for attack, it posed problems for defence. There were few convenient topographical features on which to base defence lines and, anyway, no line could be constructed that would reach the width of the Desert. The British solution was the 'box', a strongpoint based on the principle of the square, with troops facing in every direction. They came in various shapes and sizes. Tobruk is the best known, with one of its sides protected by the sea. There were similar, smaller boxes at Mersa Matruh and El Alamein.

Out in the Desert where there was no natural feature like a coastline to offer partial protection, the boxes were totally enclosed by minefields and barbed wire, behind which the infantry waited with machine-guns, mortars and anti-tank guns. Further back in the box was the artillery and, tucked away in the centre somewhere, the headquarters. A box might be built to accommodate a brigade or a division, or for that matter any sized formation, and would cover an area of several square kilometres.

A box was a position from which movement could develop. Though each box would be some distance from its neighbour, it could in theory not be by-passed, as fire could be brought to bear on an enemy trying to break through, and roving armour could engage in battle. In any case, no prudent general would press on knowing he had left strong forces behind him who could sever his supply lines and attack him from the rear, unless he himself had strong enough forces to leave some behind to lay siege, as happened at Tobruk in 1941. The so-called Alamein Line included one coastal box and several inland boxes. The great problem was that, because the Desert offered the opportunity for mobility and because the means for mobility were at hand, static defences tended to become traps, especially when Rommel forced the pace, and though they were not without their value and indeed played a part in stopping the Axis forces at El Alamein, they were seen by critics in the same way that modern cynics see pedestrian crossings - a place to concentrate victims.

Rommel and his Germans came to the Desert totally ignorant of its conditions and needs, having been told nothing by their Italian allies, and as a result they were initially badly equipped. But they adapted rapidly, and soon saw that it was no longer necessary for tanks to move in line and then fan out for action, as they did on European roads. They quickly saw that they could move in extended formation and be ready for instant battle, and their boxes were mobile squares of armour. Rommel was able to give free rein to his doctrine of moving 'damn fast', and with his practice of front line generalship, he could react at speed, too, unfettered by the cumbersome command structure that strangled British movement.

Even at Alamein in July 1942 the emphasis was on movement. It was not a shoulder-to-shoulder confrontation on the 1914-18 model, but a fluid battle given stability by only one strongpoint, the Alamein Box. It was at Alamein that Rommel showed his mastery over the Desert, and the British, veterans of the Desert from before the war, their inability to apply their long experience. Alamein was the crunch point, the place in time and space where the whole Desert ethos came together in a struggle that marked a turning point in history.

CHAPTER FIVE

EL ALAMEIN - SETTING THE SCENE

I n war seemingly unrelated events often come together.

In North Africa it was the timid advance into Egypt by the Italians in 1940 that set the stage for the defence at El Alamein in 1942.

The potential of the Alamein position as a last place to stand was known as far back as 1939, and when the Italians edged up to Sidi Barrani the following year, work was put in hand there. Three boxes were begun: one on the coast around the Alamein railway station; one about the mid-point between the coast and the Qattara depression at a place identified either as Qarat el Abd (low hill of Abd) or Bab el Qattara (Gateway of Qattara); and one on a feature called Naqb Abu Dweis (Pass Abu Dweis; it led to a track that descended into the Qattara Depression). The central strongpoint was officially known as Fortress A, or the Qattara Box, but the New Zealanders who manned it in July corrupted this to Kaponga Box, after a small settlement in New Zealand, and the name stuck. The fortress in the south was simply Fortress B, and though manned in the early stages of July, played no significant part in the battle.

The work begun after the Italian incursion was continued after the failure of the *Battleaxe* campaign in June 1941, but when 30th Corps commander, Norrie, arrived there on 26 June, 1942, with orders to get it into shape while the Eighth Army was still at Mersa Matruh, he found preparations far from complete, and he reported next day that up to ten days would be needed to make it ready. He was to have only three.

Alamein was the only place between Tripoli and the Delta that could not be turned by flank attack, except perhaps by a far-ranging loop right around the Qattara Depression through Siwa Oasis about 250 kilometres to the south. But this was hardly a feasible enterprise. Despite many references to a 'line' there was really no such thing in July, and troops arriving at their positions after hearing this term used on the BBC looked around the flat, open desert, indistinguishable from any other flat, open desert, and wondered. Continual references on the BBC to a line seem to have convinced Rommel that it existed, and it may have been this inadvertent deception, as well as the incorrect information supplied by his intelligence service, that led him to attack in the fortified north when there were large areas of open desert available to him in the south.

When Norrie arrived, there were just the three widely spaced strongpoints, none of them complete, angled across a strip of coastal plain, bounded in the north by the sea and in the south by the Qattara Depression, a massive feature below sea level said to be impassable for an army on wheels, though there were in fact restricted tracks.

Salt marshes lie on the coast, bounded on the landward side by a belt of sand dunes about 200 metres wide. The land then rises about 20 metres to a ridge, along which the coast road runs, and below this to the south is the railway line and that inconsequential yet historic station.

South again of the railway the land rises gradually to a rocky plain marked by a number of depressions and ridges that are little more than gentle humps, except for several high features in the south.

As Rommel moved forward in June 1942, moderately organised chaos reigned as reinforcements moved up and troops already on the spot toiled to strengthen the positions.

My diary:

'June 28 - Moved up main road from Amiriya last night when Jerry was bombing coast, probably Mersa. Dog tired, we camped a few miles from the main road; got a few hours' sleep before breakfast. Moved into defences (Kaponga) and worked like maniacs all day, heat or no heat. No one took seriously the info that we might be fighting here in two or three days - until Brigade advised late this afternoon that Matruh had been evacuated and the enemy was expected in 36 hours.

'June 29 - Went to Brigade last night with Charlie Jones. Bombs were pounding distantly. Planes came over twice while I was at Brigade, dropping neat sticks and rocking the dug-outs.

'We wait; heat is terrific, flies vile.'

It was bad enough sitting in an observation post all day, as I was, searching the hazy distance through binoculars, but for many, particularly troops nearer the coast, these were days of pick-and-shovel work. Mines were being laid, barbed wire fences woven, trenches dug and dug-outs covered, and where the ground was solid rock, compressor drills were chattering in the heat. Trucks were lifting 'surplus' troops, mainly those who could not be made mobile, and carrying them away, and those remaining were being shuffled and shifted.

As trucks carrying Tommies streamed past on 30 June, bottles of beer 'salvaged' from the Naafi at Daba were tossed down to sweating South Africans in the coastal positions, and one man yelled, 'Keep your chins up, mate. The Jerries are coming. They've got tanks as big as battleships.'

Among senior command, there were two generals who questioned whether the Eighth Army could stop Rommel here, and even Auchinleck was unsure, and he was uncertain where everyone was. In fact, as Rommel closed for the kill, Auchinleck's armoured forces were still in enemy territory, shooting it out as both they and their enemy raced neck and neck for points east, and indeed substantial British formations were streaming back from the west and charging through the Alamein defences like a buffalo stampede.

'Throughout 29 June scattered remnants of Eighth Army hurtled past, thickening up the desert haze until it was impossible to recognise friend from foe,' wrote 6th New Zealand Brigade commander, Clifton. ' Next morning, however, the stampeded herd had thinned to a trickle of strays and maimed; by midday for an hour or two nothing moved anywhere in sight of Kaponga - a strange, peaceful interlude before the wolves caught up.'[1]

18th Indian Brigade, slogging away to build a new strong-point, also had the inconvenience of the retreating army flooding through their positions. These stragglers moved on, usually at willing speed, to clog the coast road to the Delta, where a quite independent panic reigned. Even while the enemy was attacking in the north on 1 July, desert refugees continued to stream in through the south.

'Activity fairly intense in the OP,' my diary, written in the Kaponga Box, records for 1 July. 'Saw hundreds of MT (motor transport) milling in all directions ... MT came pouring in late afternoon, huge convoys in desert formation that wandered aimlessly about. Two comprised mainly portees and 25 pounders. Towards evening a colossal mass of trucks came pouring over a ridge line like the Grand National coming home. Excited speculation on their identity was barely quelled by a report from Battalian that they were KRRs (King's Royal Rifles).' And on 2 July: 'The flat in front of us is clear, now, save a few abandoned vehicles. To be precise there are four - a quad, a Morris PU (pick-up), a burned out derelict, and, believe it or not, a steam roller. Morning yielded nothing more exciting than a few of our armoured cars.'

These latter came driving in like lost tourists, and one, I recall, pulled up just outside the wire below our elevated OP, and a languid English voice called, 'I say, old man, is this the Alamein Line?' We assured him it was, and gave him directions for coming inside.

That's how things were as the two armies began their clash. Fortunately the troops knew only what they could see, which was disturbing enough, and in their ignorance of what was going on in high places, they awaited

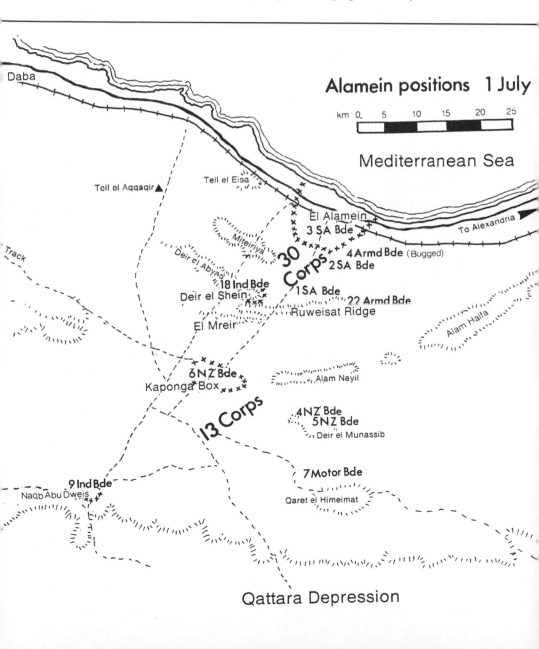

the enemy's arrival with stoic optimism, confident in the belief that although the enemy had had it all his own way so far, he had yet to deal with *them.*

The initial dispositions at Alamein were made by Norrie, but Auchinleck's subordinates never seemed to do things the way he wanted, and Norrie was no exception. When Auchinleck arrived to take command, he decided units should form battle groups based on artillery, with supporting infantry, machine-guns and mortars, all on wheels and able to respond to the fluid fortunes of desert warfare, and to this end he set about rejigging Norrie's work. When Rommel came knocking on the door in the early hours of 1 July, the front was manned mainly by South Africans, Indians and New Zealanders, some of whom were mobile, many of whom were not. The Indian units included troops from the United Kingdom, and the armour, entirely from Britain, was shuffling into place.

At the seaward end, where the cool Mediterranean contrasts with the heat of the Desert, were the South Africans, angry at the loss of their 2nd Division in Tobruk and sensitive to criticism because of it, and anxious because the Alamein Box, which was assigned to the 3rd Brigade of their 1st Division, was more or less a half-scale Tobruk, complete with undefended rear. The 1st Division had been at the northern end of the Gazala line during the June battle there, and had been withdrawn as Rommel's offensive rolled up the line from the south. Their commander, Dan Pienaar, was a general of prickly personality and an unguarded tongue that earned him displeasure from above and suspicion of wobbly resolve from his peers.

Pienaar was among those overwhelmed by the pace of events and the menacing stride of the enemy, and his lack of confidence in the Alamein positions was reinforced by unhappy memories not just of Tobruk but also other fortified boxes. Stories have been told of his wanting to pull out and retire and of having to be told to hold his ground, but the view of the 30th Corps commander, Norrie, was that Pienaar was simply saying the best place to fight was behind the Suez Canal. His outspokeness, according to Norrie, was 'a considerable source of embarrassment, both to the Commander-in-Chief and to myself', but the mood passed. One of Pienaar's senior officers, Major-General F.H. Theron, General Officer Administration, found him on 30 June to be 'pessimistic about the result, bitter about our reverses, but indominitable in spirit and determined to fight. I told him about help which was coming and felt that when I left him he had considerably cheered up'.[2]

According to his biography, Pienaar mixed with his troops, telling them, 'We've just got to win', and he is reported as telling an American war correspondent: 'You can quote me for this. Rommel will not get the Alexandra naval base; he will not get the Suez Canal; he will never dine in Cairo unless as a tourist after the war.'[3]

Of course generals do not disclose to the public their inner concerns, and the South Africans were truly not happy with their lot in the Alamein box. Norrie had intended to man it with the whole division, the formation for which it had been designed, but Auchinleck reduced the force to one brigade, giving it the support of a British medium machine-gun group, three extra companies of infantry and some extra artillery. The other two

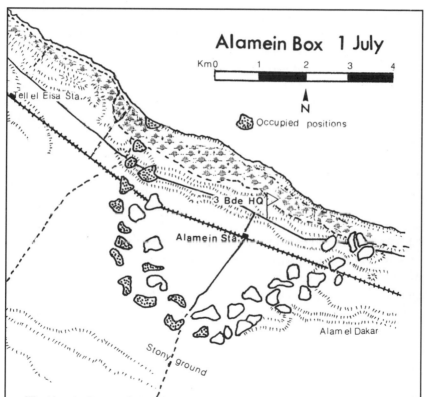

The Alamein Box was designed for a division. The South Africans had to man it with a brigade plus three extra companies, and they were able to occupy strongpoints only on the west and south faces. However, wire and minefields, not shown in this map, surrounded the box.

brigades were formed into battle groups and stationed in the open desert.

The box was a semi-circular position with its coastal base about 12 kilometres across and a circumference, coast-to-coast, of about 25 kilometres. When the South Africans moved in they found pill boxes and weapon positions concreted and roofed, but dug-outs and shelters were open to the sky and infested with fleas, which had the good sense to disappear during the first few days of battle. The wire was incomplete and there were no minefields. Thousands of mines had to be laid in just a few days, many of them in rocky ground, new fire positions had to be dug and open positions covered.

When they put aside shovels for weapons they were able to man only some of the 36 prepared positions, leaving the eastern face undefended. And despite the now substantial defences, the South Africans said there was a serious 'soft spot' in the south-west quarter, and they considered the box to be poorly placed, overlooked as it was by the high ground of Tell el Eisa to the west and two trig points five kilometres away to the south west.

Auchinleck put the 3rd South African Brigade in the box; and reasoning that the enemy would prefer to skirt around the defences, he put the 1st and 2nd Brigades, converted to battle groups and reinforced with extra artillery, into positions outside the box, in such a way that an enemy force trying to pass that way would be caught in a crescent of fire.

The South Africans' immediate neighbour to the south was the 18th Indian Brigade. Placed under South African command, it was given the task of building a new strong-point at Deir el Shein, a depression seven kilometres south west of the Alamein Box and very close to the western tip of Ruweisat Ridge. It was chosen because it was the only place where digging was possible. Ruweisat Ridge, which would have been better tactically, was mainly solid rock. And even the Deir el Shein position was not without its digging problems.

As originally conceived there was nothing but open desert in this Alamein 'Line' between the Alamein Box and Kaponga Box 15 kilometres to the south, and Norrie decided that, because he lacked mobile units, there should be an intermediate strong-point. It was he who chose Deir el Shein, a name that should be honoured in the history of the Second World War as the site of the battle that changed the course of history.

The 18th Indian Brigade, part of the 8th Indian Division, was in Iraq when the call came to move to Alamein. An army commander can only have seen them the frailest of weak reeds as they were largely inexperienced, and two of its battalions - the two, as it happened, that were to take the main weight of the German attack in the coming battle - had never heard a shot fired in anger. These were the 2/5th Essex Regiment, the English component of the brigade, and the 2/3rd Ghurka Rifles. More than this, the brigade had only a temporary commander, Lieutenant-Colonel C.R. Gray, and the brigade major had just been posted to his task after a year in a base job. Such was the formation that the Eighth Army, all unknowing, was to place at the very point where Rommel would strike with his panzers.

On the brigade's arrival, Norrie could think of nothing it could do, and said that, anyway, with no transport, carriers, anti-tank guns, artillery or ammunition there wasn't much it could do. But 24 hours later the situation was reversed with the arrival at 7.00am on 28 June of a staff officer with orders for the brigade to move to Deir el Shein. Two hours later the transport of the Essex and 4/11 Sikhs began to arrive, and all that day and far into the night a shuttle moved troops to their destination. By midnight they were all there, and at first light on 29 July they found themselves at an inconsequential hollow in the desert that the map identified as Deir el Shein.

There was nothing here; it was just a wilderness. The map said the terrain was 'very stony' and 'sand and stone'. The depression itself was described by a later Court of Inquiry as 'a sort of saucer with good OPs on the edges' - rather like Kaponga. Here this inexperienced, ill-equipped brigade was to make its stand.

The men sweated through the first day and far into the night, digging, laying mines and erecting wire, pestered by flies and occasionally blitzed by enemy aircraft. The South Africans, who were busy themselves, lent a hand, bringing over air compressors to chisel out rock.

Plenty of wire was supplied, and they encircled an ovoid-shaped box roughly 4,000 metres long and 2,000 metres wide, with a double dannert fence on the west face, facing the enemy's expected line of attack. Mines were a problem and came forward more slowly than they could be laid, and there were three different types, often supplied without fuses, and there was no sapper officer on hand to assist. However, some help came from the New Zealanders, who, though having difficulties of their own, sent up 5,000 mines and some South African sappers who had been intercepted near Kaponga Box as they drove in from the west.

Arming the box was another problem. When the 18th arrived there wasn't a gun to be seen, but eventually the commander of the 121st Field

Regiment, the brigade's own artillery unit, turned up, and after a reconnaissance, sited 18 25-pounders, 16 six-pounders and 20 two-pounders.
There was insufficient time to dig all these in. On the afternoon of 30
July, the day before the battle began, seven Matildas rumbled up to add
the weight of their two- pounders and machine-guns to the defence. The
tanks and some of the guns were manned by scratch crews only.

When 1 July dawned the work was still incomplete, and there was even
a 100-metre gap on the south-west face where no mines had been laid, and
there were other gaps at junctions of sub-units. The men of the brigade
had been working 20 hours a day, and during the previous night officers
had been complying with an army order to reorganise into battle groups.
The first enemy shells found a mass of soft-skinned transport standing
about waiting to carry away surplus troops. But at least the brigade had all
four faces of the box manned - the forward face by the Sikhs, the north and
north-east by the Essex, the south-east by the Gurkhas, and the south-west
by an engineers' unit, the 66th Field Company.

And where were the tanks to help the South Africans and Indians?

Early on the morning of 1 July, as the enemy closed in, 1st Armoured
Division materialised from the desert, but it was in a sorry state. Its 4th
Brigade, which had been on the move since moon up at 4.00am, had been
struggling through soft sand that sucked down the heavy wheeled B echelon vehicles, and when soon after first light it took up battle positions, it
found itself again in a sea of soft sand.

'Much difficulty was experienced in getting guns into position,' the
war diary reports. 'It was obvious in the event of an attack developing, guns
could not be moved and that they would have to fight it out in this position.'

They remained glued here in a position from which there could be no
withdrawal, and that night they wearily pulled themselves out again and
moved south to firmer ground.

The other brigade, the 22nd, was mobile but had only 18 runners, and
needed time to collect itself.

After moving and fighting for three days and nights, the men of both
brigades were exhausted, and their tanks and other vehicles creaked
along like cripples.

'All RHQ tanks now crocks,' the 6th Royal Tank Regiment war diary
notes cryptically.

The division had no accurate information about who was where - not that anyone did - and even if they had, their ability to find anyone would have been restricted by the fact that the only maps available to them were on a scale of 1:500,000, little better than a school atlas. The divisional commander, Lumsden, had received no orders - and that's hardly surprising - so he posted his two brigades on Ruweisat Ridge. That, at least, is what he told the Court of Inquiry, but 4th Brigade's war diary makes it plain that it was unable to reach that destination until first light on 2 July.

Only the much-jaded 22nd was on the move while the 4th languished in the sand, its guns in an enforced last ditch position.

Though together they made up little more than a division, the South Africans and Indians, with 1st Armoured Division, for what it was worth on that first day, comprised 30th Corps under Norrie. To the south lay Gott's 13th Corps in what was substantially undefended open country.

The nearest southern neighbour to the Indians was the 2nd New Zealand Division in Kaponga Box and behind it.

When the Eighth Army began to crumble in Cyrenaica in June the New Zealanders were scattered across Syria, where they had been exercising and preparing fortifications against the possibility of a German invasion of the Middle East through Russia.

Like a river drawing from its tributaries, the division's many parts began flowing in from villages, outposts and work sites to stream down the central road that formed a black bitumen strip through Syria, Palestine and the Sinai Desert, thence across the Suez Canal and eastern Egypt, through crowded Cairo streets and on to the Western Desert. A few formations travelled by train, covering the 1,500 kilometres in two days. The winding snake of motor vehicles, which continued day after day as the three brigades and divisional units followed each other down the road, took just over four days.

4th and 5th Brigades drove straight up to Mersa Matruh, where Ritchie, who then still commanded the Eighth Army, planned to make the last stand before Cairo. Here Freyberg resisted an army plan to shut up his division in the Matruh Box, and he took it into the open desert, where during the ensuing battle at Minqar Qaim it was surrounded, broke free, and returned to a position just behind the Kaponga Box, where the 6th NZ Brigade was in residence. Freyberg was wounded in the fighting and command passed temporarily to Brigadier Inglis, promoted to major-general. So like the Indians, the New Zealanders were to have a temporary commander in the coming battle.

6th New Zealand Brigade, meanwhile, had been moved into Kaponga Box on borrowed wheels, which had dropped the men and left, carrying away Egyptian labourers who had been working there and who were more than anxious to be gone. Kaponga was an oyster-shaped depression on elevated ground so that while the centre was effectively concealed from prying eyes on the outside, the perimeter was higher than the surrounding terrain, a great advantage to men in weapon pits and observation posts.

Unlike the luckless 18th Indian Brigade, the 6th NZ Brigade began with the advantage of a partly built fortress, and with its three battalions and one field company of engineers, was able to man all four faces. But all was not well. To begin with, minefields had to be laid, and the brigade had no guns, its own having been taken away for use elsewhere - borrowing and lending was common practice in the make and mend of Alamein. And of course, having no transport it was a static unit enclosed within a box that could easily be surrounded, and able to defend itself with little more than small arms and mortars.

An indignant Inglis went off to see Auchinleck, and as he later told the wounded Freyberg in a letter, 'I'm afraid I may have called a spade a bloody shovel. But it had its effect. The C-in-C was very nice about it, and with his personal say so I got 6th Brigade fixed up with the transport and anti-tank guns. Mid-East ran out of two-pounders so I cajoled 16 more six-pounders out of them in lieu.'

The division now had 65 six-pounders, Inglis reported, and the field artillery had its complement of guns.

The ebullient 6th Brigade commander, Clifton, meanwhile had found another source of supply. Barrel Track, one of the many desert tracks, ran past the northern face of Kaponga Box, and here Norrie had set up a post to collect and direct stragglers as they came in from the cold. Clifton put out a telephone line to this post, and this contact yielded a detachment of the 46th Medium Artillery, with three 4.5 inch guns - little enough, but it was something to be going on with. Another arrival at the post was the 11th South African Field Company carrying 10,000 mines which, the officer in charge of the post reported, 'they refuse to give up except to someone who is willing to fight'. Clifton, more than willing, took 5,000 mines and some sappers and sent the rest up to the Indians in Deir el Shein.

So by the morning of 1 July, the 6th NZ Brigade was strongly established in Kaponga, with the rest of the division close at hand in Deir el Munassib, and well able if called on to move in any direction.

South west of Kaponga was more empty desert, 22 kilometres of it, covered only by 7th Motor Brigade with a squadron from the 4th South African Armoured Car Regiment, but on the eve of battle it was withdrawn to Qarat el Himeimat, a raised feature due south of Deir el Munassib.

And finally, on that promontory called Naqb Abu Dweis on the lip of the Qattara depression was the 9th Indian Brigade, part of the 5th Indian Division, another remnant. The brigade had few guns and little water, and at the time no one thought it had a chance of stopping anything more menacing than a troop of Boy Scouts. As the official New Zealand historian saw it, it was 'a hostage of fortune in its isolation ...'[4]

When the battle began, the New Zealanders were the strongest force both in numbers and morale. Despite casualties suffered in their fighting withdrawal, they were a complete division, except for a few companies sent back to base, concentrated in the central area, with one brigade forward and two in reserve. After a spell of nearly six months in Syria, they were fighting fit and secure in their own self-confidence.

Auchinleck wanted the New Zealanders, too, to convert to battle groups, and when Inglis called on him to protest about the plight of his 6th Brigade, Auchinleck gave him an order to this effect. Inglis replied that he regretted it was an order with which he must refuse to comply.

'The expected explosion did not follow,' he said after the war. 'I was merely asked why I objected and what I proposed to do. The reason was that if I broke up the division and dispersed it over a wide front I had about as much chance of stopping Rommel as a piece of tissue paper would have had; and my intention was to keep the division concentrated in as central position as possible so that it could fight if it were attacked and could have at the enemy if the latter tried to bypass us.'[5]

Inglis, of course, was well aware that Freyberg had refused to accept a similar order when the division had been at Minqar Qaim.

This minor skirmish was only one of the things that troubled the New Zealanders. Pienaar's abrasive voice was just one of a small chorus of doom, and these voices sang a dirge to the harassed Inglis and a surprised 5th NZ Brigade commander, Kippenberger.

After his meeting with Auchinleck, Inglis, on the C-in-C's instructions, was given a briefing by Dorman Smith.

'This army,' he told Inglis, 'is the only effective fighting force the C-in-C has and he is determined not to lose it whatever happens. If it cannot stay here, he will withdraw to the Delta and fight there, and if necessary, in Sinai and Palestine. I am now considering whether I should advise him to withdraw on Alexandria or on Cairo or partly on one and partly on the other.'[6]

An incredulous Inglis replied bluntly that all the Eighth Army had to do was face west and fight. He considered the existence of the army useless if it did not hold Egypt and the Suez Canal. The Alamein position, he said, must be the limit of its withdrawal.

'These forthright views were not well received,' the official New Zealand war history quotes him as saying. 'Dorman Smith said they were disrespectful to the Commander-in-Chief.'[7]

They did not part harmoniously.

Inglis had another concern at this time. He was aware of the flap going on in Cairo, where headquarters units were preparing for the possibility of Rommel's arrival by burning secret documents, and he wanted to ensure that his own base units at Maadi, just out of Cairo, weren't caught up in the panic. With Auchinleck's permission he departed late at night on 28 June, leaving an instruction that his staff, then sleeping, should be told in the morning where he had gone. For some reason the message was not passed on, and a small comedy of errors developed that led Kippenberger into an alarming conversation with the 13th Corps commander, Gott.

As he tells it in *Infantry Brigadier*, Kippenberger was called by Division early on 29 June and told Inglis had disappeared, and that he was to come up and take command. At Division, Kippenberger pondered the mystery of Inglis's disappearance with the GSO1, Gentry, and then decided he had better see Gott. A pessimistic Gott came out of his armoured command vehicle to meet him, took him a few metres away from the vehicle, and said, 'Inglis has gone to Cairo.' And with this he handed Kippenberger a note from Corbett, Auchinleck's Chief of Staff in Cairo.

'I remember clearly the opening sentence: "The Chief has decided to save the Eighth Army,"' Kippenberger wrote.

The note went on to say the South Africans would retire through Alexandria and the rest of the army down the desert road and through Cairo. Kippenberger asked Gott what the first sentence meant.

'It means what it says,' Gott replied. 'He means to save the Field Army.'

Gott went on to explain that a general retirement and the evacuation of Egypt was being considered, and that Inglis had gone to Cairo to arrange for the evacuation of the New Zealand rear installations and hospitals. He supposed the New Zealanders would go home.

Kippenberger protested that the New Zealanders were perfectly fit to fight and that it was criminal to give up Egypt to 25,000 German troops and a hundred tanks (disregarding the Italians), and lose as helpless prisoners of war perhaps 200,000 base troops. 'Straffer (Gott) replied sadly that the New Zealand Division was battleworthy but very few other people were, and he feared the worst,' Kippenberger says.

As the records show, the figures Kippenberger used, taken from the latest intelligence summary, were wildly inflated, and the Eighth Army was seemingly considering buckling to perhaps 3,000 to 4,000 Germans and 55 of their tanks. But of course judgements can be made only in the light of knowledge at the time.

'I returned to Division and told Gentry of this unpleasant conversation,' Kippenberger goes on. 'We said nothing to anyone else and were both sorely perplexed and depressed. In the evening a provisional order for retirement arrived from 13th Corps. It certainly envisaged the abandonment of Egypt.'[8]

And it's true that Eighth Army operational orders 86, 87 and 88 advised that if the enemy broke through, the army would, on receipt of the codeword Brixworth, retire by specified routes to Wadi Natrun to harass him as he headed for Cairo and Alexandria. Inglis came back on the afternoon of 30 June, having battled his way against the easterly flowing tide of fleeing army survivors, to report a 'prodigious flap' was taking place in Cairo.

What was the truth of all this? Dorman Smith told Inglis only that he was considering whether to advise Auchinleck to retire - not an indicator of confidence, and not a disclosure calculated to inspire high fighting morale, but still no more than an idea in the mind. The Corbett note, as Kippenberger remembered it, was vague to say the least, and Gott appears to have put his own interpretation on it. Certainly he misunderstood the reason for Inglis's quick trip to Cairo and to have placed his own interpretation on that.

'Gott was a fine fighter,' Auchinleck is quoted as saying by Parkinson in *The Auk*, 'but I don't really think he had a lot of brains. He was undoubtedly tired. I was worried about him as a matter of fact. I was ready to retire if I had to - but I never intended to retire.'[9]

The precautionary order to retire originated not with Auchinleck but with Corbett, and an angry Dorman Smith says he did not see it before it went out or he would have stopped it.

Corbett had not spoken with Auchinleck since he left for the Desert, and, having no knowledge of his changed thinking, presumably believed further withdrawal a real possibility.

In the circumstances he would naturally have felt that something should be put in place to facilitate an orderly retreat.

However that might be, ambivalence rather than resolution seems to have marked upper echelon thinking. Auchinleck, in fact, had his doubt about whether the Eighth Army could stop Rommel, and he sent back the 10th Corps commander, Holmes, whose corps now hardly existed, to organise the defence of the Delta.

Some years later, interviewed on television by Richard Dimbleby, he branded as 'absolute rubbish' a statement by Montgomery that it had been his intention to pull back through the Nile, but agreed that he did have a plan of withdrawal. If the Eighth Army had had to withdraw from Alamein, he said it had been his intention to 'retreat as an army', and in an article in Picture Post in 1953 he spelt out his plans to deny the enemy the Nile bridges.

It's true that a separation of the army, part to retreat up the Nile, part to withdraw to the east, was on the cards. And Auchinleck's memory seems to have overlooked the serious difficulties in this plan, code-named Colonial. The reconnaissance report for the southward move was not submitted until 20 July, and this showed that the intricate pattern of poor roads and bridges among the Nile waterways would have been a great impediment to movement, and this problem would have been exacerbated by the fact that many roads and bridges were poorly maintained. The use of camels and donkeys to supplement motor transport was suggested, while a small flotilla of river craft could operate on the Nile. Villagers would be urged to stay in their homes to avoid clutter on the roads, but what a wild hope that was! Besides this, there was nothing to stop the enemy advancing in the open desert west of the Nile. All things considered, any withdrawal up the Nile in a confusion of lorries, camels, donkeys and exciteable Egyptians must be considered fanciful in its conception and catastrophic in its execution. The scheme sounds more like a film script for a farce.

If the Alamein positions had collapsed, it is likely that so, too, would have the army. And what would have happened to the great army of base troops?

Two other formations were close at hand to reinforce Auchinleck's tiny army. The 50th (Northumbrian) Division, or at any rate its two surviving brigades, was 48 kilometres to the rear reorganising into eight-gun battle groups, and these were to move up quickly to play their part in the coming battle. The 50th had seen hard fighting in the Gazala battles, and its 150th Brigade had been swallowed up in one of Rommel's more profitable coups. Then at Mersa Matruh the 50th had been involved in the chaotic break out on the night of 28 June and suffered some disintegration as a result. One of the survivors, 69th Brigade, was to appear, rebuilt, later in July, and with a composite Durham Light Infantry regiment formed from its sister brigade, the 151st, strike the final blow in the month's fighting.

Further back still, helping with the preparations of the Delta defences, was the 9th Australian Division, another recent arrival from Syria. It was the 9th that had borne the main weight of the Tobruk siege the previous year, although, like all military formations, it had absorbed many rein-forcements and its members were not all veterans. Though it was not fully equipped for the Desert, it was a complete and coherent division, and it certainly made an impact as it drove through the streets of Cairo on its arrival from Syria. The Australian war correspondent Kenneth Slessor, who rushed out to see them pass, described 'lines of lorries and trucks loaded with Australians, stripped to the waist, dark brown with sun, grinning and shouting'. They were, he said, the 'toughest and fittest' fighting men he had seen.

'The crowds waved and yelled in surprise, and there was a buzz of excitement everywhere and a genuine stimulus to the city's questionable morale,' he wrote.[10]

Though they were sent first to rear positions, Auchinleck was soon to call them forward to play a significant role in the July struggle.

On the other side of the hill there was no uncertainty though there was some misunderstanding. Rommel rode with his army towards Alamein, hammered from the air by Desert Air Force and harassed on the ground by the tanks of the 1st Armoured Division. His mind was quite clear on what he wanted to do - crash through the Alamein positions before the Eighth Army could collect itself. So confident was he that while he was still at Mersa Matruh he set up a small scratch force under Captain Briel and ordered him to drive to Alexandria, presumably expecting him to be able to weave unnoticed or at any rate unmolested through the confusion of the fleeing Eighth Army.

'Tomorrow we'll have coffee in Cairo,' Rommel told him.[11]

Alas, Briel's exhausted men fell asleep, or rather fell unconscious, according to Heckman in his *Rommel's War in Africa.* Human flesh is capable of just so much effort. It was a pointer to things to come.

Rommel was driven by two convictions. The first was that Auchinleck could reinforce his army quicker than he could. The second was his guiding principle that when you've got an enemy on the run you keep going. He was convinced that he had only to break through the defences into the Eighth Army's rear and panic would set in, sending the whole army scrambling back to the Delta. He was probably right and if his army had been stronger he might have done it.

CHAPTER SIX

25-30 JUNE - RAISING THE CURTAIN

To Auchinleck, newly self-appointed commander of the Eighth Army, the advancing Germans must have seemed the nearest thing he knew to the Mongol hordes. We who are blessed with the near omniscience of retrospection might see some aspects of the Alamein struggle as farce, but Auchinleck knew only what his intelligence service told him, and this was that Rommel could have as many as 30,000 German troops and 200 tanks, rather than the 2,000 to 3,000 men, 55 tanks and 15 armoured cars of reality. Auchinleck saw a German army that in the last five weeks had smashed a British army much larger than itself, engulfed the Tobruk 'bastion' in a day, and pursued at speed the fleeing remnants of the Eighth Army. Standing by the roadside as a morale-boosting gesture he saw for himself his tattered troops heading east in a multitudinous confusion of motor vehicles, intent on escaping from the Hun. Auchinleck knew he had to stop Rommel dead.

He took up his command at Mersa Matruh on 25 June convinced that a fixed line would be too brittle. He believed, too, that box defences invited the enemy to enclose and capture their occupants. Whatever thoughts he might have had about an Alamein 'line,' he was now resolved that the way to meet a mobile enemy was with mobile defence. Apart from the air force, his most potent weapon against Rommel and his panzers was the 25-pounder field gun, and he decided to break his formations into battle groups, strong in guns and with minimal infantry. He had, in any case, too few vehicles to put his whole army on wheels, and if his tactics were to be mobile, everyone who could not be accommodated would have to be sent back to Alamein or the Delta. Auchinleck intended that these battle groups would pound and plunder as the enemy came abreast, holding his own surviving 159 tanks, which he thought were outnum-bered, until an advantageous situation offered, and meantime shooting up everything in sight.

The decision to move to mobility was in part a response to the dispositions he inherited from Ritchie. The Eighth Army had been split between its two corps, with 10th Corps in the north pressed against the coast, and 13th Corps inland, separated from the 10th by 32 kilometres of desert covered only by two frail mobile columns. It was an open invitation to Rommel to slice through the middle.

But the genesis of Auchinleck's new policy was a discussion with Dorman Smith as they sat on the floor of a Boston bomber on their way to their appointment with history on 25 June - the assumption of command of the Eighth Army. According to Dorman Smith, by the time they stepped off the plane a whole range of tactics had been decided.

First, there would be centralisation of artillery control, right up to army level.

Armour should be regrouped to concentrate the Grants, and in battle the Grants should always have maximum artillery support and should not be sent beyond range of the guns. The lighter tanks - the Honeys and Crusaders - should be regrouped in the 7th Armoured Division, which would be called the 7th Light Armoured Division and used for flank protection. The effect of this would be to make the 1st Armoured Division the primary tank force.

Divisions and corps should be prepared to move to each other's aid as necessary and not stand idly by while their neighbour was carved up.

Infantry divisions and corps should not be placed in isolated boxes, and in defence, brigades should not be more than 10,000 yards apart, less if possible.

When Rommel had been halted, he should be forced to bring forward his Italians, who should then be attacked, forcing Rommel to defend them rather than attack the Eighth Army.

The forces should be kept fluid and moved against Rommel as opportunity offered, thus regaining the initiative for the Eighth Army.

And finally, new minefields should not protect the enemy as well as the Eighth Army, as had happened at Gazala.

All these policies were to be put into practice in the coming month, and with some important exceptions achieved their intentions. To the extent that these were Dorman Smith's ideas - and it must be supposed that they were - the coming battle belonged to him.

But it did not begin auspiciously. Trying to reorganise an army and infuse it with new ideas when it can already feel the hot breath of the pursuer was a miracle beyond Auchinleck's powers and the resilience, such as it was, of his formations, not to mention the capabilities of his signal services.

Before there was any possibility of creating Auchinleck's new mobile army, Rommel struck. 90th Light Division and 21st Panzer Division, brushing aside Leathercol and Gleecol (two mobile columns), and executing a kind of 'Prince of Wales Feathers' movement, 90th Light turning north to the coast to enclose 10th Corps, and 21st Panzer south to encircle 13th Corps. 15th Panzer, meanwhile, made a more direct approach on 13th Corps from the west. Eighth Army reacted like a trapped tiger.

The New Zealanders were attacked from three sides on 27 June, and Freyberg wounded. After much to-ing and fro-ing of discussion between Division and Corps in which the customary confusion was an element, the New Zealanders broke out that night by charging through the lines of

The initial intention was to try to stop the Axis advance at Mersa Matruh, first in static defence, then, after Auchinleck took direct command, in mobile fighting. However, Rommel broke through and encircled Eighth Army, and 50th Division and 2nd New Zealand Division escaped only by breaking through the German positions at night. Other formations also withdrew to reassemble at Alamein, where Rommel tried a similar encircling movement.

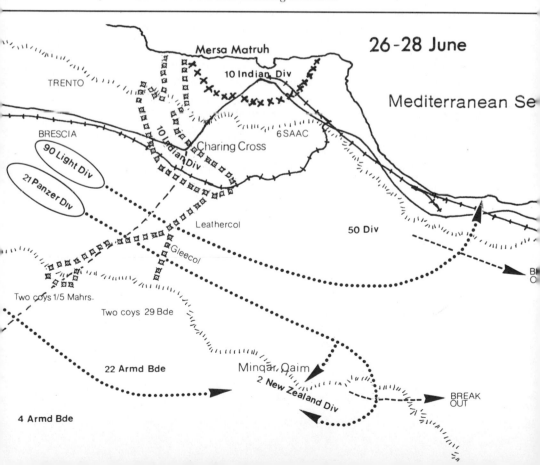

21st Panzer with bayonet, Bren gun and grenade. Motor transport streamed through the gap torn by the infantry, and the division sped east to take up a new position behind the third brigade of the division, the 6th, which was in Kaponga Box. Although the New Zealanders were not the only troops to break out, their action aroused strong passions on the German side.

'There was a somewhat whimsical idea that the division should have recognised that it was trapped, and that it had not played the game fairly in depriving Afrika Korps of the victory the Korps had arranged to garner next morning,' the official New Zealand historian wrote.[1]

Moreover, there were allegations that the international laws of warfare had been broken, and Berlin Radio spoke bitterly of 'Freyberg's Butchers', and New Zealand prisoners of war were singled out for harsh treatment. However, there was some confusion among the Germans about who was who, because when the 10th Corps, who had been left in the lurch by the departure of 13th Corps, broke through the 90th Light the following night, Rommel, who found himself in the thick of things, thought *they* were New Zealanders.

'The firing between my forces and the New Zealanders grew to an extraordinary pitch and my headquarters was soon ringed with burning vehicles, making it a target for continuous enemy fire,' he wrote. 'I soon had enough of this and ordered headquarters staff to withdraw to the south-east. One can scarcely conceive of the confusion that reigned that night. It was pitch dark and impossible to see one's hand before one's eyes. The RAF bombed their own troops, and, with tracer flying in all directions, German units fired on each other.'[2]

10th Corps, though free, was shattered in that engagement, and its fragments scattered over the Desert, taking their place among the waifs and strays who came rushing back through the Alamein positions.

There followed a wild tumbling back to Alamein with pursuer and pursued mixed up in a confusion made worse by the dust thrown up by sandstorms, wheels and tank tracks, and complicated by the fact that 85 per cent of Rommel's motor transport was British. Luckless Eighth Army stragglers seeking a ride sometimes found transport columns less than hospitable, and Italian machine-gunners peppered Rommel's convoy in the mistaken belief that it was British.

7th Motor Brigade, with 4th South African Armoured Cars, was supposed to be covering the British retreat, but it had no clear idea of the positions of either friend or foe.

The British armour had better luck and caused the enemy grave discomfort. It had two rewarding jousts with the Italian XX Corps, and wiped out the remaining 30 tanks of Littorio Armoured Division and left it with only six guns. But the British armour's most telling blow came when 4th and 22nd Brigades encountered Afrika Korps late on the afternoon of 30 June as the panzers were preparing to assemble south west of Tell al Aqqaqir for its assault the following day. A sandstorm was raging at the time, and the 4th Brigade commander, Fisher, felt the hour's engagement had been inconclusive, but it sorely troubled Afrika Korps, whose headquarters came under heavy artillery fire, and in all the chaos Colonel Bayerlein, Rommel's Chief of Staff, drove right through the British tank columns. Contact between the two groups was finally lost in the swirling sand.

But if the clash had concerned Afrika Korps, it also caused 1st Armoured Division trouble. Driven off course during the encounters, its 4th Brigade, unwilling to face the hazard of unknown minefields around Alamein or being mistaken in the dark for enemy, and with some of its vehicles caught in soft sand, laagered at Tell el Aqqaqir, just a few kilometres south east of 90th Light and actually at the place where Afrika Korps was to assemble at dawn. Afrika Korp's administration officer was startled just before first light on 1 July to find 30 tanks, with artillery, exactly on the spot for which the panzers were heading. However, after an exhausting night towing out vehicles and guns from the clinging embrace of sand, the brigade moved on, following a course parallel with that of 90th Light, which was moving up for attack. Skirting the southern boundary of the Alamein Box, the hapless 4th, with its caravan of tanks, trucks and guns, attracted artillery fire and lost some of its soft transport to shells before 6th South African Armoured Cars were able to convince the South African gunners that they were shooting at friends. It was the beginning of a bad day. The brigade pushed on to a position north east of the 2nd South African Brigade, where it ran into more soft sand that immobilised it during the first critical day of battle, though it was able to turn its guns to face the enemy.

22nd Armoured Brigade fared better. It spent the night south of the Alamein Box, and in the morning was able to move east to a position near the 1st South African Brigade. But though safely home, it needed time to rest, rearm, refuel and reorganise.

7th Motor Brigade, meanwhile, was causing more trouble for the Italians as it fought its way back east. Early on 30 June XX Corps, made up of the Italians' two armoured divisions, Ariete and Littorio, and the motorised Trieste Division, reported that an enemy attack had thrown it into confusion, and soon after it signalled that a fresh enemy force blocked its way and that attack was now hopeless. An angry Rommel signalled, 'I demand that your corps should carry out the attack, destroy the enemy, and reach its objective. The enemy is under orders to withdraw.' His fury must have continued to smoulder, because an hour later he fired off another message that in the original German was deliberately offensive to the Italians. It read: 'Trust your corps will now find itself able to cope with so contemptible an enemy.' It would not be long before similar imperatives would be directed, without the insult, to German units.

Clearly, as the two armies tumbled eastwards, anxiety reigned among the upper echelons of the defenders, frustration among the attackers.

The Italians, as it happened, were the first to breast up to the Alamein defences. South African sappers were closing the last gap in the defences of the box around midday on 30 June when the 7th Bersaglieri Regiment was sighted heading for the centre of positions held by the Rand Light Infantry. Trento Division came up on the enemy right, and the first shells came over at 12.35pm while the South Africans were still laying mines. Mines were quickly laid along the railway line, which was then blown up by the infantry, and as the 20th Field Battery of the rearguard came into the box, British guns replied to the Italian barrage, and throughout the afternoon the exchange continued.

By the evening of 30 June the Eighth Army, the armour excepted, was established in these now famous last ditch defences. The troops, according to Churchill, were 'amazed rather than depressed'.[3] Barely pausing for breath, Rommel hurled his first attack on this new obstacle to his advance, and the Battle of Egypt was on.

PART TWO

THE BATTLE

CHAPTER SEVEN

1 JULY - THE DAY THAT CHANGED THE WAR

The trucks of Rommel's 90th Light Division, growling through the pre-dawn dark into the teeth of a sandstorm, were spread across the landscape in desert formation, rolling forward cautiously, gears whining as drivers chopped and changed and peered with glazed eyes at the smudged outline of the vehicle ahead. Lorries on either side were occasional ghosts as the blind led the blind towards one of the crucial battles of history. Ahead somewhere was a guide vehicle in which someone who presumably knew where he was going was holding course with the aid of the luminescent disc of a prismatic compass, aiming the division like a slow motion projectile at a supposed gap in these last defence positions of the Eighth Army. Soon after first light they should be through and turning north to imprison the South Africans in their box, as they had done at Tobruk and again at Mersa Matruh, creating panic and promoting flight in the rest of the army.

The men jostled together as the vehicles bounced and swayed. The survivors of the past five weeks of battle and pursuit, they were tired almost beyond enduring. After the torrid days of Gazala, where they had scraped through by the skin of their teeth, there was the chase along the coast, and at Mersa Matruh there had been that explosive break-out at night by the encircled British, devastating in its suddenness, rousing men from sleep to face fire and bayonet. Sleep ... precious little time for that, and they had dozed as opportunity offered, night and day. There had been no time to refresh the mind or refurbish the spirit as companions had fallen to enemy fire or to the bombs of the droning squadrons, which had harassed their columns without ceasing.

They had been given a glimpse of the cool, cobalt Mediterranean on 29 June, the day before the assembly for the attack, and it seemed there might even be time to swim and sleep, but a hastening Rommel abruptly summoned them back to duty.

'Immediately after (Mersa Matruh) has been taken by storm the C-in-C appears at Battle Group Marcks and orders: No more vehicles will move to the west, everybody has to be ready for the attack on El Daba in the east,' says 90th Light's war diary for 29 June.

They got what rest they could as motor trucks carried them east along the coast road, not halting until midnight. Then at dawn they were up again, in high spirits in spite of their fatigue, buoyed along by the prospect of victory at last and arrival in triumph at Cairo or Alexandria, where there would be time to savour success and indulge the flesh. They were sobered by British bombs that came whistling down as their convoy threaded its way east along the bitumen strip of the coast road. A cluster engulfed divisional headquarters, and nine vehicles burned, among them a wireless van and three ammunition lorries. As they turned south into the desert they ground their way through difficult going while the wind whipped up the sand in swirling clouds that plastered sweating skin and clogged nose and ears. In the early afternoon they halted and took up outpost positions while they awaited the arrival of their Italian partners, who were also feeling Rommel's whip.

The Italians had their own problems. XX Corps, which had been halted by 7th Motor Brigade, was unmoved by Rommel's anger. Littorio Division, shaken by its encounter with the 1st Armoured Division, had been given the hurry along, too, with a message from Rommel conveying the false information that Afrika Korps was destroying the enemy as he retreated. 'Division must reach assembly area under all circumstances,' Rommel signalled the Italians.

In fact Afrika Korps was in strife, too. Bad going and the attentions of the 1st Armoured Division had consumed both time and fuel as it struggled towards a feint position deep in the desert. Its instructions were to move south east during the hours of daylight on 30 June as though to attack the south of the Alamein positions, and then move north during the night to make a parallel thrust with 90th Light, much as had happened at Mersa Matruh.

It was an inauspicious start. Basing his plans on inaccurate information, Rommel was hoping to drive through the Alamein positions without too much difficulty. Aerial reconnaissance had shown up only the Alamein and Kaponga strongpoints, but his intelligence also reported an Indian force in Deir el Abyad, a short distance in advance of the real strongpoint in Deir el Shein. He understood the Alamein Box to be manned by the 50th Division, which had actually fallen back to the rear to reorganise. He knew the New Zealanders held the Kaponga Box, but he had a firm idea

Basing his plans on a belief that he had only to bypass the Alamein Box and a supposed strong point in Dier el Abyad, Rommel planned to penetrate the British positions in the north and encircle the box and attack the southern positions from the rear. However, his information about the Alamein positions was inaccurate and the British formations were not in the position shown on this map, which is based on the one Rommel used.

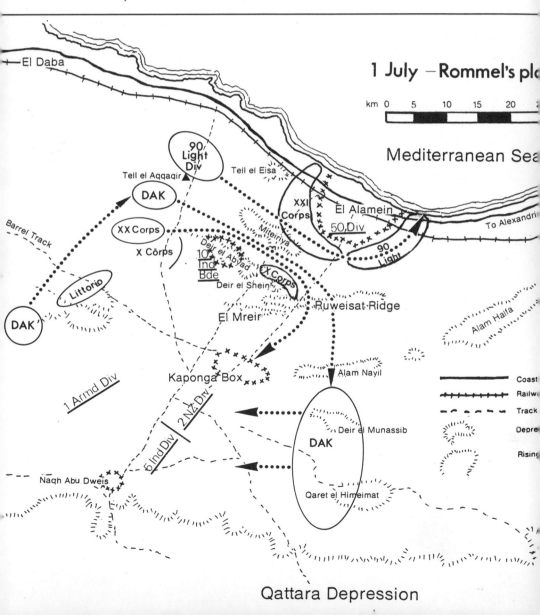

that there was a continuous Alamein Line, an impression given to him by his intelligence service, which said there were 'numerous field fortifications between the principal strongpoints', and he was reinforced in this belief by BBC references to an 'Alamein Line'. He did contemplate attacking in the south, where he would have encountered only the hapless Indians in their Naqb Abu Dweis strongpoint (if it could be called that), and had he but known it, he could have swept across open desert to the north and south of the Kaponga Box, although of course the New Zealanders at Deir el Munassib would have responded to that challenge. Instead, he chose to feint in that direction and try to battle his way through in the north with the intention of curving north and south to take the Eighth Army positions from the rear. Had he succeeded, he would have found little in the south to attack from the rear.

90th Light was to attack in a generally easterly direction north of the Miteirya Ridge, passing south of the Alamein Box and then turning north to the coast.

Afrika Korps would move north from its southerly assembly point, and then, followed by some Italian formations, turn on a parallel course with 90th Light, south of Miteirya Ridge, bypassing the supposedly defended Deir el Abyad during the dark hours of the early morning and exploding into the rear areas of the Eighth Army like a ghost from the night. With the Italian XX Corps hard on its heels, it would swing south to take the southern part of the Alamein 'line' from the rear. XX Corps would take Kaponga Box, the panzers the more southerly positions. The whole operation required Afrika Korps to make an 80 kilometre run in a wide semi-circle that would bring it back to within about 45 kilometres of its starting point.

One other force in this plan was XXI Corps, who were to attack the west and south-west faces of the Alamein Box, and who, as it turned out, were the first to move. Littorio Division also had a part to play. It was to engage the 1st Armoured Division, which was wrongly thought to be in front of the New Zealanders in the Kaponga Box. 1st Armoured was in fact up north, with one brigade bogged down in soft sand and the other on guard on Ruweisat Ridge, so Littorio had a holiday, supposing it had any thought of moving anyway.

Eighth Army's first hostile encounter was with the Italians. The Italians had exchanged shellfire with the South Africans the previous day, and around dawn on 1 July Trento Division and 7th Bersaglieri advanced on the west and south-west sectors of the wire. It was all over very quickly. In the face of South African machine-guns they withdrew with such haste that the crew of one truck towing a gun unhitched and fled, leaving the gun as a spoil of war.

90th Light, meanwhile, was in position in good time and by 4.20am (Eighth Army time) was moving forward. If the troops were lucky they would ride through to the coast on their trucks. If they were unlucky they would soon be spilling over the tail-boards and shaking out into line to face up to swathing machine-gun fire and cascading shells, and the mutilated and dead would litter the desert. It was the sort of chance any soldier takes on an average day in battle.

Further south were the two divisions of Afrika Korps, who had spent the previous night groping through the dark over unknown ground and running into all sorts of anguish. The going had been so bad that even on the flat, the rocky surface had forced a slow pace. Then they had blundered into an escarpment and found only one way down. In the darkness and congestion the two divisions became entangled: 15th Panzer Division drove clean through the 21st, inadvertently picking up 21st's rifle battalion; Korps headquarters also became enmeshed with the long-suffering 21st, and as they disengaged, the 21st's engineers and anti-tank group followed Korps instead of Division. 'No small disorder reigns,' the 21st lamented in its war diary at 1.20am. As the various parts of the divisions tried to reassemble, they filled the sky with flares with greater profligacy than even the normal German night time display, and the Korps diary remarked, 'Deutsche Afrika Korps betrays its advance by an uninterrupted display of Very lights.'

Afrika Korps warned Rommel that it couldn't hope to cross the start line before 7.00am (Eighth Army time), three hours late and an hour after dawn. An anxious Rommel urged them to cross the start line without pausing, but this was impossible. A pause to refuel was essential, and anyway, the confusion of the night had to be sorted out.

To the east, the first Bostons of the day were rising into the air and droning west. Then far below they saw a great clutter of badly dispersed vehicles - 4,000 was the estimate, but air force estimates were sometimes inflated - and released their bombs. 'A colossal bombing attack' was recorded by 21st Panzer Division, and with this introduction to Alamein, Afrika Korps at last moved east, dog tired, shaken, and like the 90th Light, just a wraith of the much feared army it had once been.

With such an army Rommel made his bid for Egypt.

90th Light pushed ahead in clearing weather, drifting a little to the north, and at dawn battle groups Breihl and Marcks on the left flank snagged the southern part of the Alamein Box. Marcks' wireless van actually ran into the wire and was captured. A vicious fire fight developed from which the Germans could not withdraw, and further out in the desert, comfortably removed from this disturbance, the rest of the division halted and considered whether to push on. They decided they would be too thin on the ground, and so 90th Light remained trapped here for the morning, unwilling to fight at this inopportune time but unable to escape. Salvation came around midday with another sand storm, beneath whose obliging veil the two trapped battle groups disengaged and moved across to the right flank of the German formations, as far as possible from the troublesome box. Around 2.00pm the division was on its way again, running now into soft sand.

Six kilometres further on the world exploded. Concealed by the sandstorm, the two South African battle groups south of the Alamein Box had lain in wait, unseen, undetected by German intelligence, and as the unsuspecting Germans approached, field guns, anti-tank guns, anti-aircraft guns, machine-guns and mortars hurled a howling cacophony of fire. In that moment the German march on the Delta stopped in its tracks and panic-stricken infantrymen spilled out over the tailboards of speeding trucks. In an observation post in front of the 1st South African Brigade an incredulous officer reached for the phone and reported the flight to his battery. 'The Jerries are on the run, man. The buggers are running!' But the news fell on deaf ears. It was obviously a case of wishful thinking. Not until the 90th Light war diary fell into Allied hands after the war did the truth become known.

'A panic breaks out in the Division (4.30pm Eighth Army time) which is stopped just in time by the energetic action of the Divisional Commander and Chief of Staff,' it records. 'Supply columns and even parts of fighting units rush back under ever-increasing enemy artillery fire.

'The commanders of battle groups however, succeed in keeping the majority of their units facing the enemy and bring back the troops which have taken flight. The division digs itself in. It is, however, impossible to resume the advance without strong artillery support. The Chief of Staff reassembles the remainder of the division, who have been streaming back, and returns them to their respective units, the operation being successful apart from a few exceptions. The situation has been clarified and a rout prevented, but the advance has broken down under concentrated enemy fire.'

The cause of this panic was almost certainly the veteran Colonel Marcks, whose car ran into the South African wire during a dust storm. In the hail of fire that followed, Marcks and his driver flattened themselves on the sand, until Marcks decided it would be healthier to withdraw. As

Instead of bypassing the Alamein Box, 90th Light collided with it, swerved to the right and ran into the South Africans' crescent of fire. XXI Corps attacked the box but made no headway. Afrika Korps, meanwhile, found its way blocked by the Indians in Deir el Shein, and although they overcame the strong point, it took them until dusk and they were unable to complete the day's assignment. 22nd Armoured Brigade counter-attacked 15th Panzer Division, which is the lower pincer of the two.

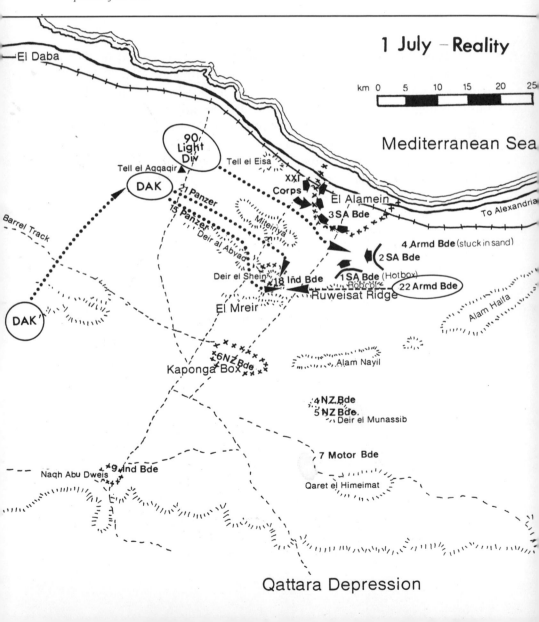

Auchinleck at Eight Army HQ in the Western Desert. IWM

Rommel (left) drinking with other officers - a toast, perhaps. War History Collection ATL

Part of a day's catch of flies. War History Collection ATL

Below: A General Grant tank (left) beside a General Lee. The main difference is the cupola on top of the Lee, carrying a machine-gun. IWM

An armoured car of the 12th Lancers on OP work near the New Zealand positions. *IWM*

Below: A British armoured car beside the railway line in the Alamein area.
LW Hutchings Collection, ATL

Destruction of German aircraft on the g round was partly responsible for the dominance of the Desert Air Force during July. This picture was taken at Fuka in November after the Eighth Army's break-through. War History Collection ATL

A low-flying Hurricane fighter swoops over a New Zealand column as the division moves from Mersa Matruh to take up a position at Minqar Qaim in June. War History Collection ATL

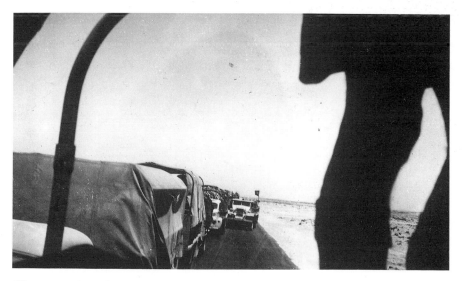

The coast road crowded with British vehicles as they flee east from Daba. R A McDougall Collection ATL

New Zealanders manning a two-pounder anti-tank gun. This gun, which was the standard anti-tank defence until mid-1942, was inadequate against the longer range German guns. War History Collection ATL

New Zealanders await the arrival of the Germans in their Minqar Qaim positions. A shell can be seen bursting in the background. War History Collection ATL

New Zealand soldiers with a six pounder anti-tank gun, which replaced the two-pounder in mid -1942. Its greater punch greatly contributed to the Eighth Army's ability to deal with the panzers.
War History Collection ATL

Men of the Rifle Brigade in positions near the Qattara Depression. In the foreground is a Vickers machine-gun, and beyond it a Bren. IWM

A South African soldier carrying mines away from a central stack. IWM

Members of the 3rd South African Brigade covering a position in the Alamein Box. The Mediterranean Sea can be seen in the background. IWM

they drove back, they ran into the following infantry trucks, causing confusion and congestion that attracted further South African fire. The result was panic.

Worse was to follow, or so it seemed to the jaded Germans. German fighters swooped over, firing lilac coloured smoke, the signal for an impending enemy tank attack, and the cry went out, 'Tank attack from the east!' Anti-tank guns were rushed forward and the artillery fired on targets to the east, and the diary records with some satisfaction that the intended attack 'is smashed while still in its assembly area...' But this was an illusion. British armour made no threatening moves that day against the 90th Light. Perhaps the airmen mistook the activity of the mired 4th Armoured Brigade for an assembly for attack, or the 22nd Brigade was seen getting itself into gear to meet the panzers.

The fire storm that had turned back the infantry also swept through the artillery, and a desperate 90th Light signalled Rommel that its guns were no longer battleworthy and help was needed. However, someone must have been shooting back at the South Africans to some effect because their 1st Brigade, in a small rocky depression close to Ruweisat Ridge, a position to become known as 'The Hotbox', caught almost continuous shell fire that afternoon. Some of this came from 21st Panzer's artillery after the 7th South African Field Regiment tried to help the Indians who at that time were fighting off Afrika Korps in Deir el Shein.

Over on the other side, Rommel responded - he always had a response - to 90th Light's cry for help by sending Kampfstaffel Kiehl, his battle headquarters troops, and he swung himself into an armoured car and went tearing to the battlefront, his first personal appearance on the field at Alamein. As he overtook the Kiehl Group, 'furious artillery fire' came down, and he was pinned down.

'British shells came screaming in from three directions, north, east and south,' he wrote. 'Anti-aircraft tracer streaked through our forces.'[1]

He was caught in the crescent of fire.

Vehicles scattered and everyone went to ground, Rommel and Bayerlein among them. Generals and privates, they grovelled in the sand, unable to move, helpless under the storm of shells. There was some small encouragement as Stukas paraded past 'time after time' and hurtled down on South African positions. But the shells kept coming. An hour went by, two. A new threat developed as the drone of bombers penetrated the din, aircraft embracing a lethal load of high explosive. In a moment they would begin their shuffle into bombing formation. And then, like the proverbial cavalry, Messerschmidt 109s that had been escorting the Stukas arrowed in and the bombers turned away. Eventually, towards evening, like the calm of dusk, the shell-fire began to slacken, and Rommel ordered his headquarters staff out, but left his Kiehl Group to help the embattled 90th Light. It wasn't much but it was something, and in 90th Light's condition, something was a large proportion of the whole. Not that there were any plans for further immediate action. For all his bustling arrival Rommel had been unable to take charge of events, his power of command having been neutralised as effectively as his infantry's best efforts to advance. For the moment it was a stalemate in this god forsaken 'gap' south of the Alamein Box.

Afrika Korps had moved at 7.45am, not in the secrecy of night but in the revealing light of day, its opportunity to slip through unseen long since gone. Though much diminished in strength, its 55 tanks formed a formidable phalanx as they churned east, aimed unknowingly at a raw infantry brigade, not yet properly dug in and still that morning in some state of disorganisation.

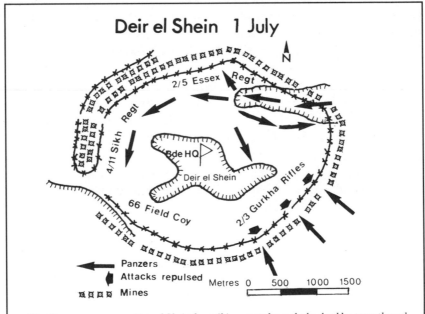

The Germans overcame Deir el Shein by striking, not through the doubly strengthened west face, but through the rear, using low ground to give a measure of cover as they broke in, first with infantry, then with tanks.

In parallel lines, 21st Panzer on the left, 15th Panzer on the right, the assorted Mark IIs, IIIs, IVs and III Specials of the two divisions drove west. Lofting above them, Bostons and Baltimores kept up a running bombardment through hazy four tenths cloud, hardly troubled by the few Messerschmidt 109s that snapped at their top cover of fighters, though the German fighters did cause damage to one unescorted flight of Baltimores. Stolidly, Afrika Korps plodded on, leaving burning vehicles in its wake. There was silence from Deir el Abyad, the anticipated strongpoint, and the Germans, finding it to be empty, moved on. Then ahead, wire.

21st Panzer saw it first as 'a wire obstacle about one kilometre deep ... facing north with an occupied position behind it. Field positions and also active guns were also seen'.

The decision was made to move south east and try to slide quietly between this position and the Alamein Box, and then turn south to meet up with 15th Panzer for the southward sweep. But it wasn't as easy as that. As the tanks moved forward it was seen that 'the positions ... formed part of a very strong and extensive fortified position ...'

21st Panzer stopped, a predator unsure of its prey. Caution was called for. How strong were the fortifications? How many anti-tank guns were there? How many tanks? What troops were inside? Best shake things about a bit and see what falls out. 21st Panzer war diary says, 'The division immediately attacked this position from the north east', but in fact it began a programme of steady escalation, attempting to conserve its slender resources and overcome this obstacle with the use of minimum force. At 9.00am the division's guns came to life, reaching across to Deir el Shein with the exploratory shells.

The Indians had known the Germans were coming, and the previous night had redoubled their efforts to strengthen their defences. Early on that 1 July morning patrols reported the approach of tanks and infantry, and the arrival of the first shells, two on the southern edge of the box and two near brigade headquarters, were signatures on a contract for battle.

It all developed with German thoroughness. For half an hour the shells droned over in systematic patterns around the box, many of them air-burst HE - a shell that explodes over the heads of troops with a flash of flame and a clap like the last trump, useful for intimidating or making infantry keep their heads down. During that half hour the Germans must have pushed forward patrols under cover of dust and shellfire because around 10.00am a concentration began falling on the Essex Regiment on the north-east perimeter, as though they had been selected for special attention. At

11.00am the pattern changed again, and the shells spread their favours more generally around the box while still holding the men of the Essex to their slit trenches. They suffered surprisingly few casualties.

The Indians decided it was time to call for help, and a message went off to 30th Corps in cypher. But no priority was given to it - presumably lack of experience - and it lay for the whole day in someone's in-tray until it was decoded about 5.00pm.

Around 11.15am the storm abated and stopped. Cautiously the Indians and Essex peered into the dust beyond the wire, and as their eyes searched the desert a Bren carrier flying a white flag approached through the haze. Nothing stirred now around Deir el Shein but wind and dust as the vehicle clattered up bearing two occupants, who identified themselves ('claimed to be', says the sceptical South African history) as officers of the 50th Division, captured in earlier fighting. They certainly wore British uniforms, though without badges of rank, but officers often removed their insignia on capture to avoid being fast-tracked through to Italian prisoner-of-war camps. A more trusting official Indian history says the visitors 'were able to leave some valuable information with the brigade (which was relayed to 1st SA Div)' but the officers were, in fact, the inadvertent carriers of German propaganda. They reported that 15th Panzer had about 60 tanks (more than the number in the whole of Afrika Korps on that day), many 25 pounders and anti-tank guns, much captured motor transport (which was certainly true) and plenty of petrol and water.

The two were sent back to Brigade HQ to convey a message from the Germans that the Indians should surrender or suffer attack, a rather desperate try-on, it might be felt, since the obvious purpose of the Indians' position was to sustain attack. In the best traditions of war, the two were sent back with a curt refusal that has been reported in two forms. One is the formal, 'Brigade will fight it out'. The other is a cryptic rebuff to the Germans to 'stick it up and be damned'. But since the British Army vernacular might not have meant much to the Germans, perhaps, sadly, the more formal version was taken.

Beyond the haze, 21st Panzer commander, von Bismark, gave the order to step up the violence a notch. He had tried without success scare tactics and an appeal to reason. Now he escalated to an infantry attack.

Renewal of shelling told the Indians the enemy was moving into the next phase. Beneath the dust, smoke and thunder of the barrage, men of Rifle Regiment 104 from 21st Panzer worked their way up to the minefield and groped around for a gap. They found one in the north-eastern corner and dashed in with Bangalore torpedoes to blow a hole in the barbed wire. The alarmed Essex summoned everyone - cooks, clerks, drivers, quarter-masters, orderlies - to help the rifle companies, and Bren and rifle fire beat around the Germans, who fell back. But as the day rolled into the afternoon the sandstorm that had rescued the battle groups of 90th Light from their entanglement with the Alamein Box swept across, and beneath this welcome cover, and aided by their artillery, the Germans blasted a hole and came through wire where the Essex right met the Gurkha left, and reached towards the defenders with fingers of tracer.

A confident message went back to Rommel, 'Advance of 21st Panzer is proceeding well', which was true if misleading. No doubt this meant that the plan of attack was unfolding nicely. Rommel's wishful thinking picture was of his panzers piercing the British line, and, much pleased, he signalled the Italians who were to follow through the gap, 'Advance goes well. XX Corps may expect to start pursuit towards 1400 hours (3.00pm Eighth Army time).' Not that the Italians were in any condition to respond. XX Corps was 20 kilometres behind Afrika Korps, and Littorio's petrol tanks were almost dry. A staff officer, Colonel Nuncenelli, took up a pencil and scribbled on Rommel's message, 'Littorio has fuel for 20 km, to Alexandria 150km!'

Though the Indians held back the intrusive infantry with mortar and small arms fire, some machine-guns became established, their tracer marking the place where they had a fingertip hold inside the box - just enough to hold open the gap in the wire. Watching and waiting to the north west, von Bismark gave the ratchet another click, and a pack of tanks and eight-wheeled armoured cars hove into view. About a dozen of them pushed in through a gap blown by the infantry and formed up behind the Essex and Gurkhas. Another eight followed them in, and with panzers now on the prowl, the Indians called again for help. This time the message was picked up by the South Africans, who sent it on to 30th Corps. Corps called on 1st Armoured Division and 2nd New Zealand Division to go to their aid.

But for the moment the Indians had to look after themselves. Some of the tanks had turned right towards the Essex, some left towards the Gurkhas. The main weight fell on the Essex who now had no anti-tank guns and little artillery ammunition. As the panzers closed in on them, some burned, but the rest came on, guns flame-flecked. German artillery pounded the weakened defending gun lines, and the panzers rolled over the Essex and moved on round the perimeter of the box to engulf the right flank of the Sikhs, who held the west face. More Panzers succumbed to gun fire, but this battalion, too, was soon scooped up.

Meanwhile, brigade headquarters, in the depression itself, and the Gurkhas in the south-eastern corner were being heavily shelled, and tanks outside the wire, probably from 15th Panzer, were battling to get in. They tried every gap in the minefield in turn, but each time were turned back.

British tanks of the 1st Armoured Division, glimpsed outside the Gurkha positions, appeared to withdraw when the panzers turned on them, although this may not have been a retreat. Unknown to the Indians the 22nd Armoured Brigade did engage German tanks, though it was too late to be of much help.

Inside the box the panzers had a duel with the seven Matildas around brigade headquarters until the British armour succumbed, and brigade staff then engaged enemy infantry in hand to hand fighting, during which the brigade commander was wounded. Panzers finally settled the issue. At 7.00pm, alone except for the 66th Field Company on their right, the Gurkhas were ordered to break out. The order did not reach two companies, which were cut off, but the remainder crashed through a gap which, while not held by the enemy, was under enemy fire, and fled east. Others of the brigade used the same route under cover of gathering darkness and, at one stage, aided by the diversion of an RAF raid.

The story is told of a medical officer, Captain V.F. Siqueira, who was of Goanese extraction, being challenged by a German while making his escape and answering in Portugese, which has some similarity to Italian. As the German approached to check, the captain floored him with a punch, bumped his head on a rock for good measure, and made off.

By nightfall the Germans held Deir el Shein.

Back at Amiriya, the Essex could count only 12 other ranks. The Gurkhas had 12 officers and 580 ORs and the Sikhs three officers and 370 ORs. One officer and 30 ORs from brigade headquarters were accounted for. Most men of the smaller support units escaped, but of the 121st Field Regiment, the record says that 'very few got away'. All told, about 2,000 men had been taken prisoner.

And what of the help that was supposed to have been sent?

4th Armoured Brigade, was, of course, still trapped in sand, though Lumsden appears to have been under the impression that its tanks were somewhere on Ruweisat Ridge. Perhaps some were there. 22nd Brigade was certainly in that general area, not far from Deir el Shein, but its regiments seem to have been flying blind in a state of ignorance and a pall of airborne sand, and there's some difference of opinion about what happened when. War diaries are of uncertain value in checking for accuracy as they were clearly written up 'in arrears', although presumably from notes taken at the time.

However, at first light 22nd Brigade was ordered to support the South Africans, an instruction that can only have originated with Lumsden, who had no orders from higher command. But by the time the tanks had refuelled, interest switched to the Indians, whose cry for help had at last reached receptive ears. The Brigade war diary says that 4th Sharpshooter were despatched, and that when they ran into 20 Mark IIIs, 1/6th RTR was ordered to assist.

8th RTR got away following receipt at 3.00pm of news that Deir el Shein had been overrun. The regiment found transport moving out of the box, and when Lieutenant Fairclough took a troop forward to see what was happening, he encountered panzers and lost two tanks.

The Queens Bays moved at 3.30pm, pushed on through enemy shell-fire, and engaged an enemy column of tanks and guns coming up from the south, presumably 15th Panzer. A tank battle developed that lasted until dark. The County of London Yeomanry lost eight tanks, including four Grants, and its commanding officer was killed.

1st RTR was immobilised, waiting for fuel and ammunition, until at last supplies were found. A rather jaunty war diary says: 'A Echelon report they are returning with enough of everything to keep us going for the present ... we may get to the battle today after all.' It was 6.30pm before the regiment did reach the battle, where it was ordered to help the CLY. 'Enemy withdrew on appearance of our tanks, who immediately commenced to follow up ... the enemy's withdrawal,' the war diary says. Even panzers, it seems, could be timid.

Whatever the accuracy of these accounts, it is clear that British armour was not impotent on that first day, as some histories suggest. Tired men pushed themselves as well as their tanks to the limit, and though they were unable to save Deir el Shein or the 18th Indian Brigade, they helped account that day for 18 of Rommel's precious 55 tanks.

New Zealand Division contributed little. A mobile column of field guns, anti-tank guns, machine-guns and Bren carriers moved north from the New Zealanders' rear position at Munassib but, nervous lest they should become too far removed from the division, which might need their help, they approached no closer than 11 kilometres to the Deir el Shein battle. A patrol sent out by the column was fired on by a tank that turned out to be British (or was it a British tank in German hands?) but, being unable to distinguish friend from foe among the moving shapes in the dust and smoke to the north, the New Zealanders went home without firing a shot.

For what it was worth, the only help to come from the south that day was fire from the 25-pounders of 6th New Zealand Brigade in Kaponga. In the late afternoon, carriers and portees were seen through a sandstorm firing back at a target that could not be seen by the observers in the box. Then about 20 tanks and a large number of trucks were seen at extreme field gun range - probably 15th panzer moving into position to meet 22nd Armoured's counter-attack - and 6th Field Regiment engaged them until dusk.

And so, alone except for 22nd Armoured's slight intervention, the 18th Indian Brigade slogged it out with Afrika Korps from early morning until the tanks crunched over the last opposition around 7.00pm. Victory in defeat is a cliche, but there is no other term for the Indian's achievement. The stand at Deir el Shein was a crucial factor in the battles that turned the tide of war in favour of the Western Allies.

Neither command was able to exercise much control of events on that first day. Rommel, ever present on the battlefield, met his match in the hail of fire from 30th Corps. And Auchinleck, though he had reason to feel confident that 30th Corps was in place and knew what it was doing, had 'lost' his 13th Corps commander, Gott. Gott turned up during the afternoon, having driven 24 kilometres across country of doubtful security. After a conference with Auchinleck, he lay down in the sand beside his car and went to sleep. He was simply too tired to drive back to headquarters.

At the end of the first day the German timetable was well out of kilter. 90th Light, which was supposed to have reached the coast and cut off the Alamein Box, was pinned down south of the box. Afrika Korps, which was supposed to have penetrated the Alamein positions and circled back to the south, had gone no further than Deir el Shein, and had lost 18 tanks. Trento Division and 7th Bersaglieri of XXI Corps, which attacked the west and south-western faces of the Alamein Box, had been repulsed and were dug in. XX Armoured Corps, which, following Afrika Korps, should have been enveloping the New Zealanders in Kaponga Box, was near Mreir Depression, to the rear of Afrika Korps, which had gone into laager on the site of battle. X Infantry Corps, which should have been astride Ruweisat Ridge, was holed up in Deir el Abyad, and Littorio Armoured Division was near Tell el Aqqaqir, some distance to the rear near the coast.

Except for the loss of Deir el Shein the British positions were intact, and incredibly some South Africans were unaware that they had stemmed an attack by 90th Light and played a decisive role in disrupting Rommel's plans. Rommel, in his papers, speaks of the British throwing in 'every gun' on that day to avert a 'deadly threat', but in fact the South Africans had merely engaged targets as they had presented themselves through the obscurity of that hot and enervating wind-blown day, and they had no idea they had prevented the 90th Light from encircling them or that they had caused so much damage to the division's morale and substance. South African troops in the box reported that it had been a boring day. 1st Brigade in the Hot Box, however, had a better appreciation of the day's events.

The return of unit strengths for the following day suggests that about 33 per cent casualties were inflicted on 90th Light as they lay impotently under South African fire on that first day of the Battle of Egypt, and the reason for its cry for army artillery support can be understood when it is seen that the ranks of its own artillery were whittled down from nine officers and 220 other ranks to two officers and 44 other ranks, a casualty rate of 80 per cent. The German artillery, of course, had to fight back from the open desert, with crews standing quite unprotected to serve their guns, while the infantry could at least flatten themselves on the ground or dig in.

In their disappointment and despair, perhaps the Indians were also ignorant of the heavy blow they had dealt the Germans. It is difficult to over-estimate the accomplishment of this inexperienced brigade, which had fought under almost every imaginable handicap and for most of the day entirely alone. It had stopped the Afrika Korps in its tracks, compelled it to commit its forces to a full-scale assault, and by holding it at bay until dusk prevented any further advance that day. This had saved the central and southern positions from attack from the rear and given the disorganised 1st Armoured Division time to get its act together; when daylight dawned on 2 July it was back in the fight. Moreover the battle had cost Nehring precious tanks, fuel and ammunition, and the customary replenishment could not be made that night because British bombing scattered the supply columns. At dawn on 2 July Afrika Korps was immobilised.

'Our prospects for victory were hopelessly prejudiced on 1 July,' Major

General F.W. Von Mellenthin wrote later in *Panzer Battles 1939-45*. 'Our one chance was to out-manoeuvre the enemy, but we had actually been drawn into a battle of attrition. 1st Armoured Division was given an extra day to reorganise, and when the Afrika Korps advanced on 2 July it found the British armour strongly posted on Ruweisat Ridge, and quite capable of beating off such attacks as we could muster. The South African positions were strong, and 90th Light never had a chance of breaking through them. The Desert Air Force commanded the skies.'[2]

But 2 July was another day, and on the night of 1 July, Rommel, unaware that he was in deep trouble, and believing that he had broken into the Alamein 'line', ordered 90th Light to continue its advance by moonlight and Afrika Korps to push on to the south and south-east. Italian units were to attack the Alamein Box again from the west and others would follow Afrika Korps through the gap as they had been instructed earlier.

Auchinleck, meanwhile, warned his forces that Rommel was likely to resume his attack next day on 30th Corps, and in the South African camp the mood was rather less than optimistic. The sappers were warned at 11.00pm of a possible withdrawal, and they were instructed to prepare demolitions of stores and petrol in the box and at El Imayid and El Hamman, the two next railway stations to the east.

'18th Indian Brigade captured. Situation serious,' the divisional engineers' war diary noted. On the night of 1 July Rommel's spirits were buoyed by a Luftwaffe report that the Royal Navy had sailed out of Alexandria, and had he but known it, 1 July was the notorious Ash Wednesday. News of the fleet's departure 'determined me to go all out for a decision in the next few days.'[3] The British, he reasoned, no longer seemed to trust their luck and were preparing to retreat.

'I was convinced that a break through over a wide front would result in complete panic,' he wrote.

And indeed, as Rommel made his plans that night, a precautionary order for Eighth Army to withdraw if necessary was being framed, but so also were orders to deal with Rommel when he resumed his attack.

Seated at his desk in his caravan that night, Auchinleck scanned through the day's intercepts and quickly assembled a picture of what was happening, and not happening, on the enemy's side. And at last he had from the enemy himself his true tank strength. It did not dispel his concern that Rommel might yet break through, but at least he had his measure.

On the Axis side, meanwhile, messages were being transmitted at several levels in the expectation that the morrow would produce the victory that had eluded Panzerarmee on the first day of battle. Panzerarmee itself sent a request to Rome for 10,000 copies of maps of the chief cities of Egypt. Afrika Korps flung a message into the ether to 'the ladies of Alexandria', asking them to make appropriate arrangements to welcome the triumphant Axis forces. When the latter message was brought through to Dorman Smith by a staff officer, he chuckled and took it to Auchinleck, where the joke fell on stony ground. Auchinleck, after all, had other things on his mind, notably the loss of Deir el Shein and the prospect that the next day German armoured forces could crash through weak British forces astride Ruweisat Ridge. His expectation, correctly, was that Rommel would drive for high ground south of Imayid railway station, the next one east from Alamein, and his own plan was that 30th Corps should oppose this 'by all possible means' while Gott's 13th Corps should strike up from the south. He wanted to talk to Gott about this so that he fully understood what was required, but communications were in 'their familiar state of semi-chaos'.[4]

There was chaos of another kind on the coast road between Fuka and Daba as almost continuous night bombing tore into the enemy's fragile supply line. Petrol and ammunition without which the panzers could not move in the morning either burned or was carried out into the desert by trucks seeking the refuge of open space.

There is no indication that 90th Light resumed its attack by moonlight as ordered, and as the new day approached, both sides had their plans, Rommel to push ahead with his original plan, Auchinleck to oppose and strike the enemy flank from the south.

What no one could have known at the time was that this first day's fighting had changed the war. Though Rommel had not yet given up, a subtle shift had taken place, not discernible as success for the British, not yet discernible as the way to success, not even seen as the beginning of hope. Indeed, the mood was still one of desperation, and defeat was still a contingency in the minds of the British commanders. Nevertheless 1 July was a seminal moment, concealing within its events the embryo of victory.

CHAPTER EIGHT

2 JULY - ROMMEL TRIES AGAIN

As first light touched the desert south of the Alamein Box the men of Rommel's 90th Light,bone weary, dragged themselves from their slit trenches and from beneath trucks, shivering off the cool of the night as they ate a little breakfast and looked with watchful apprehension around the empty landscape. The fire storm of the previous day had passed, and they were alone again in dusty space, a place without identity, a land that was nowhere, where the only shadows were their own as the sun formed a ball on the eastern horizon.

By 5.00am they were on their way again, jolting east, hunched in tired resignation as the anonymous distance slipped away beyond the tailboard. Their objective was the same as yesterday - to encircle the Alamein Box by driving through to the coast. There was no artillery preparation. Was there any artillery? The engines of the trucks whirred in the silence as they lurched across rocky ground or strained through silt-like sand. Already the heat was closing in, and dust rising from the wheels.

A kilometre goes by, two. And then the soft sibilant moan of incoming shells and the crash of their arrival. A torrent of men flows over the tailboards and melts into the ground, each form flattened into crucified fear as the deluge descends. There's a shout to get moving, and as the bodies rise, hammering machine guns sweep the ranks. They fall to the ground again, the living and the dead together.

At Panzerarmee headquarters the staff officers fretfully await reports. Communications are tenuous in 1942: radios are heavy, cumbersome and temperamental; telephone wires laid on the ground are apt to be severed by vehicles or gunfire; runners are cut down or become lost. Once infantry disappear into the sound and fury of battle they are lost to their commanders, except for whatever meagre news might filter back.

One thing is clear: only 90th Light is engaged. The tanks of Afrika

Korps, denied replenishment of fuel and ammunition during the night hours by the RAF, are stationary in Deir el Shein. Tantalisingly, the desert in front of them is open, now. No strong points lie between them and their intended sweep to the south, and given supplies they could be rolling unimpeded through the defenceless rear echelons of the Eighth Army, curving down to strike from the rear. But they must wait.

Time ticks by, and at last at 7.30am a report to Army HQ. 90th Light can't advance because it faces 'strong artillery and machine gun fire'. What's happening out there in the desert? At 11.00am Rommel learns that the division is still pinned down but will resume the advance, shifting the emphasis to the right wing after the army artillery has softened up the enemy. Perhaps he believes this because he wants to. Or perhaps he recognises futile hope. Perhaps the next message at 1.30pm is no surprise. The artillery has gone and the attack has been called off. The infantry of 90th Light are on their own, impotent in the face of scything enemy fire.

Rommel considers his map and the forces at his disposal. Afrika Korps is still in hand, not yet launched to the south. And there are Italians in several varieties not yet committed to battle. He must eliminate the Alamein Box, which blocks the coast road and rail and is a standing threat to any movement further south. He forms his plan. He will push through to the coast in an arc, using a laminate of forces. 90th Light will have the inside running in a wide left wheel that will enclose the box. Littorio will be on a parallel course on its right, and on the outside, on Littorio's right, will be Afrika Korps. When Afrika Korps reaches the coast it will reconnoitre down the road to the east to see what dangers might lurk there and at the same time 'make contact' with 90th Light, which, all going well, should reach the coast some little distance to the west. Then it will be a matter of driving west astride the road and railway across the top of the Alamein Box, opening the way to where Italian troops on the west side are dug in after a further ineffective attack that morning.

But the sweep to the south will go ahead, too. This will now be an Italian task. XX Corps (less Littorio) whose job had been to pursue the fleeing Eighth Army when the Alamein defences collapsed, will pick up Afrika Korps' original assignment and encircle 13th Corps. X Corps (Brescia, Pavia) will secure Mreir Depression with Brescia and Pavia Divisions to guard against a strike against the German flank by 13th Corps, which, as it happens, is what Auchinleck is planning.

It is all very thorough, very professional, very Rommel. It is also fantasy. Auchinleck was in fact planning a counter-attack from the south, a

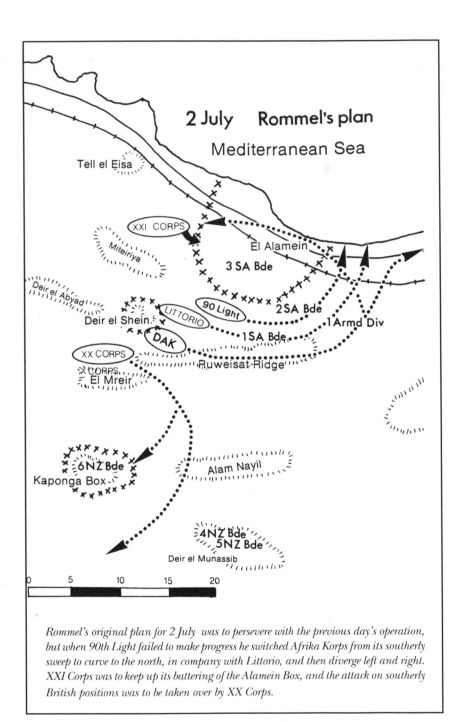

2 July   Rommel's plan

Mediterranean Sea

Tell el Eisa

XXI CORPS

Miteiriya

El Alamein

3 SA Bde

Deir el Abyad

90 Light

Deir el Shein

LITTORIO

2 SA Bde

DAK

1 SA Bde

1 Armd Div

XX CORPS

Ruweisat Ridge

X CORPS

El Mreir

6 NZ Bde

Alam Nayil

Kaponga Box

4 NZ Bde

5 NZ Bde

Deir el Munassib

0   5   10   15   20

Rommel's original plan for 2 July was to persevere with the previous day's operation, but when 90th Light failed to make progress he switched Afrika Korps from its southerly sweep to curve to the north, in company with Littorio, and then diverge left and right. XXI Corps was to keep up its battering of the Alamein Box, and the attack on southerly British positions was to be taken over by XX Corps.

scheme code-named *Latton*. He knew through Ultra just what the enemy plan for the previous day had been, and he deduced correctly that on this second day Rommel would push on again to try to cut off the Alamein Box. At midday he ordered 30th Corps in the north to prevent any enemy advance eastwards, and told 1st Armoured Division and New Zealand Division, in 13th Corps in the south, to 'destroy the enemy wherever he is met and to attack his flank and rear'. 30th Corps on this second day consisted of the three South African Brigades that the previous day had halted 90th Light and presumably could do so again, covered now on the flank on Ruweisat Ridge by a 10th Indian Division formation called Robcol made up of two batteries of Royal Horse Artillery, the 11th Field Regiment RA, and 1/4th Essex Regiment, assisted by four New Zealand batteries. Ranged behind the South Africans were columns of 50th Division, giving more reassuring depth to the defences. The way through was even more perilous for the attackers than it had been the day before.

To deliver the flank attack on the enemy, 1st Armoured Division was to move south west to Kaponga, where tanks would refuel before turning north to strike.

In their intentions at least, the two sides were like free-for-all fighters, their sight blurred by swollen eyes, circling each other, swaying and jabbing, trying to get in a blow at a vulnerable spot.

The first moves on the British side were made by the New Zealand Division and by 1st Armoured.

The New Zealanders, alerted that they might be needed, sent out two columns made up of artillery, machine-guns, anti-tank guns, carriers and infantry from 4th and 5th Brigades, which had been waiting at Munassib for just such a contingency. The columns merged at Alam Nayal, and for a good deal of the day manoeuvred around without making any direct contact with the enemy, though they shelled tanks seen advancing over the western edge of Ruweisat Ridge. The day's main diversion was to observe with incredulity crews of British tanks in evening laager dismounting in a drill movement.

1st Armoured Division was not quite ready for action as the day began. 22nd Brigade was in place, but the hapless 4th Brigade had arrived in position only at first light, after spending yet another night dragging its wheeled vehicles out of soft sand. So while Afrika Korps fretted in Deir el Shein, 4th Armoured Brigade men, who must by now have been almost asleep on their feet, re-established some sort of order. Both brigades were ordered to move south west to Kaponga Box, and then turn north to strike at the Axis flank.

While this was going on, preparations were in hand on the Axis side for the new triple assault in the north, and at 3.30pm the German artillery began a barrage. At four, the attacking formations moved forward. 90th Light ran into a shower of mortar bombs and shells and went to ground again after an advance of only 400 metres. Littorio, which was supposed to be moving up on its right, did not even stir. On the west face of the Alamein Box, where Trento Division and 7th Bersaglieri were to make another assault, shelling dowsed what little enthusiasm there was for the task.

Only Afrika Korps made progress. Released at last, the panzers lumbered east along Ruweisat Ridge, unopposed. And then, five kilometres on, a curtain of fire descended.

Such is the tunnel vision of participants in a battle that they are aware of little else but their own struggle, and while historians generally - perhaps erroneously - say British armour stopped the panzers that day, the gunners of the Royal Artillery claim credit. Specifically it was the 11th Field Regiment, the artillery component of the gun-based Robcol, who engaged the panzers, assisted by a battery of the 104th Royal Horse Artillery (Essex Yeomanry) and several anti-tank batteries. Robcol had been moved on to Ruweisat to fill the gap left by the fall of Deir el Shein, and from mid-morning on 2 July the guns needled at soft targets - anything that wasn't a tank - in the depression, where the two panzer divisions were rearming and refuelling, attracting retaliatory counter-attacks by German infantry and tanks.

The real heat came on as the afternoon push got under way, and panzers and motorized infantry became established on higher ground overlooking the gun lines, and poured in shells and machine-gun fire.

'It was a desperate situation,' says an account in *The Royal Artillery Commemoration Book*. 'But there could be no withdrawal; to fall back would lay open the road to Alexandria and Cairo.'[1]

The 22nd Armoured Brigade, with its attached Royal Horse Artillery, came up on the artillery left, fortuitously, as it happens. The brigade was beginning its south-westerly traverse when it collided, so to speak, with the battle, and as orders were to 'destroy the enemy wherever he is met' they joined in the fray, calling on 4th Armoured Brigade and New Zealand guns for help. The 4th Armoured Brigade, some distance in advance of the 22nd, had already refuelled at Kaponga and was turning north for the

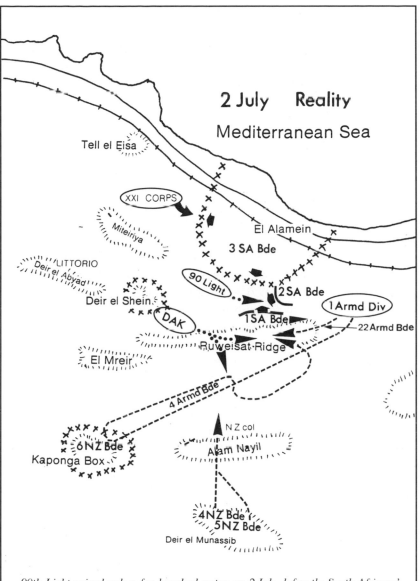

2 July   Reality

Mediterranean Sea

Tell el Eisa

XXI CORPS

Miteiriya

El Alamein

3 SA Bde

LITTORIO

Deir el Abyad

90 Light

Deir el Shein

2 SA Bde

1 Armd Div

DAK

1 SA Bde

22 Armd Bde

Ruweisat Ridge

El Mreir

4 Armd Bde

N Z col

6 NZ Bde

Kaponga Box

Alam Nayil

4 NZ Bde
5 NZ Bde

Deir el Munassib

90th Light gained only a few hundred metres on 2 July before the South Africans'
crescent of fire stopped it. Afrika Korps managed a few kilometres before a chance
encounter with 22nd Armoured Brigade. 4th Armoured Brigade, to the south west,
turned back to help. XXI Corps made a tentative stab again at the Alamein Box, but
no other Italian units stirred. The New Zealanders sent out a mobile column, but it made
no contact with the enemy. 1st South Arican Brigade withdrew a short distance.

flank attack when the call came, and it turned back, losing four Valentines and four Grants in skirmishes on the way and making a wide loop to the south to escape the trap of a wadi covered by German guns.

Desperate as it all seemed from the British side, the Germans were no less discomforted. The panzer divisions sent back a cry for help to Nehring, and each called on the other for support, refusing to move unless there was a response. The result was a great deal of radio traffic but not a great deal of constructive effort. Korps headquarters had its own problems as bombers homed in.

Note from my diary for 2 July: 'Later, battle broke out further north, and until dark the air rumbled continuously as tank fought tank and the guns poured in their share. From battalion HQ we could see a vast, smoke-shrouded plain to the north east, dotted with shadowy vehicles that to us moved as aimlessly as ants ... Hot and flies provocative.'

As dusk came and the 4th Armoured Brigade caught up with the play, the panzers made their last attempt, some tanks penetrating to within 'a few yards' of the guns that had, so the gunners say, borne 'the brunt of the tank assault'. Certainly the gunners had suffered seven officers and 80 other ranks killed out of an active complement of 300, and the battle stories include one of Bombardier Johnson who, though he had one arm shot away, continued to lay and fire, refusing all attention. He died two days later.

As darkness closed in the battle died down and the armour of both sides laagered for the night. The Germans had lost 11 more tanks in that engagement, leaving 21st Panzer with 20 and 15th Panzer with just six, though replacements were expected from the repair shops that night. The British had suffered losses, too, including seven Grants, and Afrika Korps offered itself the comfort that it had inflicted 'heavy losses' on its foe. There's more than a hint of pleading in the diary's reference to the troops having been in action day and night. 'Signs of fatigue become evident among leaders and men,' it noted.

Moreover, 'continued (air) attacks by day and night harass our troops very much; nothing is to be seen of our fighter protection'.

90th Light noted gloomily in its war diary that there was 'nothing to indicate that the enemy is considering withdrawing. On the contrary, the impression is created that he intends to halt the assault of the German-Italian Africa Army in front of the Alamein line with all the forces at his disposal.'

Wistfully it goes on, 'The German units, badly exhausted through the heavy fighting and hardships (day and night marches) during the preceding days and weeks, do not seem able to take this last fortress of the English in front of the Nile Delta with the available forces.'

The diary records that every 20 or 30 minutes 'Desert Air Force bombers, 15 to 20 at a time, fly over with fighter protection,' and though this continuous bombing and low flying inflicted little actual damage on the dispersed fighting and supply units, the morale effect on the troops 'is so much more important'.

'Everyone prays for German fighter protection,' the diary says, 'knowing only too well that the German Air Force cannot advance so very quickly. Sometimes German fighters appear singly, greeted by the roaring applause of the troops, but naturally they are not in a position to attack such heavy formations.'

And what of the Italians, 'the last hope'? X and XXI Infantry Corps and XX Motorised Corps, the diary observes, 'have seen little action and are therefore more fit'.

'However,' it adds, 'from such comrades there is little to be hoped.'

In fact, Italian units that were supposed to support 90th Light 'neither fired a shot nor had they attacked , excusing this inaction with the words that they did not want to bring down enemy fire on themselves'.

By dusk on 2 July the Axis forces had again failed to break through the Alamein defences, but rather were snagged there, like an intruder caught in a thorn hedge.

The remarkable thing about all this is that the Eighth Army command seemed unaware that its positions had been assaulted in a desperate bid to break through to the coast road, and Auchinleck reported to London that night that 'the expected attack had not developed by last night though some enemy tanks were seen'. This can hardly be true of the situation on Ruweisat Ridge, and 1st SA Brigade at least was well aware of being attacked. On the enemy side, the Italian perception was that their attack had been halted by 'violent artillery fire', and 90th Light said 'concentrated fire of all enemy weapons' and 'strong artillery and machine-gun fire' had barred their way forward 'after several hours of embittered fighting'.

So far as the South Africans were concerned, only their 1st Brigade had suffered anything worth reporting, and the divisional war diary says: 'Light shelling by both sides continues in morning, increasing considerably towards afternoon in 1st SA Brigade positions, and towards 1800 hours extremely heavy shelling of 1st SA Brigade position took place. GOC

(Pienaar) and party visited 1st Brigade HQ during the barrage and could not move from slit trenches during whole period of stay of about three-quarters of an hour. The position of 1st Brigade was on hard and stony ground, and shelling was particularly effective.'

On top of all this, 1st Brigade endured two hours' shelling by 'friendly' guns - whose is uncertain - and it was calculated that in the first two days of the Alamein battle between 15,000 and 20,000 shells fell in an area roughly 800 by 600 metres.

As the story reached the bemused but doubting Germans, British bombers and British tanks added to the woes of the men in 'The Hotbox', and Pienaar was reported to have called Auchinleck and said that if he was to be treated as an enemy he could take Alexandria within 48 hours.

A heavy bombardment hit the South Africans in 'The Hotbox' at 4.00pm, and at 4.20pm 30 tanks and infantry of 21st Panzer advanced from Deir el Shein under cover of smoke. Artillery and machine-gun fire from 'The Hotbox' and from Robcol on Ruweisat Ridge brought them to a halt, and 1st Armoured Division's artillery gave support. The Germans tried again at 6.00pm and again at 7.20pm, with 90th Light joining in from the north west. Just before last light both the South African brigadier and brigade major were wounded, and a new crisis developed.

We come here to a parting of the ways between the contemporary written record in the form of the divisional war diary, and events as they were remembered by Dorman Smith.

1st Brigade now came under command of what the official South African history calls 'a makeshift staff' of a battalion commander and an intelligence officer, who 'clamoured' for permission to withdraw, though the divisional war diary says only that at 10.00pm they asked for tanks to help ward off a threatened enemy attack. Pienaar, equally concerned, called up the 30th Corps commander, Norrie, and told him the brigade's flank was wide open and its position untenable unless flank protection from armour could be provided or some armour placed under command. He said bluntly that if help was not forthcoming he would pull the brigade back. He would not, he said, allow it to be overrun.

An unsympathetic Norrie said tanks couldn't be provided, and he saw no need to withdraw the brigade. Pienaar thereupon moved up the ladder to Dorman Smith, and from him to Auchinleck. Diplomatically, Auchinleck said he would talk it over with Norrie, and for the moment that was that. Not that it was of any comfort to the temporary 1st Brigade commander, anxiously waiting in the desert, who kept asking Pienaar for a decision, pointing out that if a withdrawal was to be carried out it should be done at night, rather than in daylight.

Around midnight Norrie came back on the line with what to him might have seemed a good compromise; 1st Brigade could be pulled back and placed in reserve, but another unit would be put in its place. At this implied slur Pienaar bridled and said that if this was to be done he would regard it as a sign of a lack of confidence and he would be forced to ask to be relieved of his command. All he wanted, he said, were some tanks or, failing this, permission to move the brigade to a position further back.

Midnight is the time when decisions are made by attrition, and a weary Norrie said Pienaar could use his discretion as to where he moved 1st Brigade, but that in any case a column of the 3rd Royal Horse Artillery would be put in its place, or just to the rear of where it had been. Pienaar pulled back 1st Brigade to a less hazardous position. At dawn South African armoured cars took a look at the old 1st Brigade positions, found some 90th Light men there and took them prisoner. At 9.30am the 3rd RHA column moved into The Hotbox, but not for long. After receiving 30 minutes' heavy shelling, it withdrew and settled down in a position to the south and a little to the rear of 2nd Brigade, where it continued to suffer from enemy shelling. South African honour was satisfied.

Dorman Smith remembered the incident differently. As he later told the story, Pienaar rang him late at night and said he intended to withdraw his division to avoid encirclement. Dorman Smith told him in no uncertain terms that he would have to stay where he was, and Auchinleck added the weight of his authority to this. Later, according to Dorman Smith, he spoke with Norrie, who said he had had a similar conversation with Pienaar.

It would have to be said that the South African version of events is more likely to be accurate, and accords with what actually happened, and the Dorman Smith version is mentioned only because it has gained some currency. Either Dorman Smith's memory is at fault - and an instance of this occurs later - or at this late hour of the night the tired Dorman Smith simply misunderstood what Pienaar was saying. And for that matter, Pienaar may not have been entirely clear in his request. If it was a misunderstanding it was another of July's small tragedies, because the incident further undermined confidence in the South Africans, who were left to fight in their static position all month, and when plans were made for the hoped for pursuit of the Axis forces they were assigned the sedentary task of staying behind to man the Alamein positions.

All in all it turned out to be much ado about nothing, but it was a pointer to the cross-currents and personality conflicts that bedevilled the Eighth Army right up to the closing days of the 'old' army.

So, looking at all that, how can it be said that one army had attacked another without the defenders really noticing, particularly when it is remembered that 1st Armoured Division and Royal Artillery had been going hammer and tongs with the panzers on Ruweisat Ridge from late afternoon? The short answer may be that despite some fairly violent exchanges, the German thrusts may have had the appearance of probing rather than attacking.

Consider the conditions, with heat haze and dust obscuring observation and objects swimming into and out of view.

In the far north the Italians were supposed to attack the west face of the Alamein Box, but the South Africans saw no great concentration of troops, merely groups who disappeared when fired on.

In the area of 90th Light's dawn attack, troops of two South African brigades would be standing to as the sky became light behind them and in a few minutes had flooded the desert with the full glare of day. Not much heat haze yet but probably a fair amount of dust, and out of the dust emerges some enemy transport. Nothing massive. Not the menacing force covering half the desert that usually precedes a German attack. Just a largish gaggle of trucks. As the shells fall among them, the enemy lorries turn about and disappear again. Then figures of men are seen. Shell bursts balloon around them and the Vickers guns chatter, and the figures disappear, too. After a while, the British artillery, denied visible targets, gives up.

Though the air force is fairly busy, shuttling back and forth across the sky and creating havoc at unseen targets somewhere west, the rest of the day is fairly quiet until around 3.30pm, when incoming shells suddenly begin to blossom. The South Africans become watchful and wait. Outgoing shells moan overhead with a hollow roar, the sound diminishing in comforting reassurance that each projectile is aimed the other way. Dust begins to rise out there and moving figures are seen. The eager Vickers gunners let go a few belts. The Hotbox receives a pasting from shell fire, but no tanks or infantry advance towards them.

Further south, British guns and tanks sight the familiar outline of panzer turrets-ten, twenty, maybe forty of them, not the usual hordes that intimidate the infantry and terrorise rear echelons. Turret covers clang shut and the single band radio communication network buzzes with orders, requests and information. Everyone can hear so everyone knows what's happening. And then it's all on. Solid shot flies, bouncing off hulls or plunging a white hot lance through toughened steel and into explosively receptive shell racks and petrol tanks. A tank glows and smokes as the men inside cook, and then a blast tosses off a turret, which falls to the ground beside the blackened hull like some grotesque, huge egg cup. Other crews are luckier. Their tank slews and stops, and they know they've lost a track. The hatch is thrown open and they clamber out with frantic haste, and run for dear life.

There's something odd here, though. The Jerries don't seem as aggressive as usual, not quite as pushy, not really wanting to come through. They usually fight as though they own the place. They don't seem to be trying too hard today.

And then at last the sun goes, a red ball that slips with visible haste behind the western horizon obscured by the dust of battle. There's little twilight and no cool of the evening, just a rush from day to night as though darkness, the only decency left, should not be delayed.

Tanks still burn, and occasionally there's an eruption from within. The survivors move away and form into laager and signal their supply columns to bring up more fuel and ammunition.

And what was it all about? Where were the Jerries going, if anywhere? Were they just testing, looking for a weak spot?

At his spartan headquarters, Auchinleck writes a review of the day's events, and tells London that 'the expected attack had not developed by last light though some enemy tanks were seen'. And the truth is that the German thrust was not what the Eighth Army was used to.

Timid infantry and tentative armour were not the stamp of the German army, not the bold assault expected of a general reaching for Cairo.

Rommel's perception was rather different and his optimism less assured.

He wrote of the British falling back in the south and then launching a heavy counter-attack on his open flank, and of 'violent defensive fighting'. He still hadn't given up, but his orders for the next day, 3 July, were more restrained. He instructed his army to attack from daybreak to 10.00am to seek out weak points - an order to probe and search. Not his style at all, though he did not abandon his southern encirclement plan and he ordered Ariete and Trieste to carry out the drive to attack 13th Corps in the rear. But if there had been little of 13th Corps in the first place, there was even less now as the Eighth Army, preparing for the next day, carried out some minor reorganisation. The Indians in their remote outpost at Naqb Abu Dweis in the far south were doing no good there and were totally exposed. Auchinleck sent them back to Qarat el Himeimat to reorganise as a battle group under 5th Indian Division. He felt, also, that Kaponga Box might now become a liability, and the New Zealanders were instructed to withdraw, leaving a battle group to hold out for another day to destroy the defences and stores. Some of the brigade pulled back under cover of darkness, leaving two battalions in charge. Auchinleck wanted 6th Brigade infantry sent back to the New Zealand base camp at Maadi because under his battle group policy he considered them 'surplus'. But a cautious Inglis decided to keep them with the division until the situation became clearer.

One day remained in this first attempt by Rommel to break through the Alamein defences - a day in which the pattern of battle changed ominously for Rommel, hopefully for Auchinleck.

It was on this day, 2 July, that it had been planned to despatch the first troop convoy from Taranto to Alexandria to make secure the Axis occupation of Egypt.

CHAPTER NINE
3 JULY - THE TIDE TURNS

S leepless Alamein offered rest for few on the night of 2-3 July as the armies gathered themselves for the third day of battle.

The Royal Air Force droned through the flak to bomb ammunition and petrol dumps near the coast. Spectacular explosions flared and flamed, one so violent that it blew the Wellington responsible clean out of the sky. For the 23 hours to dusk on 3 July the RAF flew 900 sorties, four times as many as the enemy, and the DAF 770. Bombs were dropped at the rate of ten tonnes an hour, not all, alas, on the enemy. Air crew were having a great deal of trouble locating the interface between the armies, and around midday on 3 July, 2nd SA Brigade was ground strafed by British aircraft and during the afternoon 3rd SA Brigade was twice bombed by Baltimores. One officer was killed and 12 other ranks wounded. The aggrieved South Africans lodged suitable complaints.

The armoured units of both sides spent the night attending to maintenance and minor repairs, and replenishment with fuel and ammunition. As German custom was to remain on the site of battle, they carried out these tiresome tasks on the spot, going into laager where they had fought that day and awaiting the arrival of the supply convoy. British custom was to draw back some distance, an added strain on exhausted crews. On this occasion some tanks became lost on the way back, and though they all turned up in the end, the night's work was not finished until the early hours of the morning. The Italians were active that night too. Ariete and Trieste moved up in readiness for a daylight advance to Alam Nayil.

At dawn on this third day 90th Light was still trapped in the sand and flies south of the Alamein Box and west of the two South African brigade groups, bogged down in its own inertia and with not the slightest chance of making headway.

Afrika Korps was astride the western end of Ruweisat Ridge, with 21st Panzer on the northern slope and 15th Panzer on the southern and in the shallow dished valley to the south. Ariete was to the south of 21st Panzer, with Trieste on its left, behind the Germans.

The Germans on this day had only 26 tanks and 1,200 to 1,500 men. The Italians had perhaps 70 tanks, 40 in Ariete and 30 in Trieste. The number of men is unclear, but there were large numbers of non-motorised Italian troops still far to the rear and not yet able to play any part.

On the British side the South Africans stood firm in the Alamein Box and in their two brigades groups to the south, except that the 1st Brigade had drawn back from 'The Hotbox'. They faced 90th Light.

1st Armoured Division was on the eastern end of Ruweisat Ridge, still with orders to make a south-westward then northward sweep to catch the enemy flank, the move it had begun the previous day. Having been reinforced, it had 120 tanks, 38 of them Grants, giving it a substantial majority over the combined German and Italian forces. But it was not a well integrated formation, being made up of bits and pieces from broken units.

Two battalions of the 6th New Zealand Brigade were still in Kaponga Box, and the major part of the division at Munassib. The mobile column formed the previous day by 4th and 5th Brigades had its guns on the southern slope of Alam Nayil, eight kilometres to the north of Munassib, with observation posts on the crest.

The Indians had been withdrawn from the south and were reforming.

So on this day the only fortified position still held in strength was the Alamein Box. Deir el Shein had, of course, fallen to the enemy on the first day, and Kaponga Box was only lightly held and would be given up that day. The south was wide open, watched only by small roving battle groups identified by the names of months - monthly columns as they were called - but no one was taking any interest in that part of the Desert.

Afrika Korps and 1st Armoured Division set out at first light on a collision course and again met by accident. Ariete moved off in the direction of Alam Nayil to protect Afrika Korps' flank and in the hope of completing that southward curve behind Eight Army's non-existent defences, and it, too, became embroiled in the armoured struggle.

It was absolutely critical not only that British armour and guns not allow the enemy through, but also that they be permitted to take no more territory.

'If the enemy had gained the ridge he would have had observation for about 13 miles to the north east,' notes the war diary of the 4th Armoured Brigade.

As the 8th RTR war diary tells the story: 'At first light ordered forward ... Tanks were in poor shape. Wireless practically nil. Replenishment did not arrive until we were in battle position ... At about 0630 enemy tanks started to advance along ridge ... and valley to south.

'We engaged them with some Honeys of 1st RTR. They greatly

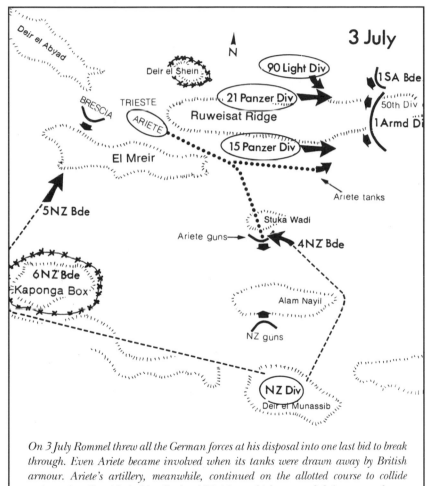

On 3 July Rommel threw all the German forces at his disposal into one last bid to break through. Even Ariete became involved when its tanks were drawn away by British armour. Ariete's artillery, meanwhile, continued on the allotted course to collide unintentionally with the New Zealand Division, which captured their guns and most of their transport, and then sent one brigade off to El Mreir to cut off the fleeing remnants. But the brigade found itself faced with another Italian division, Brescia.

outnumbered us being about 30 Mark IIIs. They moved southwards into the valley and we were ordered to cover them there. We were engaged strongly. 6th RTR came up to the ridge and we were sent into the valley. One troop of Grants later sent to help us. Enemy still came on and moved on to south ridge. We were ordered there to hold them up. Though they had 10-20 Mark IIIs we held them up long enough for 6th RTR to come up on south ridge, and 22nd Armoured Brigade took over the north ridge. The battle continued off and on all day with very heavy shelling at times ... Just at dusk 22nd Armoured Brigade made a quick thrust down the valley, returning under cover of smoke.'

In the midst of the scuffle, orders came through at noon to repeat the attempt to encircle the Axis forces from the south. It might have been thought that the armour had their hands full, but somehow the move was begun at 4.00pm (or so the 22nd Armoured Brigade war dairy says), with 4th Armoured Brigade leading.

'Met eight Mark IIIs ... and went into action,' the diary says laconically. 'The enemy was held until last light without much damage to either side.'

There is something almost ritualistic about all this as thrust is met by counter-thrust, defence by attempted evasion, and finally the defenders make a late charge and quick withdrawal like some territorial animal warning off an intruder.

Ariete became embroiled when it brushed against 4th Armoured Brigade, and most of its tanks peeled away to the north east while the artillery and one or two tanks plodded on to the south east to an unexpected rendezvous with the New Zealanders.

As throughout the day the tanks engaged in this vaguely mobile slogging match, Afrika Korps headquarters existed in an atmosphere of mixed desperation and hope.

'21st Panzer attacks again at 1600,' its war diary says. 'It is requested that Littorio, which has so far only followed 21st Panzer Division, should join forces in the attack ... The Korps commander is instructed to see the C-in-C. The question is discussed whether the continuation of the attack holds out any possibility of success. 1600 hours, both divisions renew the attack. If the tanks can now push forward, the attack may succeed after all ...'

An irritable Rommel spent the day at his headquarters firing off admonitions to both 90th Light and Afrika Korps. Poor 90th Light, a spent force, was moved across with its anti-tank guns, to help 21st Panzer, but as Rommel later noted 'was equally unable to force a decision', and an order to 'co-ordinate ... attack' meant little. Afrika Korps was told in mid-afternoon, 'I demand energetic action by the whole DAK.' Korps passed this on to 21st Panzer as, 'The C-in-C orders that the attack must be carried out with the utmost energy', and to 15th Panzer as 'The C-in-C demands that 15th Panzer carry out the attack at all costs to the very end. Exert yourselves to the utmost'. One imagines that the C-in-C must have been characterised that day by some choice German expletives that called his ancestry into question.

The fantasy of the orders contrasts with the realism of the 21st Panzer's diary, which records bluntly, 'In spite of new instructions and orders the attack does not gain further ground. The fighting power of the division is exhausted. The battalions of Rifle Regiment 104 have suffered many casualties. Numerically the enemy tank force is superior to ours. The enemy throws in everything he has to stop our attack. For 1600 hours (5.00pm Eighth Army time) a new attack is ordered ... The following order is issued to all units: "Attack will commence at 1600 hours. You will advance non-stop until the target is reached".'

But the Germans had gone as far as they were ever to go, except for minor swirls in the ebb and flow of battle and their ill-fated venture against Alam Halfa in September, which was, in any case, a trap into which they were drawn. The great advance that had elated the Axis and cast a pall of gloom over the Western Allies had come to a dead stop on this barren hump in the desert, in the face of the guns of the 1st Armoured Division and two small supporting columns from 50th Division - the Tynesiders. If you want to put a finger on the exact time and place when the tide of war turned against the Axis in North Africa you could say it was here on Ruweisat Ridge, at dusk, on 3 July, 1942.

What might have been in Rommel's mind that day can only be guessed at because his own account fudges events, and even his contemporary reports to GHQ in Rome tend towards fiction, though he may well have been misinformed or made wrong assumptions. It is hard to see, for instance, how he could have reported that 'On 3 July Panzerarmee widened its breach in the enemy's defence system in a north-west direction'. North west is perhaps a mistake - or translator's error - for north east, but there was in fact no breach because there was, in effect, no defense system outside the Alamein Box. Auchinleck was using the box as a peg on which to hang a loose defence chain that could yield and swing back. And on that day the tail end of the chain flicked up and caught Ariete a shattering blow. It may have been this set-back that infused Rommel's orders to his Germans with just that touch of desperation, as though he believed he might succeed by the power of his will.

Ariete led itself to destruction, though Trieste must take some of the blame. Ariete and Trieste, it will be recalled, were to advance to Alam Nayil, but at daybreak only Ariete moved off, and this without making the 'aggressive reconnaissances' ordered by Rommel. A prudent look ahead would have told Ariete that the New Zealanders were already in residence at Alam Nayil, well equipped to deal a deadly blow.

The Italians lost most of their tanks to the armoured battle soon after they set out, and only artillery, with about 48 heavy guns, and the few remaining tanks continued on course, thankful no doubt to be leaving behind the clamour then taking place on Ruweisat. Blissfully unaware of what lay ahead, they paraded across the shallow basin south of Ruweisat, trailing the customary trail of dust that attracted the attention of the New Zealand observation posts on Alam Nayil. Around 7.00am they were framed in the watching binoculars, and the New Zealand guns were alerted. Breach blocks clumped shut on shell cases, and at 7.15am, when Ariete was just over six kilometres away to the north west, the 25-pounders came to life and shells whooshed over the observers' heads and erupted among the advancing columns.

Ariete halted, and in frenzied haste swung around its own guns, and counter-battery came flying back. But as the New Zealanders had observation and the Italians did not, it was a weighted contest, and with the New Zealand guns clearly gaining the upper hand, the NZCRA, Weir, called on Division to settle the matter with an infantry attack.

Back at Munassib 4th Brigade, already getting ready to move out, hastened preparations, and by 9.15am the infantry were on their way north, steering a course just east of Alam Nayil. Five kilometres on, reconnaissance disclosed the Ariete guns to be six kilometres away, and 4th Brigade despatched its 19th Battalion at speed on trucks, led by carriers, to launch a surprise attack.

They pounced first on a small outlying group, through which the speeding carriers charged like cavalry as they headed for the main concentration. Italians from this group promptly began waving pieces of paper and white cloth at the following infantry, now advancing on foot with fixed bayonets. While the rifle companies were sorting out this lot, word came back from the carriers that they were pinned down by heavy fire and needed help. Two companies fanned out along a ridge, 1,000 metres south east from the Ariete concentration, and a third took up position further south. An exchange of machine-gun and mortar fire followed, and the New Zealanders brought up four two-pounders which, together with small arms fire, persuaded the Italian artillerymen they would be unwise to attempt to man their guns. Three Italian tanks went scurrying back through the gun lines. Then as the two companies advanced from the south east, bayonets gleaming in the sun, and the third made its appearance from the south, the Italians gave up. Dust rose from the wheels of speeding vehicles as some men managed to scramble aboard and head away to the north west, but there were about 350 prisoners left to be counted, together with 44 heavy and medium guns, five of them 25-pounders, together with a swag of anti-aircraft and anti-tank guns, mortars and small arms of various descriptions, two tanks, and a great mass of motor transport, which the New Zealanders didn't bother to count - or to send on to Army as obedience to Army orders required them. It was a case of finders keepers. Also welcome booty were medical stores and goods the Italians had picked up from abandoned Naafi and YMCA stores. Some of the enemy guns and four serviceable 25-pounders went back into service, pointing the other way.

The difficulty the historian has in trying to establish facts even from primary sources is illustrated by the official Italian General Staff account of the encounter, which says Ariete was attacked from the east, south and north by the New Zealand Division, supported by 4th Armoured Brigade, which is a confusion of two separate actions.

'After strenuous resistance, with ammunition exhausted and practically all guns lost and the left wing completely open, the remnants of Ariete withdrew ...' the reports says.

Panzerarmee's report to Rome took a different line, and even this flatters Ariete. 'The Italians fighting value is so small that on 3 July an attack by a very weak tank force captured 360 prisoners from Ariete without any resistance worthy of the name,' it said. 'The Division lost 28 guns and 100 MT.'

The New Zealanders, of course, had no tanks, only Bren carriers, but Ariete tanks had been in action against 4th Armoured Brigade.

The true significance of what was an elegant but not, after all, great victory, may be seen in Rommel's comment that 3 July began to show 'signs of disintegration among the Italians.'[1] The Ariete reverse, he wrote, took the Germans completely by surprise, because in the weeks of fighting around Knightsbridge, Ariete, covered, he conceded, by German tanks and guns, had fought well against every onslaught by the British and suffered heavy casualties.

'But now the Italians were no longer equal to the very great demands being made of them,' he lamented.[2]

A jaunty Inglis, writing to Freyberg several days after the event, expressed the elation and confidence of the New Zealanders.

'As you know,' he wrote, 'we made rather a mess of Ariete some days ago, destroying its complete artillery. I have eight 4.5s and four medium hows at the moment in addition to the divisional artillery. Am managing to keep them fed with shells and use them to advantage.'

But this was only the beginning of the story. There were still those fleeing Ariete fugitives, and New Zealand Division decided to run around the block, so to speak, to catch them in their expected refuge in Mreir Depression. 5th Brigade was despatched on this enterprise, moving west from Munassib at 11.15 am and executing a right wheel around the southern and western faces of Kaponga Box, still occupied by the 6th Brigade rearguard. An inquisitive fast-moving Me 110 hurtled low overhead as the column moved north, watched from the comfortable elevation of the 6th Brigade observation posts in Kaponga. It was curiously like a circus caravan, strung out along kilometres of desert, with the carrier screen up front, the infantry and other arms following, and the artillery at the tail, literally hours behind the rest. Sucked along, in effect, by the advancing carrier screen, the infantry were obliged to keep up, and as they topped a low ridge, their trucks eased out into desert formation and moved on Mreir, about six kilometres to the north. Shells began to fall among them as they approached, and just short of the depression the trucks swung about to allow the infantry to debus and go forward on foot, left to right in line. To the rear, their own artillery was coming into action, battery by battery, as it came around the Kaponga corner and over the top of the ridge.

In Kaponga Box, the two battalions that had been left behind as a cover for the attack were pulled back, and they watched in awe as the developing battle at Mreir stirred up its own local sandstorm, from the midst of which came the great clanging and banging of gunfire. 5th Brigade, far from merely rounding up the fleeing survivors from Ariete, found itself locked into a full-scale battle with Brescia Division, and at dusk the outcome had still not been resolved.

In the opposing headquarters, the two army commanders surveyed the day's events in different frames of mind.

An elated Auchinleck signalled to all ranks of the Eighth Army: 'Well done, everybody. A very good day. Stick to it.' And for the first time his operation order for the next day considered the possibility that Rommel was beaten. To avoid defeat, he thought Rommel might withdraw, and Auchinleck ordered a 'pursue and destroy' operation, ebulliently code-named *Exalted*, an indication of optimism that doesn't quite square with the reservations he was later to express about the Eighth Army's ability to hold the line.

But Rommel had no intention of pulling back, and this may or may not have been fortunate for the Eighth Army. Scoullar says scornfully that *Exalted* 'was indeed an exalted idea of the possibilities'.[3] He considered the army unfit to pursue and destroy the enemy, and that had it occurred to him, Rommel's smartest move would have been to entice Auchinleck out of his defences by withdrawing. With its superior recuperative powers, Panzerarmee, he considered, would have turned on the Eighth Army 'with every prospect of a decisive victory'. Perhaps he had the Battle of Hastings in mind.

Well, he may be right, although Rommel's tanks were now few and his men exhausted. Eighth Army still had superiority in tank numbers and a proportion of these were Grants, and tired as some formations were, there were reasonably fresh troops on hand. New Zealand Division alone outnumbered the Germans, and so far had hardly been dented. It was fully equipped, fit and well rested, and thanks to its triumph over Ariete, had some extra wheels and guns. The South Africans were in reasonably good shape, though committed to static defence. 1st Armoured, while not in peak condition, was better off in every respect than Afrika Korps, and that night the first formations of another fresh infantry division, the 9th Australian, came into the line, and it, too, was fit and ready for a fight, though still short of some equipment.

But then might-have-beens have no place in war. Auchinleck's judgement was not put to the test and we shall never know whether his optimism was misplaced. However that might be, this was the forerunner to a succession of orders that flowed from Eighth Army headquarters in the weeks that followed stating as their objective the destruction of the enemy where he stood. This the army might have done.

Rommel surveyed the outcome of 3 July more soberly. He knew now that he had failed to break through Alamein, and he knew, also, that for the moment he could ask no more of his men. Though he realised that a pause would give the British the chance to reorganise and build up their strength, he felt he had no alternative but to go over to the defensive. But he was not prepared to surrender a metre of ground.

'Enemy counter-attack must be expected tomorrow ...' he signalled all formations just before midnight. 'Corps and divisions will organise themselves for defensive action and will hold their positions. DAK is responsible for the defence of today's line of attack. Regrouping during 4.7 (7 July) can be anticipated.'

He told Rome his own decreasing strength and his 'precarious supply situation' compelled him to break off large-scale attack for the time being. He gave the fighting strength of his German divisions as no more than 1,200 to 1,300 men, and the 'Italian units are also very low regarding fighting strength'.

'The bulk of the infantry,' he said, 'are still in the rear army area and unmotorised.' He gave his urgent need as 'a rapid moving up of personnel and equipment'. Besides the weakness of his forces, Rommel had to contend with the problem of bringing up what supplies were available.

'The supplying of the army cannot be carried out at night without difficulty,' he said, 'as the roads are almost completely blocked by the enemy air force.'

Already a new plan was forming in his mind. He would switch to a frontal attack in the south.

CHAPTER TEN

4 JULY - THE ARMY THAT WAITED

4 July marked the difference between the Germans and the British. One can imagine Rommel, in Auchinleck's position, breathing in the morning air at first light, listening to the silence of the battlefield, and saying, 'The bugger's given up. Let's go and get him.' Or whatever they say in German. Almost within the hour, panzers would be moving, the infantry rolling forward in their trucks, and the artillery laying down fire patterns. The whole army would be focused on the commander's demands.

Nothing like this happened on the British side that day, though Auchinleck did nurture such thoughts.

He and Dorman Smith, pondering their next move late into the previous night, concluded correctly that the Germans had shot their bolt and that an opportunity to clobber them might now present itself. As midnight approached, Operation Order No 89, the first to contemplate decisive action at Alamein, went out through the signals system, coded 'most secret', setting the scene for 4 July under that confident title *Exalted*, chosen, perhaps, with the eye to history but not one that might be considered appropriate for an order in which the operative word was 'if'.

The first two sections read:

Information

1. This order governs the action of Eighth Army in case the enemy attempts to withdraw from his present positions to avoid defeat.

2. It will be difficult to judge the moment of the enemy withdrawal but the best indications will probably be

a. if the enemy gives up his positions in the former 18 Inf Bde area*.

b. If the enemy tries to remove his AFVs** from contact. The enemy, when he withdraws, will probably go far and fast.

* i.e. Deir el Shein   ** Armoured fighting vehicles, usually tanks

Intention

The enemy will be pursued and destroyed.

'Far and fast' ... how little they knew their enemy! Withdrawal might have been the prudent thing to do, but clearly the generals were carried away by having stopped the unstoppable Rommel and they expected him to comply with the rational options of received military wisdom. And both this expectation and the order based on it marks the difference between Auchinleck and his opponent. For Rommel, a door open just a chink would have been opportunity enough. Auchinleck liked the door to be open and the room inside clearly in view. Though he knew Rommel was in trouble, his orders were to 'pursue and destroy' only if the enemy tried to pull back. From this developed a fatal inertia on a day when Rommel could have been caught off balance and desperately short of ammunition. Though British armour did move forward in response, mistakenly, to perceived withdrawal, the operation never came together and the threat to the enemy evaporated in the Desert sun. All the Germans suffered was a fright.

This was the day on which Rommel planned to regroup and, hopefully, rest some of his forces. He had only 36 tanks, and those in 15th Panzer had only two shells apiece, and his German units were down to a strength of 1,200 to 1,500 men. But this did not inhibit his aggressive intentions and in particular his desire to get rid of the division that the previous day had carved up Ariete. Not for him a patient wait for opportunity, opportunist though he was branded. He resolved to eliminate 'the standing threat from the south' in the form of the New Zealand Division, and he signalled Rome: 'Our intention is to hold our front line positions and regroup with a view to encircling and destroying 2nd NZ Div, and also to occupy Siwa Oasis with a mobile force. I request the Italian Supreme Command to send forward all possible forces to the front as soon as possible to thicken up our very thin front line.'

Siwa? A mobile force? Where could he find the men, vehicles and resources to send a group of any significance 320 kilometres to the south? Or was this just flannel to impress higher command?

Rommel, well served by his intelligence service, learned that day that Operation Order No 89 required the New Zealanders to be launched across his rear while 30th Corps kept him busy in the north - if the opportunity offered, of course. The stage for such an operation was set thanks to what Tuker calls 'the enterprising New Zealanders'[1], whose 5th Brigade had the previous day installed themselves on the southern rim of

Mreir Depression, facing north. Auchinleck's plan proposed that 13th Corps formations - New Zealand Division and what was left of 7th Armoured Division - would, in the event of a German withdrawal, carry out a pursuit 'with the greatest vigour', racing for Daba and Fuka respectively and strike against whatever enemy columns were encountered.

Whether coincidentally as part of his regrouping or in response to this threat from the south (it's hard to tell which), Rommel pulled back 21st Panzer from its Ruweisat position, where the previous day it had waged a futile battle with 1st Armoured Division, and 1st Armoured, sensing this withdrawal, came tramping on its heels until its ardour was cooled by a line of anti-tank guns.

For British tank crews, it was a relaxed, sporting kind of a day as, relieved of pressure, they enjoyed shooting up a now defensive enemy.

22nd Armoured Brigade caught one enemy group in laager and had a 'first class shoot' that incinerated a number of trucks. A few light tanks, encountering some anti-tank guns, skilfully put down a smoke screen that enabled them to close to a range where they could machine gun the crews, who were put to flight. This gave encouragement to other British tanks to join in, and the artillery added its share. However, the enemy was able to retain some cohesion, and withdrew behind tanks and anti-tank guns, and the advance fizzled out after several kilometres.

But though 1st Armoured's advance came to nothing and there was no fleeing enemy to pursue, 7th Armoured Division in the south sent about 40 armoured cars haring west, almost reaching Daba. German artillery, its ammunition exhausted, could only watch impotently until, according to Rommel, one battery with shells was found in Zech Group, and the adventurers were turned back with 'its last few rounds'.[2]

Another cause of excitement that day was a report that went through the Eighth Army like wildfire that 600 Germans - Germans, indeed! - had tried to surrender to 22nd Armoured Brigade and had been dissuaded from this folly by one of their own 88mm guns, which opened fire on the British tanks. To this day the event is a mystery. Six hundred would have been about half Rommel's German army, and Scoullar questions whether so many could have been found in one group. Afrika Korps diary refers to a lorried infantry regiment as having been overrun, and Dorman Smith wrote in his singularly spasmodic diary, 'First batch of Germans surren-

---

* 'noted much as a naturalist would have recorded the first primrose as a sign of advancing spring,' comments Connell[3]

dered*.' But Auchinleck's evening signal to London reported that an apparent surrender 'seems to have been a ruse and no prisoners fell into our hands.' All this is confused by another report of 100 to 200 men of 115th Lorried Infantry Regiment surrendering to Robcol, a 50th Division group.

For the men of the Eighth Army, who hadn't heard any good news for a long time, this apparent crack in the facade of German militarism was welcome indeed. The uncertainty of the event, though, is symptomatic of the day's confusion, and academic though it might now be, it is of some interest to consider whether the men who failed to press on with Auchinleck's plans were themselves confused or were the cause of the confusion. The South African historian considered that in Eighth Army's failure to push on 'one of the great opportunities of the war had been missed'[4] and Connell blames Norrie and Gott, whom he says were too tired to respond.

Von Mellenthin, too, put the blame on Auchinleck's corps commanders, who, he says, could not be stirred into action.

'We survived 4 July,' he wrote 'with no real damage except to our nerves.'[5]

Rommel, who now knew that his opponent was Auchinleck, took a more reasoned view. He wrote later: 'General Auchinleck ... was handling his forces with considerable skill and tactically better than Ritchie had done. He seemed to view the situation with decided coolness, for he was not allowing himself to be rushed into accepting a second best solution by any moves we made.'[6]

Second best? One swift blow that brought down the Germans would hardly have been a second best. But truly, did the Eighth Army have the capacity, even against such a weakened enemy? Though it certainly had the weight of numbers, there was a heavy psychological burden of defeat and misconception on the British side, and the corps commanders, not to speak of the troops themselves, were tired men. Some of them had endured weeks of battle in the sweltering heat, with no opportunity for rest and often little time for sleep, and they had seen all their best efforts crumble into failure. Besides, although the Eighth Army just might have knocked out Rommel with a blow, had he eluded them an extended pursuit would have been out of the question. Unlike Rommel, for whom a break-through would have led to an Aladdin's cave of stores and equipment, Auchinleck would have fought his way literally into a desert, and massive improvisation would have been necessary to maintain supplies. And being cynical, it might be asked whether, in view of what took place later in the month, the Eighth Army would not have botched it, anyway. 4 July might be considered an opportunity missed or a disaster averted.

More than this, the Australians, who had also been chosen for pursuit, had only that day begun to arrive, and their commander, Morshead, was proving to be as bloody minded as Inglis.

The 9th Australian Division, recently arrived from Syria, was in reserve in a defensive role at Amariya when an instruction came by telephone at 3.00am on 3 July from Eighth Army Headquarters to reform into battle groups and send forward at once one brigade group less one battalion. This was not well received. The 9th was now the only Australian division in Egypt, the other two having gone home to deal with the Japanese threat, and before their commander, Blamey, left he advised Morshead that piecemeal employment of Australian units should not be permitted.

So taking the precaution of ordering his 24th Brigade, less one battalion, to be ready to move forward at 5.00am on 4 July, provided deficiencies in equipment and transport could be made good, Morshead took himself off to Eighth Army Headquarters for an interview with Auchinleck. It was more or less a re-run of the discussion Auchinleck had had with Inglis several days earlier.

Auchinleck said he wanted the Australian brigade right away. 'You can't have it,' Morshead replied. 'Why?' 'Because they are going to fight as a formation with the rest of the division.'

'Not if I give you orders?' 'Give me orders and see,' said the obdurate Morshead.

'So you're like Blamey,' said a resigned Auchinleck 'You're wearing his mantle.'

Auchinleck had to yield or wait while the question was handed over to the Australian Government. But there was no time for that sort of carry-on, and Morshead was allowed to order up his whole division. With that agreement, he released the one brigade group requested, to be temporarily attached to 30th Corps, and on 4 July the 24th Brigade group came forward.

There must have been times when Auchinleck felt he was fighting his Commonwealth generals as well as the enemy.

The net result of all this is that while there was some restless shuffling on the Alamein front that day, the two armies were more or less locked into their positions of the previous day, although the line between them had developed a distinct dog leg.

The South Africans in the Alamein Box and south of it still faced the inactive Italians and whatever elements of 90th Light remained there after they had lent a hand in the previous day's armour battle. 1st Armoured Division was astride Ruweisat Ridge from where it made its short-lived pursuit of 21st Panzer.

From Ruweisat Ridge the battle line took a right-angle turn to the west where Brescia and the 5th NZ Brigade faced each other across Mreir Depression. It was a stand-off situation here; on that open ground no one on either side could move without bringing down artillery, mortar or machine-gun fire.

South of this, again, there wasn't a lot to be seen, apart from mobiles roving loose on watch for enemy movement, and during the day Rommel moved to fill this vacuum.

In the rest of the New Zealand camp, 4th Brigade was back in Munassib with the booty captured from Ariete, and the itinerant 6th Brigade was at Himeimat.

Most of the day's mayhem was contributed by the opposing air forces, Stukas to pound 5th NZ Brigade's rear echelons, Desert Air Force to do the same to the enemy from a higher altitude.

The airmen, who knew as little about what was happening on the ground as the soldiers knew about the air war, received Auchinleck's 'well done' message as a sign that the tide had turned, and in mid-afternoon there was great jubilation when the story of the surrender of 600 'bomb happy' Germans reached them. In the air force version, the enemy had 'walked in with their hands up'. Beyond this, there was talk of an advance, planned for 6 July, and the commander of 233 Wing gave orders for squadrons to organise into stripped-down groups, able to move forward rapidly taking only the minimum number of men and the bare amount of equipment necessary. Clerks, even ground gunners, were to be left behind, and only blankets were to be taken. 'No beds, razors, washing kits or extra clothing will be carried,' the order said. 'Every inch of space, every pound of weight and every effort must be made to cut down the amount of transport used to carry personnel as I intend to use the bulk of wing transport as a private S and T column.' A commendable order, it might be thought, if a little over-zealous. After all, a man might carry a razor and soap in his pocket. During the day, Kippenberger, with his 5th NZ Brigade at Mreir, became uneasily aware from reports sent by the patrolling NZ

Divisional Cavalry that enemy vehicles were moving into Mungar Wahla, a position eight kilometres west of his open left flank, and he decided he must go for a quick decision at Mreir with an attack that night.

He had reason to be nervous. As part of his regrouping, Rommel had despatched three reconnaissance units to the south to operate against any British turning movement - 580 Recce to Mungar Wahla, and 3 and 33 to a location near El Kharita, about 16 kilometres west of Kaponga. This was his first diversion of troops away from the centre of action in the north. In the north itself he spread his other German troops more thinly, moving 21st Panzer as we have seen, to counter the New Zealanders at Mreir. 90th Light and 15th Panzer, nervously awaiting British counter-attack, extended left and right to fill the gaps. To support Brescia at Mreir, a detachment from Kapmstaffel Khiel was ordered across.

At nightfall, 5th NZ Brigade was in a salient, with Germans to the west, south west and east, and Italians and Germans to the north. Kippenberger, in search of his quick decision, sent his 23rd battalion on a circular foray through the Italian lines that night, and though everything did not go according to plan, partly because of poor leadership, the battalion made a fighting intrusion into the Italian positions and came back with two prisoners from Pavia Division, and a Breda machine-gun for good measure.

A 'tired and fagged out' Rommel had little to tell his wife, Lu, that day. 'Resistance is too great and our strength exhausted,' he told her. 'However, I still hope to find a way to achieve our goal.'[7]

At Auchinleck's headquarters the lamp burned late into that night. Again as midnight approached, Operation Order No 90 was put to paper, signed and sent off. This time the wording was less Churchillian, and a touch of fatigue might be seen behind the more moderate language. The plan for 5 July was to be the same as for 4 July - 13th Corps to attack Rommel's flank from the south while 30th Corps kept him busy in the north. But it was all very vague. The opening paragraphs read:

Situation

Today the enemy suffered considerable losses in equipment and prisoners.

Appreciation

Best evidence shows that the enemy hopes to gain time to recover from his reverses of the last three days. It is not impossible that he will attempt to withdraw though there are no signs of this yet.

Intention

Eighth Army will attack and destroy the enemy in his present position.

Nothing now about fast and far. Nothing now about pursuit. Now it was 'destroy the enemy in his present position', and this was to be the theme to run through operation orders for the rest of the month. Enemy flight was always kept in mind, but the strategy was to keep him bottled up and demolish his army where it stood. And God knows, the Eighth Army tried.

CHAPTER ELEVEN

5,6,7 JULY - PORTENTS OF DISASTER

As the air force understood it, 5 July was to be the day that the enemy's 'withdrawal' was to be turned into retreat. Doubt crept into this resolve when returning aircraft reported little movement on the coast road, certainly no sign that the Axis army was giving up. Finding no juicy targets there, the aircraft turned their attention to whatever could be found in the desert.

Down on the ground, as the army made plans for counter-attack, the desert wind carried straws of disaster to come. Eighth Army headquarters became aware on 4 July that changes were being made on the Axis side of the line. It looked as though Rommel might be regrouping to outflank the coastal positions, as well as planning for a rest period while reinforcements and supplies were gathered in. Auchinleck thereupon issued an order on 5 July: 'Our task remains to destroy the enemy as far cast as possible and not to let him get away as a force in being ... The enemy should be given no rest ... Eighth Army will attack and destroy the enemy in his present position.'

With 1st Armoured Division comfortably supplied with tanks, Auchinleck ought to have been able to carry this off. By Liddell Hart's reckoning Rommel had only 15 tanks that day, but German war diaries on 6 July indicate that there were then 44 and it might be questioned whether the field workshops could turn around 29 repaired tanks in 24 hours.

Whatever the number, the British had clear superiority. But behind this seemingly secure armour position lurked the concealed hazard of what might be seen as burn-out. Dorman Smith was in Norrie's caravan that day when the 1st Armoured commander, Lumsden, arrived and 'immediately and brusquely' demanded that his division should be relieved; his men had been fighting for weeks on end and were exhausted. Nothing Norrie could say could calm him, and as the 'over-excited and emphatically undisciplined' Lumsden carried on, Dorman Smith watched 'in fascinated horror' and wondered why Norrie did not place him under arrest.

Dorman Smith does not tell us how Norrie eventually overcame this high-level rebellion, but of course 1st Armoured Division stayed in place under Lumsden, though with a change. 2nd Armoured Brigade came up on 5 July, and on 7 July took over from 4th Armoured Brigade, absorbing its vehicles and signals. 4th Brigade was withdrawn and converted into a light armoured brigade group. 2nd Armoured Brigade, which assumed the major role in coming operations, then consisted of 3rd County of London Yeomanry (ten Grants, 25 Crusaders), 3/5 Royal Tank Regiment (24 Grants, 14 Honeys, three Crusaders), 6th RTR (13 Grants, 17 Honeys), 1st Royal Horse Artillery (22 25-pounders, 13 six-pounders), and 1st KRR (nine six-pounders).

In its new role, 4th Armoured Brigade consisted of two armoured car regiments (11th Hussars and 12th Lancers), a regiment of Honeys (two squadrons of the 4th Hussars and one of the 8th Hussars), 104th RHA and the 9th Rifle Brigade.

In fairness to Lumsden, he spoke no more than the truth to Norrie. The armour had been fighting without pause for weeks on end, and it might be wondered how much of what occurred later in July could be attributed to plain battle weariness.

Norrie's surprising calm in the face of Lumsden's bluster might, perhaps, be attributed to his knowledge that he himself was to be relieved of his command in the next two days. Norrie's departure early in July at a time when it might be thought the Desert crisis would demand his retention was accomplished without fuss, and no one could say whether he had been sent home or had gone of his own volition. In fact Auchinleck was not happy with the way he had handled his corps and so replaced him, though Dorman Smith took a different view of his performance.

And so it came about that the 50th Division's former commander, the Luger-toting Yorkshireman Ramsden, stepped in as corps commander, and a new point of friction was created in the command structure - or it might be seen as another fracture in an already fragmented army. Pienaar had a strong antipathy to Ramsden and thought him a poor commander, and Morshead resented the fact that he was now subordinate to a general who was his junior. Of such temperamental material are senior officers made. According to Brigadier Cilliers, GS01 of the South African Division, Ramsden was showing signs of strain and found it hard to handle awkward personalities like Pienaar and Morshead. He describes seeing these two divisional commanders at orders groups waiting tensely while Ramsden gave out his orders, and then 'descending on him like a pair of wolves'.

What was needed in the Eighth Army was an army commander who would knock a few heads together.

Meanwhile, on the real battlefield not a lot happened on either side.

5th New Zealand Brigade had already established one jaw of a nutcracker movement, and Auchinleck's counter-attack was to build on this. Three variants of how this was to be done emerged on 5 and 6 July, and in the end none was implemented.

All this time, 5th NZ Brigade held its position south of Mreir, and the intention of the final plan was that 4th NZ Brigade should move up on its left flank, facing north, which meant taking over the area in which Mungar Wahla lay - the position into which 528 Recce had moved, as well as Littorio Division, as it was to be discovered. 1st Armoured Division, with two Australian companies and Australian anti-tank guns in attendance, was to make a night attack along the now well-tramped territory of Ruweisat Ridge, and the two New Zealand brigades were to be ready to exploit from the south. The New Zealanders were also to co-operate by providing an artillery bombardment ahead of the intended 1st Armoured advance. 6th NZ Brigade was brought back on to the scene and returned to the Kaponga Box, where it would provide some security from the south while the rest of the division was busy in the north.

There were, though, three unsettling elements in this 'destroy the enemy' plan.

The Eighth Army chose what must surely have been the most inappropriate moment to issue a new order on 5 July on action to be taken should the British defences collapse. It came with the lame warning that it was not 'to be interpreted as a weakening of our intention to hold the present position or as an indication that our efforts have or are likely to fail'. Well! This is a long way from the 'far and fast' order.

That was straw number one - ambivalence.

Moreover, in its orders for the counter-attack, 30th Corps told Morshead that if he thought there was not enough time for his Australians to prepare he should ask for a postponement. This is surely an unsettling element to inject into a battle plan, and as things turned out the assembly of the Australian Division was not completed until 8 July, and the attack was postponed. 30th Corps told 13th Corps of this, but word did not reach the New Zealanders.

That's straw number two - poor communications.

On 6 July, Kippenberger, with his 5th Brigade south of Mreir filled a quiet day, as he tells it in *Infantry Brigadier*, writing a blow-by-blow account of what was going on. At 5.31pm he noted that a message was received that 1st Armoured Division was to attack that night, with the New Zealanders to exploit success in the morning. 'Fanciful,' he wrote.[1]

Then just over an hour later, recording that the New Zealand artillery was shooting simply at a map reference on a windy, dusty evening as a prelude to the planned (but now aborted) attack, he wrote, 'Show doesn't

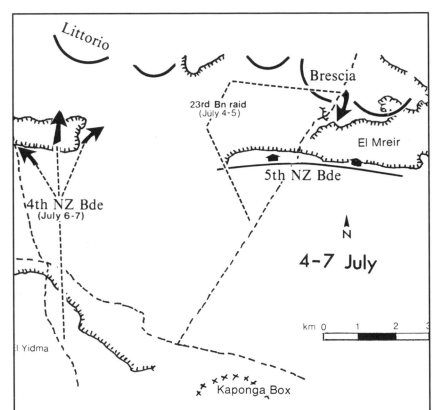

While Eighth Army grappled with the Axis army on and around Ruweisat Ridge, New Zealand Division engaged in a little private enterprise south of El Mreir Depression. 5th Brigade went there originally to cut off fleeing remnants of Ariete, and 4th Brigade ranged alongside to take its place in an intended army attack that never came off. However, 4th Brigade did shoot up an unsuspecting Littorio, and 5th Brigade sent a battalion on a night raid through Brescia's positions.

look very hopeful. Feel certain the tanks won't attack at night whatever Corps may order.'

Straw number three. In that last sentence he put his finger on one of the causes of the Eighth Army's repeated failures in the weeks to come and a prime reason why Rommel, his army tottering on the brink of ruin, was able not merely to hold Auchinleck at bay but also to snatch away some of his most prized troops.

On 5 July, though, it was all on, and 4th NZ Brigade made its approach march by moving west to make a turn, as had 5th NZ Brigade, around the southern and western sides of Kaponga Box. The dusty column was moving west when enemy aircraft howled out of the sun and a plaster of bombs flashed red amidst their own dust cloud. When the aircraft turned away, Brigadier Gray and his brigade major were dead, as well as a number of other officers and men. As the graves were filled in, Lieutenant-Colonel Burrows assumed command, but in these days security in the Eighth Army was so tight that not even he knew where the brigade was going or what it was to do when it got there. Fortunately there was one survivor who did, 20th Battalion's intelligence officer, and the brigade moved on, completing its round-the-corner move and reaching a modest feature west of Kaponga known as Qarat el Yidma at 3.00pm where it was bombed again, this time with little effect.

5 July brought Operations Order No 91, which said that 'enemy resistance increased during 5 July', and that '13th Corps made good progress during 6 July'. It served notice that the Eighth Army would shortly 'attack and destroy the enemy', but added, 'The C-in-C will decide later if this attack is to be made or not'.

This waffle was unsettling, and it was during the course of 6 July that the three successive plans filtered down from above. With a curious biblical touch, the first was known as *Luke*, perhaps because it was a Sunday. It was a repetition of the flank attack from the south. The second, known as *Revelations*, changed the emphasis to the north. Then at 3.30pm the third plan came through, providing for the armoured drive along Ruweisat Ridge with Australian support and with the New Zealanders being required to fire a barrage ahead of the tanks, the plan Kippenberger thought fanciful. At the same time 4th NZ Brigade would move up to a position level with 5th NZ Brigade, so that the two would be side by side, facing north, ready to strike. It was this plan that was cancelled without the New Zealanders being told.

As evening fell, New Zealand guns, together with 64th Medium Battery of the Royal Artillery, pasted the designated area, and though Inglis noted later that this turned out to be a waste of ammunition, at least it gave Afrika Korps headquarters, then in Deir el Abyad, 15th Panzer and Breihl battle group from 90th Light an unpleasant time, and astonished Rommel with the profligacy with which the Eighth Army fired off shells.

4th NZ Brigade, meanwhile, prepared on this 6 July to set out on a night advance to a feature overlooking Mungar Wahla, where it would be in a position to make Auchinleck's intended strike north. It set out at 3.00am on Monday 7 July and by a nice piece of night navigation covered the designated 3,000 metres to arrive right on target. With an hour to go to first light, units dug in and artillery was placed in position.

As light came into the sky, the New Zealanders found themselves looking down on an enemy formation 600 metres away to the north. Unaware that they were being watched, men of Littorio Division stretched and yawned, folded their blankets and went about preparing breakfast - the usual comfortable routine of soldiers set back from the immediate line of fire. In an earlier war it might have been thought unsporting, and in today's more pacifist climate rejoicing at the sight of human targets might be thought barbaric, but 1942 in North Africa was another time and another place, and the men of the 4th NZ Brigade felt no qualms as they lined up their sights, and as the signal was given a hail of fire tore into the unsuspecting Italians. Rifle and machine-gun fire ripped through troops within closer range, and mortars and machine-guns so effectively saturated an area of four 75 mm guns that not one shell went into the breach. From behind the New Zealand riflemen the field guns cracked into life, and shells fell among the more distant trucks and tanks.

It was not until about 8.00am that the enemy gathered themselves enough to send back mortar and small arms fire and to begin assembling a counter-attack - a move reported by carrier patrols. All available weapons turned on the assembly area, and the enemy infantry dissolved. Head haze and the inevitable dust of battle began to cloud vision as the morning went on, and by midday firing had died away, and the antagonists could only peer towards each other in anxious frustration.

Over at Mreir, 5th NZ Brigade had also had an active night with fighting patrols, and in the early morning hours there was a warning that the enemy might be withdrawing westwards. But daylight brought the news that 1st Armoured Division had not advanced during the night (as Kippenberger had foreseen), and the two New Zealand brigades now found themselves 'sticking out like a sore thumb miles from any other substantial part of the army,' as one senior officer put it. That day both brigades were pulled back from the positions they had so hopefully taken up, ending any chance of a counter-stroke from the south. 6th NZ Brigade was yet again taken out of Kaponga Box and sent back to Amiriya for a quiet loaf. In 13th Corps it was one step forward, one step back. In 30th Corps nothing was happening at all. But it was 13th Corps that was to be singled out by a post-war critic.

'Throughout this period, 13th Corps had evinced the all too familiar inertia and lack of enterprise that had undermined the army at Gazala,' Tuker wrote[2]

The minor attacks that had swung the corps 'left flank up to Mreir had been instigated,' he said, 'by the lively impulses of the New Zealand Division,' but the corps did nothing further and pulled back these forces from positions 'threatening Rommel's whole stability between Ruweisat and the sea'.

Rommel, though, hardly seems to have been disturbed by all this activity, let alone been aware that his stability had been threatened, and Panzerarmee reports are dismissive.

British activity, Rommel wrote in his journal, was restricted to small scale sector attacks, which is true. He was surprised by the 'astonishing amount of ammunition the British expended in their preliminary barrages', and said that during the night 6-7 July, 'British guns fired 10,000 rounds into a five-kilometre sector of the 15th Panzer Division'. This would have been the New Zealand barrage put down for the aborted armoured attack. He also records that British infantry worked their way forward and flung 'explosive charges' into defence posts - 5th NZ Brigade's fighting patrols, perhaps, or a company raid sent out by the 2/43rd Battalion of the 34th Australian Brigade, which destroyed four 50 mm guns and captured one 25-pounder, four gun tractors and two large troop carriers, and which also recaptured a Bren carrier, besides inflicting 40 casualties and taking nine prisoners. German accounts inflate the Australian incursion into a frontal attack supported by tanks, and an irritated Rommel ordered that officers of forward units must stay awake all night to avoid being taken by surprise. 21st Panzer war diary, which had shrugged off the raid as just one of those things, recorded that Rommel's instruction was received 'with pained surprise'.

Rommel wrote later that the Australian attack had been 'preceded all day by tank thrusts against my exhausted troops who had lain all the time in their trenches and fox holes exposed to the full blaze of the sun'. The British had succeeded in taking over part of the line, he wrote, but were 'thrown back by a spirited counter-attack'. The attack on Littorio could hardly go unnoticed, either, though it was seen as only a minor engagement.[3]

Rommel's real worry was supplies and reinforcements. Italian infantry was gradually coming forward and taking over in the front line from German motorised units, allowing them more mobility. But for 'some unaccountable reason' the few ships crossing the Mediterranean were berthing at Benghazi or Tripoli so that supplies had to be brought forward by motor transport or meagre coastal shipping, 1,120 kilometres from Benghazi, 1,824 from Tripoli. (Paris to Warsaw is about 1,560 kilometres in a direct line.)

'This, of course, is more than we could manage,' Rommel wrote.

A measure of the Axis problems is an entry in 90th Light's war diary for 6 July: 'The division tries to get one battery of Littorio through army channels, which, however, proves impossible as Littorio allegedly has only one gun left. Instead of this, Army grants leave for Battle Group Briehl and Recce Detachment 3 artillery to operate under one staff.'

It was this combination, according to the division's diary, for 7 July, that thwarted an attempt by New Zealand Division to make an encircling move.

And for the time being, that was that. The first phase of the Battle of Egypt was over. Rommel had been repulsed and was now settling in to build up his forces and devise a new plan. 21st Panzer Division, also giving some thought to what should be done next, says in its war diary of 5 July: 'The enemy must be cured of his zest for offensive.'

One proposal was to 'build in' heavy weapons and, playing on British respect for the 88 mm gun, create a number of dummy artillery positions using telegraph poles.

'This must be done on a large scale but no conspicuous exaggeration must occur,' the diary says. 'Mobile 88 AA guns will fire from such dummy positions.'

It was not until 26 July that British patrols recovered two Bofors with poles wired to them to resemble 88s. Angle iron had been fixed to the gun to support a tarpaulin, and 25-pounder shell cases and ammunition strewn about. The patrol reported that it was five metres from the dummy before the deception was discovered. A wrecked Chevrolet truck, similarly treated, was less convincing. As a matter of record, the two Bofors were repossessed, and one put back into action.

Nothing as ingenious as this was being considered on the British side. The Eighth Army had gone through the motions of counter-attacking without actually consummating, and Auchinleck was now bringing up reinforcements and considering his next move.

The air force was also turning its mind to changes, though for a very different reason. Throughout these three days the hapless South Africans continued to suffer the hostile attentions of friendly aircraft.

'1845 hours (6.45pm) the 3rd SA Infantry Brigade in Alamein Box again bombed for fifth time by RAF bombers,' says the 1st SA Division war diary for 5 July. 'As in the other cases, a strong protest was put to 30th Corps.'

'Our air force active, but inclined to over-do the close support bombing, the ILH (Imperial Light Horse) and the RDLI (Royal Durban Light Infantry) areas being bombed five times in the past two days,' reports the 1st Rand Light Infantry.

'Our air force continued to do very good work but unfortunately we again had two Boston raids, which landed very close to Battle HQ's area, at least too close to be comfortable, and the ground around shook,' says the report from the ILH. 'We certainly felt very shaken.'

As the airmen saw it, they had bombed 200 to 300 stationary vehicles and tanks 11 kilometres at their closest from the Alamein Box, and though they were at 7,500 feet and there was a haze caused by a dust storm, they saw enough to be able to claim a direct hit on a gun pit. But aerial photographs the next day confirmed that the 12th and 223rd Squadrons had indeed bombed the Alamein Box.

The official response when the error became known was that the airmen faced enormous problems in determining where they were. There was frequent dust haze that obscured what features there were in a 'featureless' desert, and this difficulty was exacerbated by a bomb line (the line beyond which it is safe to attack from the air) that frequently wove 'a devious course'. And the problem of recognising individual vehicles from a height of 7,000 to 8,000 feet was 'insoluble', particularly as the enemy was using so much captured British transport. These arguments might have served if the bombing errors had occurred far out in the desert, but the South Africans were in and near the Alamein Box, the perimeter of which was starkly clear from the air. Besides this there were many natural features near the coast, not to mention the man-made features of a bitumen coast road, a number of tracks, and the railway line.

'That bombs could fall seven miles from where they are reported to have fallen must have done nothing to reassure Air Headquarters of the utility of the light bombers to render really effective close support,' says a thesis by E V Axelson.[4]

True enough, and a reminder of the handicap the British laboured under for want of a dive bomber.

Air Headquarters decided on 6 July that in future, rather than have the army define the bomb line, it should tell the air force where its forward units were and allow the air force to set the bomb line. Forward units were also to put out markers about 200 metres across to indicate positions. But of course, if the air crews did not know where they were, the position of the bomb line was immaterial.

The air force reported 'an air of quiet on the front' on 7 July.

'No major activity is in progress or seems to be pending,' 3 Wing recorded. 'The battle has dragged to a standstill ...'

The bombing went on, though, and Afrika Korps said of this day: 'Enemy air attacks continue, the fighter bomber attacks being particularly irksome.'

There was a remarkable moment of unintended co-operation between air and ground when bombers hit a group of vehicles just as a field battery was preparing a fire for effect on the same target.

At midday on 7 July, Operation Order No 92 set a new direction for the Eighth Army. It read in part:

Summary

The enemy is now over-extended and he has been forced to bring his Italian formations into forward positions.

Eighth Army is reorganising so as to secure our positions firmly while preparing to take instant advantage of any opening which the enemy may afford us to take the offensive or pursue.

Intention

Eighth Army will hold its ground and continue to wear down the enemy while preparing for decisive action.

The order went on to warn both corps to be ready to act 'at very short notice' on receipt of the code word *Exalted*. It was a blend of uncertainty and hope, and the stage was being set for a kind of ritual dance of war in which there were to be forward steps, backward steps and sideways steps, with men being trampled underfoot at every move.

CHAPTER TWELVE

8-13 JULY - THE AUSTRALIANS STRIKE

The great question was who would dance to whose tune. This was resolved by a touch of farce that left Rommel claiming a victory in the south while Auchinleck rocked him with a blow in the north that took back the first modest piece of territory in the great reclamation of whole countries that was to follow over the next 2 $^1/_2$ years.

8 July was a quiet sort of day as both sides completed their regrouping. Auchinleck, now with about 200 tanks at his disposal, moved all his Grants into the 1st Armoured Division (as he and Dorman Smith had agreed) on the assumption that they corresponded to German types, and gave the division the task of neutralising the panzers and working with the infantry and Valentines. To the dismay of tank crews there, the Crusaders and some Honeys went south to 7th Armoured Division, which was to strike at Italian armour and infantry, and range like cavalry deep into enemy territory. This division was not to become involved with German tanks except under favourable circumstances, presumably an indication of Auchinleck's lack of confidence in his Crusaders. 4th Armoured Brigade, which was now with 7th Armoured Division, was also to harass the enemy flank and rear in armoured cars, and to carry out reconnaissance. And so the planning made on that 25 June flight up to the Desert fell into place.

On this day the 9th Australian Division completed its move to the front, adding one complete division to the Eighth Army, and as the only substantial loss to this point had been the 18th Indian Brigade, this was almost all clear gain.

On the other side, a stocktaking showed that despite the arrival of reinforcements, Rommel considered his formations 'no longer merited the title of divisions'. Afrika Korps had 50 tanks, mainly Mark IIIs, with a few Mark IIs and IVs, with about 600 men and 20 anti-tank guns in the rifle regiments and an artillery regiment of seven batteries. Normal strength would have been 371 tanks and 246 anti-tank guns.

90th Light was more or less holding its own with 1,500 men, 30 anti-tank guns and two batteries, but this compared with a normal complement of 12,000 men and 220 anti-tank guns.

Then there were three reconnaissance battalions with 15 armoured cars, 20 armoured troop carriers and three captured batteries - about 27 guns.

The Germans also had an army artillery group in addition to those attached to individual divisions (something that Auchinleck emulated with his reorganisation). This army group had 11 heavy and four light batteries, together with 26 88 mm guns and 25 50 mm guns.

Total German strength that day would have been perhaps 3,000 men.

The Italian troops consisted in the main of XX Motorised Corps made up of two armoured and one motorised division, with 54 tanks and eight motor battalions. The motor battalions had an overall strength of 1,600 men. There were 40 anti-tank guns. Normal complement of the corps was 430 tanks and 120 anti-tank guns.

There were, finally, what were listed as 'elements' of X and XXI Corps, consisting of about 2,200 men, with some light and heavy batteries. There may have been about 15,000 Italian present, all told.

Rommel distributed this inadequate force along his front. He gave the north and the gap that 90th Light had penetrated to the Italians. South from here were mixed German and Italian forces, with a particularly strong German cluster consisting of 15th Panzer and heavy artillery astride Ruweisat Ridge. 21st Panzer was prowling around the area between Mreir and Kaponga, and 90th Light, with several recce units, was testing the water around Gebel Kalahk and El Taqa Plateau in the far south, where there were columns from the 5th Indian Division and South African armoured car squadrons. In this southern fastness both sides were content to keep a wary watch.

More than anything else, the Axis forces needed rest, but this they were denied. From his Derna headquarters, Mussolini had ordained on 6 July that if there was no further attack in the following 10 to 14 days all chance of exploiting the Eighth Army's weakness would be lost and the slight force at Rommel's command would be insufficient to push through to the Suez Canal by way of Cairo. He suggested as an alternative that the shorter jab to Alexandria would bring greater prestige, but Rommel and his Italian superior, Cavallero, decided that if anything was to be attempted it should be a drive through to the Red Sea via Cairo. The coast route via Alexandria, they agreed, would mean a traverse of the many obstacles of the Nile Delta.

The new Axis plan was to attack in the south, where Rommel would strike 'a heavy blow on the New Zealanders on 9 July, capture their position (Kaponga) and use it as a base for a breakthrough'. From here the Axis forces would advance to Alam Nayil and then turn north. What he did not know was that Auchinleck was planning an attack along the coast with the recently arrived Australians and the South Africans with the intention of capturing those Tell el Eisa mounds that overlooked the Alamein Box. He would then push south west against Rommel's communications and headquarters area. Zero hour for this offensive was 3.00am on 10 July. The stage was being set for the Eighth Army to seize the initiative.

There were a number of things Rommel did not know, in particular that the 4th and 5th NZ Brigades had withdrawn from their exposed positions to Munassib, and that 6th NZ Brigade had evacuated Kaponga, leaving only a rearguard of a platoon, because it no longer fitted into Auchinleck's plan for maximum mobility. The Germans did not discover the disappearance of the New Zealanders from Mungar Wahla and Mreir until about 3.45pm on 8 July, just as Stukas were about to launch an attack on the Mreir positions.

During that afternoon a German patrol approached Kaponga and turned away when fired on by the rearguard. From this point onwards the Germans appear to have become confused, and Rommel never seems to have discovered the truth of it all. At 10.45pm 21st Panzer told Afrika Korps the box was empty, and it was instructed to install a reconnaissance troop there. This was not done, although a patrol did go out.

When he phoned Afrika Korps the next morning, Rommel was told the box was empty and he exploded in anger because no move had been made to occupy it in strength. 21st Panzer put the wheels in motion, but reported soon afterwards that its recce troop had retired north 'under strong pressure' of superior enemy forces. This deluded report changed the operation from a peaceful take-over to a full-scale assault.

Rommel stirred things along again when he arrived at Afrika Korps headquarters at 10.00am. The Korps diary records that he 'starts nagging because the enemy strongpoint is still not occupied'.

Towards noon a formidable force began its approach march towards an inoffensively empty Kaponga Box. A phalanx of Mark IIIs of 21st Panzer led the way, followed by the light tanks of Littorio. Behind them came infantry, engineers and heavy artillery, and as this force came up to the fortifications towards evening, Stukas pounded Kaponga with a massive weight of high explosive. As the engineers moved in to lift mines and cut gaps in the wire, the artillery joined in and the infantry stormed through. This neatly executed text book assault was watched in astonished fascination from a safe distance by some New Zealanders and a column from 7th Motor Brigade.

At 6.15pm 21st Panzer signalled Afrika Korps that the position had been taken, 'with the enemy falling back to the east', which was deceptively true. Perhaps someone misfiled this message, because at 10.03pm Afrika Korps signalled Panzerarmee: 'Last night's recce in force discovered the Qel el Abd (Kaponga) was still firmly held by the enemy. Since midday today 21st Panzer has been attacking with considerable success against gradually stiffening opposition ... Div ... is to continue attack at 0500 10 July.'

But Rommel must have learned from somewhere that Kaponga was now in German hands, because his message to Rome, which incorporated news of some cautious probing by 90th Light, said: 'On the morning of 9 July Panzerarmee attacked the southern end of the Alamein Line, and during the day made a break-through and drove strong enemy forces back on a wide front from the Qattara Depression to the previous breach in the line. A fortification system strongly built and protected by numerous fieldworks and minefields was taken and occupied.'

And so the truth is embroidered as at each level commanders seek to placate those above them and gain merit for themselves.

A finally satisfied Rommel took himself to Kaponga, where he set up his headquarters in a concrete bunker in preparation for his new offensive.

'It was a quiet night,' he recorded. 'Seeing that 5th Indian and 7th Armoured Divisions had been thrown back by our striking force during the day, we planned to thrust on next morning with all our strength.'[1]

And in what must go down as one of history's famous last words, the keeper of the 90th Light war diary concluded his entry for 9 July with the observation: 'The enemy shows no intention of attacking in the north sector.'

At 5.00am the next day, 10 July, Rommel was awakened 'by the dull thunder of artillery fire in the north. I at once had an inkling that it boded no good'.[2] He was right.

The guns in the north, the heaviest drum roll German veterans of the First World War could recall, marked the start of Eighth Army's counterattack. They heralded a new phase in which British guns would play the tune to which the Germans would dance.

Rommel called off the major part of his thrust in the south and hastened north to see what was happening and what could be done about it. What was happening was that the 9th Australian Division and the 1st South African Division were executing Operation Order No 93, issued on 8 July, which gave as its intention:

'Eighth Army will continue its efforts to destroy the enemy in his present positions, breaking through his northern flank on 9-10 July'.

The attack has been hailed as the Eighth Army's first advance since its long series of disasters, a step forward from which there would be no turning back, and the South Africans conclude their official history, *Crisis in the Desert*, at this point in the belief that it signified the turning of the tide.

'... Eighth Army was never again to know the anguish and humiliations of defeat,' it says[3]

In a symbolic way perhaps it was the first step forward, because although the Australians did not break through (and the South Africans

The attack by the Australians on 10 July was heralded as Eighth Army's return to the attack after its long retreat to Alamein. Although its scope was modest, the offensive seized a finger of territory along the coast and the Axis never succeeded in recovering this. One of the objects of the attack was to secure the Tell el Eisa mounds. This was partly achieved in the first few days, but enemy counter-attacks pushed the Australians off again

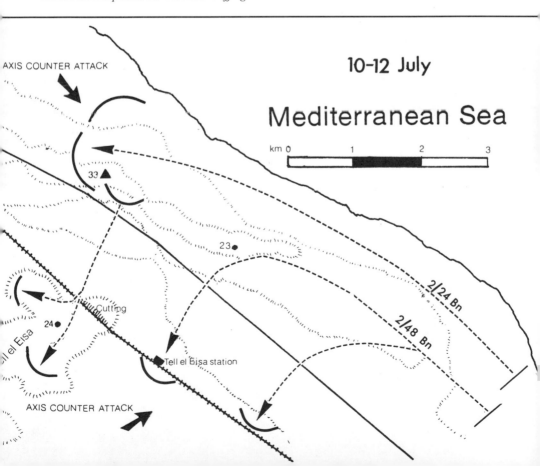

turned back), they secured and held territory that remained theirs, and carved out a fiefdom in the north that they held against all comers. Territory as such was not all that important, and in fact it was to the Eighth Army's advantage to hold Rommel in the Alamein constriction, but the Australian objective contained the Tell el Eisa mounds which, in enemy hands, permitted observation into the Alamein Box as well as other Eighth Army territory. More than this, the salient became a base for attack. When the pressure came on in the centre or south, Auchinleck could activate the north; when the Australians were threatened, he could stir more vigorously in the south. Between these two poles Rommel danced in frantic desperation, and he never again regained the initiative.

On the other hand, the Eighth Army, having seized the initiative, failed to use it to achieve a conclusion. The 10 July attack by the Australians and South Africans, in fact, established a pattern for every other operation to follow - a successful break-in by the infantry, and the collapse of the follow-through. Not once was the Eighth Army to grasp the victory that lay within reach.

Operation Order No 93 on 8 July stated:

'Eighth Army will continue its efforts to destroy the enemy in his present position by breaking through his northern flank.'

The order goes on to require 30th Corps to secure and consolidate a line from Tell el Eisa to El Makh Khad, for battle groups to roam and raid, for 13th Corps to deceive the enemy and prevent him sending reinforcements north by keeping up pressure in the south, and for 13th to be ready to attack north 'immediately a favourable opportunity offers'. 13th Corps was to be a dog on the leash, required to bark furiously until its commander saw an exposed rump to savage. For the moment, 30th Corps was to do the real biting.

The code name for this operation was *Reefknot.*

For all the thunder of its guns, the attack in the north was a modest affair of only two Australian battalions and a South African column. The Australians were to advance along the coast for five or six kilometres, then turn inland, seizing a length of railway line and, more importantly, the Tell el Eisa mounds, comprising a twin-peaked feature, with each height identified by the number 24. To distinguish one from the other, one was known as East Point 24 and the other West Point 24; these two peaks were to cost the Australians many lives in the coming weeks.

The South Africans were to sally out from their box and secure Tell el Makh Khad, another hill generally south east of Tell el Eisa.

To help things along, Morshead, the Australian commander, had 32 Valentines of 44th RTR under his command, and the South Africans were given six Matildas. These were, of course, infantry tanks, to be distinguished from the cavalry types with which the New Zealanders were to have an ill-fated liaison later in the month.

The offensive began, in fact, not with a roar of guns but in silent stealth.

The 2/48th Battalion of the 24th Australian Brigade was the first away in the pre-dawn dark of 10 July, though not without trauma. During the approach march their trucks became bogged in the salt marshes beside the track, and they arrived at their start line only after the exertions of heaving their transport into motion again, and were too late for the planned few hours' sleep. In the cool early morning darkness they moved forward on foot at 3.40am, silently, following the line of high ground. An aircraft droned unseen above them, and then suddenly a parachute flare blossomed in the sky and hung, all-revealing, over the leading companies, drenching the landscape in harsh white light. The Diggers froze in their tracks and waited for the storm of fire that must follow. But nothing happened; nothing. They moved forward again, and soon darkness closed in, and they broke in a steel-tipped khaki wave over the first Italian positions. In a turmoil of confusion, they engulfed the four surviving battalions of Sabratha Division, catching many men still asleep. Others took to their heels. An embittered Rommel later wrote that some Italian batteries did not fire because they said they had no orders, and the infantry who were not captured ran away, throwing aside their arms and ammunition as they went.

And then the barrage began.

If it roused Rommel and pummelled the Italians, it also had a shock effect on the gunners. 'The damn thing's terrifying at this end. I hate to think what it must be like at the other,' an officer in a troop command post, megaphone in hand, shouted to his assistant. One gunner was to write after the war, '... we felt ... a creative, a spiritual force.'[4] Strange words, but then a weapon of almost any calibre confers a great sense of power on its user, and at last these men were using that power to strike back at an enemy who had bested them and nearly broken them.

The poor Italians on Point 23, the first major objective, were hit with devastating force. As daylight came and the barrage lifted, the 2/48th pushed on, screened now from the enemy further west by smoke shells, and Point 23, more than 4,000 metres west of their start line, fell without a casualty. Prisoners included the commander of the 7th Bersaglieri

Regiment, caught in his shirt, but pugnaciously confident for all that. One man captured 14 Italians with a shovel. Prisoners were found to be carrying maps of Cairo showing the hotels designated for headquarters, and text books on the British Army. They expressed surprise at finding themselves facing real Australians.

With Point 23 in their possession, two companies of the 2/48th swung south towards the railway line, where German artillery batteries succumbed only to direct bayonet charges, firing right to the end. The Aussies then dug in around the Tell el Eisa railway station and a position to the east, and for the rest of the day crouched under a series of dive bombing attacks.

The second battalion in the attack, the 2/24th, which was to advance on a parallel course close to the sea, also became bogged down on their way to the start line, but got there in time to be away by zero hour, 4.30am. They moved forward first across country cleared of the enemy, and then, remarkably, considering the hullaballoo caused by the Australian guns and other infantry, encountered Italian troops still in their night attire - a luxury at any time for British troops, who normally dossed down in their clothes, and an astonishing neglect of common sense on an active battleground. But the resistance began to stiffen, and the Australians threw forward their Bren carriers like light tanks. In one charge they overcame machine-gun posts and anti-tank detachments without being fired on, although the guns were found to be loaded.

The 2/24th's objective was a position known as Trig 33, some distance west of where the 2/48th had swung south. They were there by 6.35am and were to have done a left turn to move on East Point 24, supported by tanks and machine-guns, but these were bellied in the salt marshes some distance to the rear, and the Australians dug in where they were, beating off several infantry and armoured counter-attacks in the course of the day and suffering the attentions of Stukas.

If from the Australian point of view all this sounds fairly mundane, if reasonably dangerous, on the German side there was high excitement, not to say alarm. The 2/24th thrust brought it to within three kilometres of Panzerarmee Headquarters on the coast near Ras el Shaqiq, and the German perception was that the Australians had been halted only by the desperate efforts of the machine-guns and anti-aircraft guns of the headquarters defence force, aided by the small arms of elements of Infantry Regiment 382, reinforcements who had been flown across from Crete and who were only then just arriving in the front line.

If the German report smells of panic, it's not surprising. Sabratha had been swept away and its survivors seen rushing back past Panzerarmee Headquarters.

But worse, much worse, was the capture by 2/24th Battalion of Long Range Recce Company 621, the Germans' radio intercept unit. This highly efficient company under Captain Seebohm had established itself near the coast not far from a feature known as White Knoll. Called 'the circus' because of its accumulation of trucks and tents, it included in its establishment an intercept platoon, an analysing platoon, and medium and short wave direction finding platoons. It was reputedly so efficient and British radio discipline so poor that it sometimes had British messages in Rommel's hands before they were received by the officers to whom they were addressed. Besides this, they were for a period able to listen to information about British plans radioed to Washington by the United States Military Attache in Cairo, Colonel Fellers, a clerk at the embassy having stolen a copy of the code.

Of course, the Australians knew nothing of this when, on their plunge along the coast, they came upon this collection of vehicles and tents. Seebohm, busy trying to burn papers, turned on them with a pistol, and was cut down. The Australians gathered up all the paper they could find, together with equipment, and sent it to the rear, with a haul of prisoners, Seebohm among them. He later died of his wounds.

A furious Rommel, told of the unit's location, exploded 'Then it's lost!'

And indeed it was. Apart from depriving Rommel of his eyes and ears, it alerted the British to their own shortcomings, and revision of procedures followed.

Rommel had come racing north with his Kampfstaffel Kiehl, that so useful headquarters group of last resort, together with its three or four tanks, and a battle group from 15th Panzer with 12 German and two Italian tanks.

The first counter-attacks fell on the 2/48th in and around Tell el Eisa station as Rommel sought to sever the salient from its base in the Alamein Box. Australian infantry resisted with anti-tank guns and, as the tanks passed among their slit trenches, with sticky bombs, and 'terrific shell fire' from the box gave them strong support. But the tanks kept coming throughout the day, and in the fifth and final attack, ten penetrated to Australian positions near the station. Anti-tank guns knocked out six, and the survivors fled. As the crew of one of those destroyed tried to follow on foot, screened from an Australian Vickers by a slight rise, one man lifted the gun, tripod and all, a total weight of about 42 kilograms, while another man fired. The tank crew surrendered.

Around 5.00pm there was another attack from the west on 2/24th Battalion, dug in around Trig 33. Eighteen Italian tanks came floundering across the salt marshes, most becoming bogged down. Fourteen were knocked out by anti-tank guns and artillery. Then another nine tanks appeared on the southern slopes of Trig 33, and the Australians disposed of five before the survivors withdrew. The battalion's 'take' for the day was 800 unwounded prisoners and a great deal of equipment for the loss of six killed and 22 wounded.

Altogether it was a successful day for Auchinleck and a hopeful start to the Eighth Army's counter-attack, though the Tell el Eisa mounds were still in enemy hands and providing observation for fire into British positions. But this was soon to be put right. At long last the Valentines caught up with the infantry, and at 4.30am the next day, 11 July, 2/24th Battalion moved on East Point 24 under cover of another massive artillery barrage provided by Australian, South African and British guns. Without so much as a single casualty, they overcame two Bersaglieri strong points and a battalion from Trieste, and while eight Valentines from 44th RTR provided cover in an exemplary manner, they dug in on the elusive Tell el Eisa height.

Rommel reacted as he always did. He turned his whole army artillery on the Australians, and beneath that deluge of shells the casualties began to mount. To dampen down any further Australian ambitions, the rest of Trieste was pulled in to put up a barrier to the south west, and a German unit, Recce Detachment 3, was posted out to the west. At the same time he summoned 'every last soldier out of his tent or rest camp up to the front for, in the face of the virtual defeat of a large proportion of our Italian fighting power, the situation was beginning to take on crisis proportions'.[5]

An instruction issued on 11 July was an indication of Rommel's mood and a measure of the man.

'The place of every man of the Panzerarmee is at the front,' he said. 'Recreation homes, recreation camps and such like institutions will be disbanded immediately. There is no such thing as replenishment behind the front.'

And to the Italians corps commanders he fired off an even more threatening note: 'Cases where soldiers leave the battlefield without a fight are becoming more frequent ... You must not shrink from inflicting the death penalty.'

Rommel was desperate, perhaps shaken, but the Australians were now vulnerable, wedged far out in a salient of their own making.

A short distance to the south, meanwhile, there were two sorties from the Alamein Box.

At 5.30am on 11 July as the 2/24th was mounting its attack on East Point 24, a force called Daycol, a joint British and Australian enterprise of tanks, artillery, infantry in Bren carriers, six-pounder anti-tank guns and Vickers guns, ventured towards Miteiriya Ridge. Hardly had the leading infantry got their carriers through the minefield and into open country on their exit from the box than they found their way blocked by hundreds of Bersaglieri wanting to surrender. It was all very embarrassing. The following artillery and tanks were threaded along the track through the minefield, and the unscheduled halt, with the rising sun behind, made them a target for enemy gunners. As the shells came in, the British guns scrambled through in great haste, dropped their trails and fired back, and infantry winkled out less forthcoming infantry at the point of the bayonet. Then the column pushed on to become enmeshed in gun duels. Stukas added their attentions, and the long, hot day dragged on without any real tactical achievement, although eight Italian field guns and other weapons destroyed and 1,023 prisoners brought home made it a reasonable day's work.

Another force with more ambitious plans to sally out from the box that day was a South African battle group called Matie Column (it was commanded by Brigadier C.L. Matie du Toit) The Matie Column episode must rate as a military curiosity.

It had its origins in that antipathy by Pienaar towards his new corps commander, Ramsden. Not only did Pienaar dislike him, but he also thought him incompetent and nursed a whole catalogue of grudges from events that occurred during the Gazala battles.

According to Major-General Theron, a close friend of Pienaar, there were arguments whenever Pienaar and Ramsden met, and it was tactless, to say the least, for Ramsden to turn up in the South African positions on 11 July and criticise the small take of prisoners achieved by Pienaar's men. Pienaar responded with a complaint that the attack just made by the Australians had been 'his' battle. He and Norrie had planned it together.

Ramsden replied that he had given it to the Australians because they were fresh and strong enough to exploit initial success. By way of placating the irate Pienaar, Ramsden suggested an alternative adventure, promising him some tanks to go with it - 16 Valentines and six Matildas. The result was Matie Column, a gesture to pride, and a fiasco. Even its commander had no faith in it.

The force consisted of infantry (2nd Botha), artillery, anti-tank guns, three light anti-aircraft troops, C Squadron of the 6th Armoured Car Regiment, C Squadron of 44th RTR, and a detachment of Matildas. Its task was to establish a base on Miteiriya Ridge and from there to exploit to the south west. But the operation quickly came apart. In the end only nine tanks were starters, radio communications broke down, and the tanks turned back. The column did clear enemy from Tell el Makh Khad, but to everyone's displeasure was then taken back.

The fighting continued around Tell el Eisa for a few days without a result either way as Rommel attempted to throw the Australians out of their salient. The battle brought both army commanders to new resolutions. Rommel decided that the Alamein Box must go, and he ordered up 21st Panzer from Kaponga to do the job. Auchinleck decided that, with German attention focused on the north, now would be a good time for his 13th Corps in the south to strike a decisive blow. Rommel struck first.

The Alamein Box was the key to the British defence. Without it Auchinleck's position would be immeasurably weakened. Rommel had tried to eliminate it by the time-tested method of encirclement and had failed. Now, with time ticking away and his worries increasing, he decided he must face up to a head-on assault.

Rommel's main concern was that the British were reinforcing faster than he was. He was also disturbed by the 'considerable enterprise and audacity' his enemy had been displaying, and he had no doubt that the British would continue to attack his Italians, whom he described as 'easy meat'. And we might suspect that a fair measure of frustration was setting in. One lucky break and he could be on his way again.

For the attack on the Alamein Box, 21st Panzer was told to move up under cover of night. Rommel also marshalled every gun and aircraft he could find.

'... the air is still electric with crisis,' he wrote to his Lu on the day before the attack. He thought his enemy in the box was the Australians, but in fact the South Africans were still there, now strengthened by Australian batteries.

Rommel assembled his forces on 13 July behind a morning mist that turned to wind-blown dust as the day heated up. Around midday the Stukas paraded in line-ahead over the box and plunged into screaming dives, a disturbing sight for the Australians clinging to their Tell el Eisa salient and reliant on the Alamein defences for their security. The

German artillery weighed in with a barrage, and then the panzers and infantry moved forward.

But it all came to pieces.

Anti-tank guns and dug-in tanks held the panzers outside the outer defences, although an Australian gunner claims there was an 800 metre gap 'without a man covering it' where the tanks could have come through. 'The tanks did no more than cruise up and down the forward defence lines straffing the South African defence lines ...' he wrote.[6]

The infantry did not even approach the wire. They assembled two or three kilometres too far back, and shell fire from Australian and South African guns rained down on them. One regiment alone, the 1st South African, pumped out 8,000 shells and by day's end the ears of the gun crews bled. Under this weight of fire the German infantry advance crumbled before it passed through the Italian front line.

A bad-tempered Rommel decided that evening that he would have to call off the operation, and he lamented the lost opportunity of a stormy day that would, he claimed, 'have robbed the British of all visibility'. But this sounds like a desperate general looking for excuses.

It made no difference, though, to his resolve to oust the Australians from the salient, and during 14 July German tanks broke over the 2/24th battalion, holding East Point 24 and Trig Point 33. The tanks were driven off, but on Tell el Eisa the two companies on East Point 24 became dangerously isolated, and that night they were withdrawn. They had the consolation of leaving 10 enemy tanks burned out on the battlefield

15 July would have been another torrid day for the Australians had not events further south intervened.

The outcome of the first phase of the Australians' northern offensive was a good-news, bad-news situation. Though they had failed to take the whole of the Tell el Eisa feature and then lost the piece they had, they still held their salient, which the more imaginative saw as a finger pointing west.

Their demolition of further Italian units had also weakened what little confidence the Germans had in their allies, and a policy was introduced of interweaving German forces through Italian held positions, thus diluting German strength - another victory for Dorman Smith.

Beyond this, Rommel, chastened by his defeat outside the Alamein Box, now accepted that there could be no question of launching any large-scale attack in the immediate future. He had surrendered the initiative.

The air force, meanwhile, was poised, with some reservations, to follow a confident Eighth Army.

'Everyone is sleeping in the open, near slit trenches or anything, and the squadron is fully mobile,' 5th Squadron recorded on 12 July. 'It will not take more than half an hour to start the convoy when the squadron has to move. The army is still confident and advise that they have the initiative at El Alamein. Unfortunately we have learned by recent experience that such advice usually precedes movement in the wrong direction.'

While the main action was in the north, in the south 13th Corps had been exchanging unpleasantries with the enemy though not to any particular conclusion. Although Rommel had been compelled by the Australian attack on 10 July to call off his major offensive down there, he kept urging his units to press ahead and both 90th Light and 21st Panzer, which was not called north until Rommel resolved to attack the Alamein Box, probed forward with no great show of enthusiasm.

So the Germans struggled on with their plans to attack in the south. Of course, it wasn't the grand slam Rommel had intended, but nonetheless he drove on 21st Panzer, 90th Light and Recce Detachment 33 with his customary remorseless demands. Opposing them were 5th NZ Brigade, some of 7th Motor Brigade's 'monthly' columns and tanks of 1st Armoured Division. In this dance of war it was rather like a gentile quadrille. The Eighth Army had no enthusiasm for battle in these parts and was content to step back as the Germans stepped forward, and move forward in turn to harry them as the opportunity arose. It's difficult not to feel sorry for the Germans, in particular for 90th Light, whose weak punches met mainly empty air, and units became mixed up.

90th Light war diary made the following summary: 'Final appreciation of the day's events: Owing to bad leadership and to supply difficulties the attack of 90th Light on 10.7 progresses only hesitantly. As a consequence of considerable losses of vehicles (through bombing and artillery fire) Battle Group Marcks was no longer in a position to detach vehicles to ensure the bringing up of supplies during the attack ... Battle groups were held up without fuel, ammunition and water as early as 9.7 ...'

The much frustrated 90th Light made a feint attack on 13 July, the day Rommel attacked the Alamein Box, and the Eighth Army responded by stepping back. The same thing happened the next day, the 90th Light diary noting that the Eighth Army 'has declined to be involved in infantry action and has only attempted to halt the advance of the Div by means of heavy weapons'.

90th Light gave the 13th Corps commander, Gott, so little trouble that he was able to devote his thoughts to how he could exploit the developing situation in the north, and from this emerged an operation code-named Bacon. The plan was for New Zealand Division and 1st Armoured Division to attack Ruweisat Ridge while 30th Corps penetrated to the rear and developed the second stage of the attack. The New Zealand commander, Inglis, who was privately conveying to his wounded Commander-in-Chief, Freyberg, some reservations about Eighth Army command, asked Gott if he could have tanks under his command, as the Australians had. Gott's response was that there were none available and that 1st Armoured Division had been trained to act independently, not in close co-operation with infantry, a curious commentary on an action that was supposed to employ a joint infantry-armour force, and yet another portent of things to come.

Inglis was truly not a happy man, and he wrote to Freyberg on 11 July that what the army needed was 'a commander who will make a firm plan and leave his staff to implement it, crash through with it; and once the conception is under way, move about the battlefield himself and galvanise the troops who are looking over their shoulder ... I feel that penny packets of enemy who could easily have been destroyed have been allowed to make progress instead, and that time has been frittered away over and over again'.

Such a cry for leadership from an army longing to be led.

As Inglis saw it, both sides conception of attack 'seems to be shoot with artillery and stop when suitably shot up'. And he viewed with disfavour the numerous mobile groups - the monthly columns - that were 'scattered all over the landscape so that their own divisional headquarters never seem to know where they are or what they are doing'. He considered them too weak in infantry and too tired after so much retreating, and when approached they had 'eastward leanings' all the time.

It was in this atmosphere that the New Zealanders approached their first major entanglement with the Germans in the Alamein positions, the infelicitously name *Bacon*. *Bacon* proved to be a moveable feast. It was postponed once, twice, and then as the Tell el Eisa operation sputtered inconclusively out, it was third time lucky, and *Bacon*, conceived as a diversion, was promoted to the main event. Operation Order No 96, issued on 13 July, gave this intention: To break through the enemy's centre and destroy his forces east of the track El Alamein-Abu Dweis and north of Ruweisat Ridge.

Bacon in fact nearly cooked Rommel's goose. As things turned out it became one of the might-have-beens of the Battle of Egypt.

PART TWO

CHAPTER THIRTEEN

14-16 JULY - RUWEISAT, THE FIRST DISASTER

Ruweisat Ridge was a highway of impervious rock 13 kilometres south of El Alamein along which armour could advance and descend into the enemy's rear. It was along Ruweisat that Rommel's panzers had attacked at the beginning of July in their bid to break through and cut off the Alamein Box. Now Auchinleck's armour was to attempt to reverse the flow of battle by the same route.

The outcome was to strip bare the weaknesses of the Eighth Army and give cause to fear for the future.

Ruweisat is a modest height running east and west, with three spot heights: Point 64 on the El Alamein-Himeimat track, more or less in the centre; Point 63 about five kilometres, away to the west; and another Point 63 about the same distance to the east. Like all ridges, it is not a simple hump, but has folds that provide some limited cover, but it is one of the most exposed locations in this part of the Desert. Though clearly visible from the south across a shallow basin that some war diaries refer to as a 'valley', it is only a gradual rise that in the dark might be crossed without being noticed, and its claim to be called a ridge rests on the contrast between its gentle contours and those of the surrounding terrain. Among similar humps and also the depressions that pit the Desert, it was a focal point that governed the planning of the Battle of Egypt. On the night of 14-15 July it was the Eighth Army's first objective in an offensive that was to burst through the Axis defences and shatter their army with superior tank numbers.

The declared intention was that two infantry divisions, the 2nd New Zealand and 5th Indian, should attack in a generally north-westerly direction and seize the ridge as a jumping off point for 1st Armoured Division to strike through to the enemy rear. Rather than have the armour bat its head against the brick wall of Rommel's formidable anti-tank guns, the infantry, advancing under cover of night, would dismantle the wall and open a way through. And the time to do this was now, while Rommel had concentrated his forces in the north to contain the Australians - a left hook, so to speak, to follow a right cross.

The code name of *Bacon* was a curiously mundane divergence from the loftier titles used at other times during the month. Perhaps it was felt that a name that did not imply an expectation of success would not tempt the fates.

The immediate enemy on and in front of the ridge was 15th Panzer (less the battle group sent north to deal with the Australians), with Pavia and Brescia Divisions. But of course these were, as Rommel kept lamenting, only shadow divisions. 15th Panzer had no more than a dozen or so tanks at its disposal that night, and the Italian infantry were too few for anything but a shallow defence line. All that was necessary was for the Eighth Army to thrust with determination and purpose and the job would be done.

So simple a task, yet not so simple that it was beyond the competence of the army to scramble it into confusion. The central problem was that the Eighth Army was acting as though it was still a force of substance, and although its numbers were few it retained a two-corps structure. On this night the Indians were under the command of 30th Corps, the New Zealanders under 13th Corps and each seems to have had a different perception of what was expected from the operation. Moreover, the Indian 'division' in fact consisted of only one brigade, the 5th, of two regiments, the 3/10th Baluch Regiment and the 4/5th Rajputana Rifles; the New Zealand Division consisted of two brigades, the 4th (18th, 19th and 20th Battalions) and the 5th (21st, 22nd and 23rd Battalions). Between them, therefore, these two so-called divisions actually made up the equivalent of only one division, divided between two corps. Besides this there was 1st Armoured Division, which had a tendency to be a law unto itself whichever corps it happened to be in at the time, and whatever expectations the infantry might have of the armour's intentions, the understanding given to the armoured brigades was that they should wait on the start line until someone told them they were required.

1st Armoured Division's orders said the division would co-operate in the attack, stating specifically: '2nd Armoured Brigade will be prepared to move on centre line of the inter-corps boundary with the tasks (a) of exploiting success of the NZ Div to the NW, (b) countering any counterattack by enemy armour against NZ Div which may develop from the NE, north or NW.' 22nd Armoured Brigade was to be prepared to move from Deir el Hima to an area north of Deir el Dihmaniya to protect 'the southern and western flank of the NZ Div from first light 15 July particularly against attack by enemy armoured forces'. This latter brigade actually moved away to the south west to Alam Nayil on the evening of 14 July to deal with enemy tanks reported to be approaching from that direction, and while this action confirmed to its flank protection role, it also removed the 22nd from a position where it could quickly support 2nd Brigade.

13th Corps Operation Order No 140 also clearly defined the 1st Armoured's Division's task as: to protect the southern and western flank of the New Zealand Division attack from first light on 15 July; and to be ready to exploit north west with armoured forces if a favourable opportunity occurred after first light on 15 July.

On top of all this, Corps orders gave three code words: *Faith*, indicating that the New Zealand Division had captured its objective; *Hope*, indicating that it had been delayed and would not capture the objective by first light; and *Charity*, signalling that 1st and 7th Armoured Divisions were to be in readiness to exploit in the directions named.

The important point to note in all this is that while the New Zealanders believed they had a rendezvous with the British tanks at first light, come hell or high water, the orders to the armour said only that the brigades 'will be prepared to move', so that clearly the tanks would not roll until someone told them to, and this seems to be in accord with the policy of armour command - to await developments before sending in the tanks. And corps orders spoke of protecting New Zealand Division's flank and of being ready to exploit, and makes no reference to joining the division to help repel an enemy counter-attack.

There were therefore three commands in one small force, each with a different perception of what should happen, with all the potential for confusion this implies.

This was not all. Yet another ingredient of potential chaos was the incorrect information British intelligence had of the enemy dispositions. In a fluid situation like that at El Alamein that's not unusual, and both sides worked under this handicap, but the problem was compounded by the absence of aerial photographs, which the New Zealanders had repeatedly requested. In the end they got them - a set of over-exposed prints in which no detail could be discerned and which came to hand as the attack was about to begin.

There was one deficiency, though, that was obligingly made good by the enemy. Kippenberger, reflecting on the expectation that tanks were to follow the infantry through, says he does not recall any orders to clear and mark gaps in the minefields for the armour. 'Fortunately,' he says, 'the Italians had left some gaps on their own initiative and had also gone to the trouble of marking them.'[1]

The New Zealanders were to attack with two brigades, shoulder to shoulder, almost a division. 4th Brigade was on the left, and in the morning would be at the 'sharp end' nearest any hostile enemy intentions; 5th Brigade was on its right, and in the centre of the attack; and 5th Indian Brigade on its right.

A desert night attack has its own particular pattern. The infantry advance on foot, first the fighting troops, then the reserve troops who stay a little behind, ready to be called forward if they are needed. After them

The events of the night of 14 July, with the New Zealanders striking through to objectives on Ruweisat Ridge and the Indians meeting resistance that held them back.

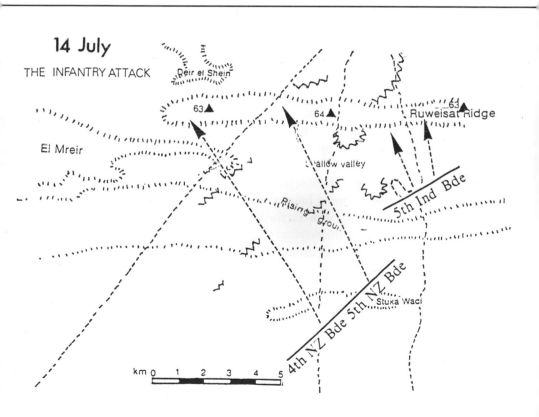

14 July

THE INFANTRY ATTACK

Deir el Shein

63▲

64▲

63▲
Ruweisat Ridge

El Mreir

hallow valley

Rising ground

5th Ind Bde

4th NZ Bde 5th NZ Bde

Stuka Wadi

km 0   1   2   3   4   5

come the battalion and brigade support columns, consisting of fleets of motor vehicles - wireless vans, Bren carriers, mortars, artillery, anti-tank guns, and trucks carrying ammunition, mines and all the paraphernalia needed by the foot soldier to defend himself against a morning counter-attack.

The New Zealand infantry got away on this night in reasonably good shape, though some anti-tank guns that should have accompanied the infantry were late and had to move forward with the supporting arms.

5th NZ Brigade commander, Kippenberger, who had a close affinity with his men, describes how he and his brigade major, Fairbrother, having missed the leading battalions before they set out, went to talk with the men of the reserve battalion, the 22nd.

'Monty (Fairbrother) and I walked along the line, always a poignant experience before an assault,' he wrote in *Infantry Brigadier*. 'The men were quiet, those I spoke to cheerful and resolute. Most were veterans, for the 22nd had seen much hard fighting without ever being involved in a disaster ... The battalion stood up, there was a jingle and rustle of equipment, and then it moved silently forward, hearteningly orderly and resolute looking. We waited ten minutes and then moved, a solid mass of cars, trucks, carriers, portees, wireless vans at less than walking pace, Monty leading, with my car immediately behind him.'[2]

It was a still night, cold and quite dark. There was no barrage, the artillery having scaled down their shooting programme as zero hour approached, and the infantry tramped into the shallow valley in silence. Overhead an RAF plane flashed its navigation lights to draw fire and disclose the enemy's location. Flares lit the desert as nervous Germans and Italians sensed or saw movement, and then chattering machine-guns reached out with flowing fingers of tracer. Following the flying stream of lights back to their source, the infantry swooped in, bombing and bayoneting, turning this way and that as the opposition revealed itself, and then moving on, leaving prisoners to be taken back to the rear by detached riflemen.

The sound of battle rumbled to crescendo as they fought through strong points, punching holes in the defence for those following to use and leaving for reserve units the task of mopping up any they had missed. What they did not know was that these were not the lightly held forward posts they expected but the more strongly held main defences, and they left behind more than they knew.

Tanks of 8th Panzer Regiment, aroused from their slumber, shuffled around nervously, half blind in the dark. One hosed the ground at random with machine-gun fire, and was asked by an exasperated New Zealander, 'Why the hell don't you go home? You're spoiling the whole show.' Two collided and in panic sprayed each other with tracer. Others were dealt with by riflemen, who under cover of night could creep up and shoot any commander unwise enough to have his head out of the turret, and finish the job with a grenade down the hatch or a sticky bomb on the hull. Some men aimed at the drivers' slits, and one fired inside at point-blank range with a Tommy gun, causing the beast to roar, rise on its haunches, and move off at speed. Tanks fleeing from infantry was a sight to behold ... but then night was the time of the foot soldier.

Beyond the tanks were the artillery lines, where Italian gunners gave up with alacrity, and the infantry were in open desert again.

While this was going on, the 4th NZ Brigade reserve group was caught in heavy mortar and artillery fire. As the fire lifted, it moved on through 'vast quantities' of abandoned Italian guns and equipment.

The forward troops moved up onto the ridge in various states of cohesion and assumed their positions. Some were too far one way or the other, some had lost sub-units which had gone astray during the confusion of attacking strong points or tanks, some sub-units became attached to other battalions. But the job had been done.

4th NZ Brigade held the west end of the ridge and the westerly Point 63. 20th Battalion was on the western tip, not far, as it happened, from 15th Panzer battle headquarters. Due east of the 20th were 19th and 18th Battalions, with some elements of 21st Battalion (of 5th NZ Brigade) attached.

To the east again, near Point 64, was 5th NZ Brigade in a moderately dismembered state. 23rd Battalion was complete, but it had another part of 21st Battalion attached to it. The remainder of the 21st was still further east, actually too far east. The two New Zealand brigades had thus established a chain of positions, aligned from west to east, along Ruweisat Ridge. 5th NZ Brigade's other battalion, the 22nd, was in reserve just south the of ridge. The 5th Indian Brigade was coming up on the eastern end of the ridge, in the area of the other Point 63, though at this stage with only one battalion, the 3/10th Baluch Regiment. Its companion, the 4/5th Rajputana Rifles, had gone astray before it reached the start line, run into an enemy strong point and been pinned down by heavy fire, and at first light was still lagging behind.

But the pieces were falling into place. Large numbers of Italians had been taken prisoner, many senior officers among them, and thousands more were fleeing in disorder. The Germans, the real opposition, had been caught off guard, stretched between the Australian threat in the north and this new incursion in the centre. All that remained to be done was to dig in and await the British tanks in the morning. Dig in ... shovels and picks clanged on unyielding rock. The first niggle of concern. As the night hours slipped away, the troops did what they could to scratch shallow cover or build up low sangars with loose rocks. There were to be few comfortable slit trenches when daylight disclosed them to the enemy. But then that's when the tanks were due. Everything was taken care of.

There was a little fighting on and around the ridge in the last hours of

After the infantry attack on the evening of 14 July, first light on 15 July found the New Zealanders on Ruweisat Ridge and the Indians still battling to get there. 22nd NZ Battalion was being scooped up by 8th Panzer Regiment. 2nd Armoured Brigade was still at the start line.

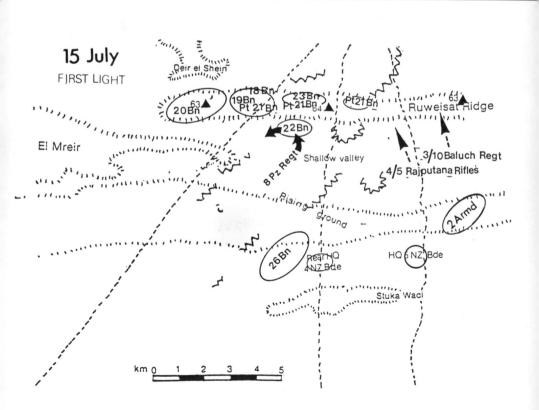

the night, including a bayonet charge into German artillery positions led by Captain Charles Upham, whose leadership here compounded earlier exploits at Minqar Qaim to earn him a bar to the VC he won on Crete.

4th NZ Brigade's six-pounders had a skirmish with panzers to the west when it became light enough to see them. Three were knocked out and the rest withdrew to a safe distance, from where they sulked for the rest of the day, tossing shells on to the northern and west faces of the ridge.

First light found 5th NZ Brigade's reserve battalion, the 22nd (the one Kippenberger had seen off), snugged down out of harm's way on the southern side of the ridge, preparing a defence position while it awaited whatever call might come from the battalions on the exposed crest. They had four six-pounders of 33rd Anti-tank Battery on portees, and when it became light enough they would be taken off and dug in. But there was really no hurry, and anyway, Kippenberger was there on a fleeting visit and that was some reassurance.

Well satisfied that events were shaping up as planned, Kippenberger clambered into his Bren carrier, a clapped-out vehicle with a top speed of 20 k.p.h., and limped off in the direction of his brigade headquarters to the south east. As the roar of his struggling engine diminished into the distance another sound came from the south, the unmistakeable clank and squeak of tank tracks and the guttural chatter of exhausts, and turreted shapes took form. 2nd Armoured Brigade, right on time? Well, no ... Tracer came streaming towards the men of the 22nd, and they went to ground. Now it was day, the time of the panzers. 8th Panzer Regiment were about to take revenge.

One tank flung a shell at the departing Bren carrier, and as the shot 'screeched overhead', Kippenberger poked up his head to see 'five tanks ... heading towards us all shooting hard, spitting flame like dragons'.[3]

One 22nd platoon sergeant, Keith Elliott, who was also to earn a VC that day, recalls that when he saw the tanks coming he correctly identified them as panzers and warned nearby platoon commanders, who were new to the Desert and had never seen German tanks before. They disregarded his alarm, and Elliott, after a democratic conference with his corporals, pulled out his platoon and moved up on to the ridge to join the front line troops.

As the tanks closed in, enemy anti-tank guns and Italian infantry in strong points by-passed during the night, joined in the fray. The six-pounders, still vulnerable on their portees, were swung about and replied at 1,000 metres range. They hit three tanks and set at least one on fire, but though the crews stayed at their guns even when they were hit, the odds were in favour of the panzers. They closed in to gather up most of the battalion and the nearby headquarters of the 23rd Battalion as well.

This early morning coup by 8th Panzer sounded the alarm bells. As the day's events unfolded it became clear the troops on the ridge were enclosed within a hostile circle, with enemy in front and behind them and on their left flank, and there was a pocket, too, on the ridge between the New Zealanders and the Indians. While there were gaps in the enemy positions, the New Zealanders had, in effect, fought their way into an enclave within the Axis defences. They were almost surrounded.

While the 22nd Battalion fought for its life, Kippenberger was struggling across the desert in his defective carrier in search of British tanks. 'Almost frantic with helplessness', he crawled on, passing the debris of battle - prisoners being herded back, bodies lying on the ground, abandoned weapons strewn across the desert. But no sign of tanks. At brigade headquarters in Stuka Wadi he switched to a car, but 'nothing whatever would go right in this battle'. The vehicle was down on one cylinder and chugged along at a maddening 16 k.p.h. At New Zealand divisional headquarters he found only the general, Inglis, who, because communications with the brigades had failed, had no idea what was happening at the front. Kippenberger brought him up to date, took his direction to the location of the armour, and sputtered off in his ailing car. 'Ages' later - actually about 20 minutes - he came upon the tanks of the 2nd Armoured Brigade, with every turret occupied by a man with binoculars watching the smoke rise from Ruweisat Ridge, about six kilometres away. He located the brigadier, Briggs, who, he says, received him coolly. Doing his best not to seem agitated, Kippenberger introduced himself and said that when he had left his brigade an hour earlier it was being attacked from the rear by German tanks. Would the British armour move up to help?

'He said he would send a reconnaissance tank,' Kippenberger wrote later. 'I said there was no time. Would he move his whole brigade? While he was patiently explaining some difficulty, General Lumsden drove up. I gave him exactly the same information. Without answering, he walked around the back of his car, unfastened a shovel and with it killed a scorpion with several blows. Then he climbed up beside the brigadier, who was sitting on the turret of his tank. I climbed up beside them, and McPhail (Captain E. A. McPhail, 5th Brigade intelligence officer) stood within hearing. The general asked where we were, and the brigadier pointed out the place on the map.

'"But I told you to be there at first light," General Lumsden then said, placing his finger on Point 63. I jumped down and did not hear the rest of the conversation but in a few minutes the general got down and in a soothing manner which I resented said the brigade would move as soon as possible. I asked for urgency, which both he and the brigadier promised, and drove off.'[1]

Kippenberger went back to his brigade headquarters, and tanks arrived soon afterwards. According to Kippenberger, they drove off the tanks of 15th Panzer, 'without difficulty' and settled down a couple of kilometres ahead 'apparently without any clear idea of what to do next and certainly with no idea of exploitation'.

The various accounts on what happened at this time confuse rather than enlighten, and it is not even clear which German tanks these were that Kippenberger says were driven off. What is certain, though, is that the British tanks ran into unsubdued strong points, and it would have been these, rather than indecision, that caused them to halt in view of the anxious Kippenberger.

The panzers that rounded up the 22nd Battalion would, by this time, have already gone, taking their prisoners with them. Eager to be clear of the area, they hurried the New Zealanders away.

While all this was going on, Rommel was busy on his side gathering together bits and pieces from everywhere to plug the gap. At daybreak the initiative lay with the British, and the tanks, if they could have joined the infantry, could have gone through, but the opportunity soon slipped away.

From the German point of view there was vast confusion, magnified by the swarms of Italians fleeing to the rear. 21st Panzer was hastily despatched, together with two recce units and Baade battle group from 90th Light.

So while the Germans gathered their forces and the British armour dallied, the New Zealanders on Ruweisat Ridge waited for something to happen. Most exposed was 4th Brigade, at the western end of the ridge. On the gentle downward slope of the inhospitable rock, the men could look on to the enemy's rear and observe his guns and vehicles, but the corollary was that the enemy could see 4th Brigade, which could do little to dig in. Any movement attracted fire.

Though considerable numbers of prisoners, mainly Italian, were rounded up and sent to the rear under light escort, some managed to escape and others were released when the parties ran into enemy pockets. The number of prisoners taken was estimated into five figures, but by the end of the day the count was much diminished. One group claimed to have captured four Italian generals and ten colonels.

Like the British tanks, the New Zealanders' own support groups found their way to the ridge barred by enemy strong points, and the infantry battled on as best they could, and Sergeant Elliott was out among the enemy earning his VC. He took his men in search of an officer who had been wounded while leading a patrol, and in the course of the sortie, Elliott, although wounded in the thigh, led an attack with only two men against a battalion of Pavia Division, and himself made a solo bayonet charge across 100 metres of open ground on a machine-gun position. He was wounded a second time, in the knee, but helped beat off a counter-attack, and eventually returned to 4th NZ Brigade with 130 prisoners, leaving 30 Italians killed or wounded.

As the morning wore on, the heat on the ridge grew intense, and the exposed troops, who moved at peril of their lives, could only wait and hope - for tanks, for the support of their own artillery. But communication with the guns had been tenuous, and finally had failed.

As it happens the New Zealanders were not entirely alone, although they had no way of knowing what else was happening around them. Indeed, reconnaissance aircraft were bringing back information that would have been of value if it could have been transmitted, but the bombers, at least, were able to give practical help by plastering the enemy to the west and north west.

In the South African camp there was a moment of wild optimism when 30th Corps advised at 3.45pm that about 2,000 enemy were walking in to surrender and that a good push might bring about complete collapse. Pienaar dropped everything and began planning.

Late in the afternoon there was a glimmer of hope on Ruweisat Ridge when an ammunition column turned up at 4th NZ Brigade after slipping by a strong point while attacking tanks distracted it. 5th NZ Brigade also got some relief from a column that came in through the neighbouring Indians. The Indians had, with the aid of 2nd Armoured Brigade tanks, cleared away the strong point separating them from the New Zealanders at about 2.30pm.

There were also at this time reports that British tanks were on the move, and as the enemy braced for counter-attack there was a tension between hope and alarm. The New Zealanders were well aware of their danger. Experience had taught them that the Germans followed the doctrine of either immediate counter-attack or delayed counter-attack in greater strength. And a German general held by 19th NZ Battalion offered the information that a counter-attack could be expected at 4.00pm, and he lent authenticity to this intelligence by energetically improving his slit trench. Shelling that portended an approaching counter-attack began falling on 4th NZ Brigade about mid-afternoon.

And then at last an officer of the 2nd Armoured Brigade drove up to 18th NZ Battalion with the news that a strong force of British tanks was about four kilometres way and making its way west along the south side of the ridge. The cavalry, so to speak, was coming.

The cavalry had found it no easy task to reach the ridge. Minefields and strong points had barred the way, and one, Strong Point 2, included German-manned 88s among its anti-tank guns. The New Zealanders, in fact, had not so much pushed the enemy back as burrowed into them, and neither their own support weapons nor the tanks could, for some time, traverse in daylight the territory over which the infantry had attacked the previous night.

But now the tanks were on their way, indeed were close at hand, and when the situation was explained to the armoured brigade officer, he went away, so it was thought, to bring tanks forward. But with the Germans clearly about to strike, Brigadier Burrows sent a liaison officer after him to accelerate their response. He found tanks about two kilometres away, and explained the situation to the regimental commander, and returned to the New Zealand positions with a British liaison officer.

By this time enemy fire was intense, and the armoured brigade officer thought it prudent to return to wrap himself in a light reconnaissance tank so that he could make a detailed survey. Burrows said bluntly that there was no time and that armoured support was needed now. The officer left to return to his regiment as the German attack fell on 20th NZ Battalion.

Perhaps we should not be surprised at the seeming lack of enthusiasm on the part of the armoured brigade officers. They had come forward to find a killing ground on which there was little cover even for infantry, far less for tanks, and it was a fair assumption that the Germans would by now have set up a line of anti-tank guns that could devastate any armour that dared brave the forward face of Ruweisat Ridge. Of course, it's not a point of view the infantry could be expected to appreciate, and if the tanks had arrived when they were supposed to in the early morning the situation would not have arisen. All things considered, the information the officers took back can hardly have been calculated to encourage tank command-ers to charge forward into the fray, and anyway, they had other things on their mind that conformed more to their expectations of what British armour was supposed to do. This may explain the temporising experience of 5th Brigade's signals officer, Captain Dasler, who had come across to 4th NZ Brigade with the news that a supply line was now open through the Indians, and had then gone in search of tanks.

He found a squadron in cover not far away, but his request for urgent action was met with a response that no orders to advance had yet been received. An offer was made to send forward an officer to reconnoitre. Always this seemed to be the armour's standard reply.

By now the threat from the west was making itself evident. Artillery, mortar and machine-gun fire scythed the 4th NZ Brigade positions, and smoke from burning vehicles around Point 63 swirled up with the dust in a dark cloud. Men of the 20th NZ Battalion, in the most exposed position, replied with their Vickers and six-pounders as targets could be found through the atmospheric clutter and against the glare of the late afternoon sun. Around 5.00pm armoured cars came tearing in like a whirlwind from the south west, machine-guns chattering as they dashed around at speed, creating more dust and confusion. At the same time tanks, half-tracks, self-propelled guns and captured British portees, many of them carrying men of 104 Regiment, advanced from the west.

New Zealand anti-tank guns fired at the panzers through the dust and smoke. But the guns fell to enemy fire, and as the attackers overran infantry positions, soldiers rising to surrender sometimes masked targets. There was a brief moment of chivalry when New Zealand gun C1, having knocked out two German tanks, began siting on a third when a group of captured New Zealand soldiers walked between the gun and its target. The tank, for its part, was laying on the gun. Both held their hand. Then as the last man cleared the line of sight, the tank and the gun fired simultaneously. The tank shell hit a metal plate of the six-pounder just below the shield and sprayed pieces of metal among the crew. All except the driver were wounded. The six-pounder shell smacked into the tank, and as the gun drove away the tank burst into flames.

As the anti-tank guns fell silent, there remained only the Vickers. The enemy came inexorably on, rounding up the 19th and 20th NZ Battalions and the Vickers gunners too, though some men escaped. Armoured cars and panzers pressed on along the ridge, threatening to engulf 4th NZ Brigade headquarters, a part of 18th NZ Battalion and a company of 21st NZ Battalion that had just eluded the Germans. There was some general skirmishing during which some troops were taken prisoner and others

Australians using a captured Italian Breda machine-gun in an anti-aircraft role. The gunner is wearing captured German boots. L W Hutchings Collection ATL

Above: A Messerschmitt 109 fighter shot down by Australian anti-aircraft fire while straffing the coast road. L W Hutchings Collection ATL

Below: The pilot of the German fighter shot down by the Australians being given a cup of tea by his captors. L W Hutchings Collection ATL

Australian troops on the way back to the Desert on July 9, 1942. IWM

The stony desert, with vehicles scattered in the background. The hump in the distance is Ruweisat Ridge. L W Hutchings Collection ATL

A Valentine bogged in the soft salt flats near the coast. ATL

No, this is not a natural dust storm but smoke and dust stirred up by enemy shelling as the Germans advance on Ruweisat Ridge on July 15. IWM

B Company, 6th Field Ambulance, ADS in action at El Mreir on July 22. The fact that men are standing around in the open desert suggests that the action was over when this picture was taken, and the smoke would be from fires in the depression. War History Collection ATL

Below: A German Mark IV knocked out in the fighting on Ruweisat Ridge on July 16. War History Collection ATL

A German mortar crew. This picture was taken from a German prisoner. War History Collection ATL

slipped away. Some who were able to cross to the south side of the ridge found British tanks whose crews said though they were willing to help, they had not yet received orders.

5th NZ Brigade now received the attention of the enemy guns, and stragglers from 4th Brigade began arriving with tales of disaster and a warning that panzers and armoured cars were not far behind them.

The day's movements can't be accurately plotted, but the four armoured regiments reached forward positions by divergent courses, with three joining forces to meet Axis tanks approaching from the south west. It is difficult to say just where 3 CLY was in relation to the others. While the armoured regiments battled with the enemy tanks, the German counter-attack slipped past them to the north, overrunning one NZ infantry brigade and driving the second away. By the time the enemy attacked the next day, the Indians, dug in tanks and artillery were able to beat them back.

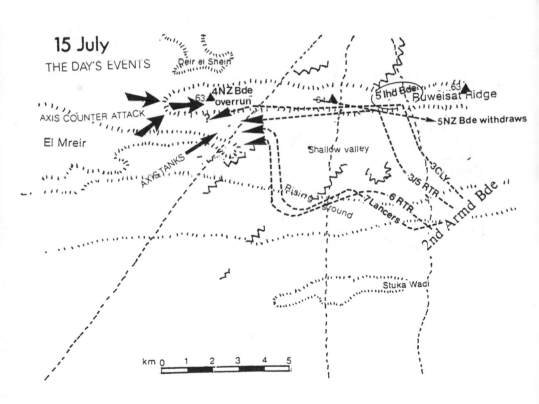

At about 5.30pm, about the time 5th NZ Brigade was falling back to new positions, the New Zealander commander, Inglis, received a message, thought to have come from 1st Armoured Division, that 4th and 5th NZ Brigades were 'quite happy on the ridge'. But by this time 4th brigade had all but ceased to exist and 5th Brigade was withdrawing.

And what on earth had the British armour been doing all this time? Oddly enough, they thought they were doing their job, not in the way the infantry expected but in the manner in which they had been trained.

There is no doubt at all that the armour knew its task was to support the New Zealanders. Unreliable though war diaries can be, this is quite explicitly stated in several regimental diaries. After Kippenberger's distraught appeal, the tanks did move forward, as he relates in *Infantry Brigadier*. But what did they actually do all day? The story can only be pieced together, and to follow what happened, it has to be understood that there are five accounts: the brigade war diary, and those of 9th Lancers, 3/5th RTR, 6th RTR and 3rd CLY.

3rd CLY seems to have been the odd man out as it claims to have moved off at first light. The regiment ran into anti-tank guns and turned north, where it found the Indians near the east Point 63 still trying to secure their part of Ruweisat Ridge. 3rd CLY joined in the fray and took 700 prisoners and several guns.

Though this regiment appears not to have contacted any other part of the armoured brigade, it pushed west, and concludes its entry for the day: 'The NZ Div were pushed off Point 64 by tanks, and the battalion took up battle positions at 878279 and held off the enemy attack which also comprised many armoured cars.'

3/5th RTR, away at 8.00am, encountered opposition, and on Briggs' orders shuffled to the right and reached the ridge at midday. It followed the ridge west for three kilometres and took up battle positions. 3/5th was almost certainly the regiment who sent an officer to 4th NZ Brigade with the glad tidings that tanks were coming.

6th RTR, meanwhile, advanced on the centre line of the attack, followed at 7.00am by 9th Lancers, accompanied by E Battery, 1st RHA.

At 7.15am Brigade heard that the New Zealanders were being attacked from the west by panzers, and ordered 6th RTR to contact them on the objective. Easier said than done. 6th RTR bumped into an enemy minefield and a defended box, which yielded 200 Italian prisoners, at the cost of one Crusader blown up. 9th Lancers, ordered to help, also ran into an enemy strong point, 'mined and wired in', and shelling winkled out between 700 and 800 prisoners from this position.

6th RTR ran into more minefields and lost three tanks and three others damaged. By 11.35am both 6th RTR and 9th Lancers had reached high ground from where they could look north to where the battle clamoured on Ruweisat Ridge, four kilometres away. Still the way was not clear. Twelve anti-tank guns could be seen and were shelled, and the enemy replied with a Stuka attack, during which a bomb narrowly missed Lumsden's armoured car.

Moving slowly toward Ruweisat, the regiments encountered 12 enemy tanks. They destroyed one and repelled the rest. But then enemy anti-tank guns accounted for two more British tanks.

While this was going on, 3/5th RTR on the southern slope of the ridge became engaged with a formidable array of Panzer IIIs and IVs, artillery, and 88mm and 50 mm anti-tank guns. At 5pm the regiment advised Brigade that the New Zealanders on Point 63 feared an attack from the west and requested assistance.

At 6.15pm 2nd Armoured Brigade heard that the New Zealanders' forward defence lines had been overrun by 13 tanks. At least three of its regiments, 9th Lancers and 3/5th and 6th RTR, which had now joined up, were at that time engaged elsewhere with 29 other enemy tanks, an enemy ploy, perhaps, to draw them away from the infantry. The opposing groups indulged in a 'shelling match', which went on until dark.

So as dusk came, infantry and tanks fought their individual battles. It was as if they spoke different languages.

Nehring called off his Afrika Korps at 8.30pm, reasoning that in the dark, and with the mix up in units that had taken place it was useless to continue. Troops were ordered to hedgehog for the night and press on next morning. The crises of the day, he noted in the Afrika Korps war diary, had been mastered 'by throwing in the last forces available'. The 15th Panzer diary recorded its astonishment that the British had not exploited their break-through, and wondered whether this could be because they did not realise the extent of the success gained in the night action, whether it was intended as an action with only a limited objective, or whether the Eighth Army did not have the troops to exploit.

The South Africans moved forward in the early evening to topple the supposedly tottering enemy, but when it became known that the only collapse that day had been the New Zealand positions on Ruweisat Ridge, they bounced back, and by 4.00am on the 16th all three brigades were home again.

It was not, however, a night without casualties. The Rand Light Infantry was bombed that night for the sixth time by British aircraft, leaving a casualty list of one dead and five wounded.

'As on every other occasion, GOC made strong protests to Corps about this,' the divisional war diary says.

5th NZ Brigade was withdrawn from the ridge that night, but the Indians, with tanks dug in and with the help of New Zealand artillery, stayed to meet the renewed attack next morning, 16 July, by 15th Panzer on the southern slope, 21st Panzer on the northern slope, and 33rd Recce along the crest. German tank strength was little more than 20, and with the Australians now putting in a diversionary attack from their Tell el Eisa salient, the enemy had more than he could handle. Nehring tried again that evening, with the setting sun behind him and strong Stuka support above, unaware that careless use of radio had disclosed his plans to the defenders. Around 6.30pm clouds of dust rising over a ridge less than 2,000 metres away warned 5th Indian Brigade of approaching trouble, and panzers streamed into sight. They ran into fire from hull-down British tanks and dug-in six-pounders, and what the divisional history calls 'a furious engagement' took place over the heads of the infantry. The battle clamoured on into the night, with light tanks and armoured cars skirmishing out to meet the enemy, creating a spectacular criss-crossing display of tracer. At 9.00pm the enemy decided he had had enough and broke away.

Daylight revealed bodies sprawled on the ground 800 metres from the Indian positions, and behind them a graveyard of wrecked tanks and guns reaching back as far as Deir el Shein. There was reason to believe several tanks were shamming dead, and a few shells among them sent them scurrying for safety. Demolition parties of engineers dealt with the debris. The division claimed to have destroyed 24 tanks, six armoured cars (described as 'scrap metal') and a large number of guns, including six 88s.

'For these kills, the six-pounders were largely responsible,' the history says. 'In a day these venomous little cannon became the pride of the Eighth Army.'

At least something had been salvaged from the ruins of Ruweisat.

Rommel, meanwhile, had been able to hold the Australian attacks in the north but at the cost of his striking power on Ruweisat, and at the cost, too, of rest time for his troops. Rest had been his immediate plan - rest and then a fresh assault. The one benefit to the Eighth Army from Ruweisat was that it again snatched away the initiative.

5th Panzer Regiment had been needling the Australians on 15 July when Rommel called them away to help chase the New Zealanders off Ruweisat Ridge. The way was now open for another bid to complete the capture of Tell el Eisa, and this the 2/23rd Battalion did in daylight on 16 July, aided by tanks from 8th RTR. The Australians demolished the remaining battalion of Sabratha Division and part of 1/383 Regiment, sending back 601 prisoners, of whom 41 were Germans. There were three colonels in this tally, one of them German; some small compensation for the disaster on Ruweisat the previous day.

The success was short-lived but it kept Rommel dancing. As the situation quietened down on Ruweisat, he put 9th Panzer Regiment on hold, moved 33rd Recce Battalion, Briehl Group from 90th Light, and a battalion from 104 Regiment north to meet yet another 'critical' situation. It was the same old story - left foot, right foot, left foot, with hardly time to draw breath. What might have been accomplished if the Ruweisat break-through had been exploited!

On Tell el Eisa the situation was now too hot for the Australians. The area was swept by fire, and they had no artillery, no Vickers guns and no anti-tank guns, and casualties were mounting. They withdrew again.

The Australians marked this as the end of the first phase of 9th Division's drive west from Alamein, during which they had taken 3,708 prisoners and inflicted 200 casualties on the enemy, caused mainly by artillery and machine-gun fire. According to the divisional report: 'This was the first time the divisional artillery and machine-guns had fought beside their own infantry, and for most it was their baptism of fire.' It was also the first occasion on which direct air support had been available to them.

In his daily report to Rome on the morning of 17 July, Rommel said that on 16 July, following heavy artillery preparation in the early morning, the Australians had attacked west, south of the coast road, supported by tanks. They 'overran a battalion of Sabratha Division in dug in positions and took over 400 prisoners. By midday the position was restored by German troops. Eight tanks were destroyed'. Always, it seemed, Rommel could find Germans somewhere to plug a gap.

His report on the southern part of the line said that 'during the last few days' his enemy had destroyed nearly four Italian divisions.

'This has lowered the striking power of the Panzerarmee so far that no offensive operations can now be undertaken, especially as the enemy has reinforcements continuously in infantry, tanks and artillery,' Rommel wrote. 'If he succeeds in making any more breaks into our line, the Alamein positions will no longer be tenable.'

And very likely someone in Rome said smugly, 'I told you so.'

Rommel followed with a breakdown of Italian strength that showed just how weak his army had become. It looked like this:

X Corps: Brescia Division, one battalion, no artillery; Pavia Division, two battalions, little artillery.

XXI Corps: Sabratha Division, no complete infantry battalions, no artillery; Trento Division, no considerable losses.

XX Corps: Ariete Division, 15 tanks, one battalion, one artillery unit; Littorio Division, 20 tanks, one battalion, one gun; Trieste Motorised Division, three battalions, one artillery unit. Italian Army Artillery: one heavy battery.

Even before the report was despatched, fresh news came in, and Rommel added a postscript: 'In the early morning of 17 July the enemy made another breach from the north in the area Bir el Makh Khad (seven kilometres west north west of El Alamein). Army heavily engaged.'

There was to be no rest.

Ruweisat should stand in history as a victory. It was a shambles.

At the time it was offered up to higher authority as a moderate success. 'Our tactical position in this very important part of the front was improved by this operation,' Auchinleck signalled London, referring presumably to the line held by the Indians. 'Moreover we took some 2,000 prisoners, mostly Italians.'

But what about the 1,405 New Zealand casualties? Of these, 1,115 had been killed, taken prisoner or were missing. Most of them were languishing in forward prisoner-of-war cages and in the following days would be trucked back to Benghazi, thence Italy.

What about the fact that two battalions of 4th NZ Brigade, the New Zealand Division's veteran formation that had been the first on the scene in 1940 and had fought in Greece, Crete and Libya, had been wiped out, and that this brigade was not to appear again on the field of battle for the rest of the North African war? What about the fact that one battalion of 5th NZ Brigade was also a prisoner, making the German haul the equivalent of a complete brigade, a third of the division's fighting strength, a third of this de facto national army that Rommel was so keen to eliminate from the scene?

And what about the bitterness and ill-feeling that began to corrupt the Eighth Army, and the loss of confidence in the armour and higher command?

'The Ruweisat Ridge show provided a wonderful opportunity for exploitation by armour at first light,' Inglis wrote to Freyberg. 'The enemy was properly rocked. Had the opportunity been seized (and the whole purpose of the operation was to make the opportunity) no question of armoured counter-attack would ever have cropped up.'

No understanding of these crucial days in North Africa can be complete without knowing this. And this was just the beginning. Worse was to come. Much worse.

It would have to be said that the Germans were seen at their best on that day. The night before and the early morning were chaotic, with Italian troops high tailing it to the west. There was no clear information. And there was no reserves. Simply to contain the Australian and South African offensives in the north Rommel had had to grasp at reinforcements as they arrived and throw them straight into battle. On 15 July, with his line penetrated at a critical point, he faced catastrophe.

Of course, Rommel was lucky. He always had been. However stretched he might be, however stupid his own mistakes were, he could always rely on the British to fumble and allow him to recover. So it was this day. The devastating drive through the centre never took place. While his guns and mortars dealt with the New Zealanders, he had time to pull together a scratch force.

He had few panzers and if there were as many enemy tanks on the battlefield as 2nd Armoured Brigade reported most must have been Italian. His infantry was thin on the ground and stretched to the limit, and he was able to assemble a force to counter-attack only by weakening his formations in the south. Indeed, he could do nothing without robbing some other part of the line. This makeshift force descended on the New Zealanders like a whirlwind, demolished their few anti-tank guns, and in a few hours delivered to their general his most cherished prize - a great haul of New Zealanders.

At a superficial level, the failure of Ruweisat can be simply stated. The New Zealand Division was denied tank support and was isolated from its own guns. Without these it could not hold off an enemy counter-attack. By contrast, the attack in the north four days earlier by the Australians succeeded, in part at least, because they had tanks under their command (actually under their command not merely as accompanying friends), and they had massive artillery support. The Indians on Ruweisat were able to withstand counter-attack because they had tanks and guns in support.

The kindest thing that has been said about this disaster is that it displayed a failure in infantry/armour co-ordination, which says everything and nothing. The harshest critics blamed the armour, and some post-war writers have continued this vilification. Tuker, for instance, says that New Zealand Division was denied close tank support, a decision that was 'clearly contrary to the spirit of the instructions of the Eighth Army'.

'It explained the dismal failures of 13th Corps throughout July and, as the policy was repeated by the 1st Armoured commander, it also explains the indifferent showing of that division,' he says.

'On the other hand, although opportunities to act independently had presented themselves, they were not taken. The division hung about the Ruweisat Ridge while the enemy stabilised his front and the sands of the days of manoeuvre battle ran out.'[5]

But this is not entirely fair to the armour, and an analysis of Ruweisat shows much more deep-seated flaws that weakened the whole army. Ruweisat, in fact, was doomed before it started. Four factors contributed to the failure.

The first was inadequate information about the enemy. To attack without knowing where your enemy is invites disaster, and so it was. The main enemy positions were not where they were thought to be, and aerial reconnaissance failed to reveal the true position.

The second was that the objective was inappropriate. Norrie had rejected Ruweisat in June as a place to build a strong point because of its inhospitable surface, but no one had thought to tell the New Zealanders this. In the light of day they were presented as an easy target.

The third was that there were insufficient troops for the operation, though there were uncommitted reserves. In an extensive review of the tactics of night fighting, Tuker says: 'At night, especially on a moonless night, the attacker should fill the defence system with men so that by dawn not an enemy will remain unaccounted for. If trenches are missed, then at first light their occupants will raise their heads, and only a few automatic weapons are needed to make immense trouble for the attackers, even to drive them out again.'[6]

This is exactly what happened. The situation was in fact worse than Tuker's scenario; the unaccounted-for enemy had several 88mm guns, and a secondary battle had to be fought behind the infantry before help could get through.

The fourth and most serious defect was a failure in command. Part of this failure lay in the absurdly complex structure - two corps to conduct an infantry attack by the equivalent of one division. Tuker writes that it was 'ridiculous' that so small an operation should have been handled under 'the full panoply of two corps commanders'.[7] Scoullar remarks that 'there were three commands on one battlefield - 13th Corps, New Zealand Division and 1st Armoured Division.'[8] But of course, 30th Corps was in on the act, too.

This command failure manifested itself in part in the different expectations of infantry and armour. The infantry expected the tanks to arrive automatically on cue. The armour merely held itself ready for the propitious moment. And when the tanks advanced they expected to hunt panzers, not fight with the infantry. Scoullar's comment on this is that Corps command failed to co-ordinate armour and infantry, and this, as he sees it, was the basic cause of failure.

How could such an incompetent army *ever* beat the Germans?

CHAPTER FOURTEEN
17-20 JULY - THE POLITICIANS STEP IN

While generals fight their battles, they have always behind them the politicians, for whom success is not merely the bread of life but also the substance of survival. It would be too cynical to suggest that they think only in terms of how events might effect them, but they cannot ignore the fact that when things go wrong those who elect them hold them responsible. They have to deliver.

Besides this, Auchinleck had looking over his shoulder a Prime Minister who was conscious of standing in succession to Marlborough, and who liked to translate his imaginative and sometimes romantic notions into stirring calls to battle. During June, as the Eight Army fell back into Egypt, Churchill told Auchinleck: 'You have 700,000 men on your ration strength in the Middle East. Every fit male should be made to fight and die for victory. There is no reason why units defending the Mersa Matruh positions should not be reinforced by several thousands of officers and administrative personnel ordered to swell the battalions on working parties. You are in the same position as we should be if England were invaded and the same intense spirit should reign.'

Auchinleck replied with characteristic patience: 'Your instructions regarding fighting manpower will be carried out and in fact are being observed. Working parties on El Alamein position are being reinforced from base depots in Delta so far as maintenance limitations and especially water will permit ...'

Of course, this fell far short of every fit male being herded forward to 'fight and die', and the mind boggles at the prospect of the Eighth Army filling the Desert with clerks, quartermasters and mechanics, who of necessity would have to march there on their own two feet and be supplied by who knows whom, to form a human wall against the invader.

Apart from this, Churchill was always urging that armoured units should be thrown into battle as soon as their tanks touched sand. No doubt the military were often less than efficient in trimming time from necessary preparations, but there are nevertheless limitations on what can be accomplished in moving up complex mechanised forces to face the enemy. They cannot be marched forward like men with rifles, and prudence requires that even infantry should have some time to acclimatise and learn the ways of this totally alien environment.

Now, as the battle moved into the second half of July, the politicians intruded yet again into the fray. To be fair, they responded to a request, not from Auchinleck, but from the Middle East Defence Committee. While the battles of the early part of July were being fought, the committee was viewing with alarm the progress of the German 6th Army in southern Russia as it plunged towards Stalingrad. As the committee saw the situation, if it kept up its momentum the Germans could be threatening Persia by 15 October, and if they took a short cut through Anatolia they could be approaching Syria and Iraq by 10 September. As this northern front had been sucked dry of the best divisions to fight the Battle of Egypt, the committee asked London which front, Egypt or the north, should have priority.

Churchill replied soothingly that there was no need to assume that the Russian front would break or if it did, that substantial forces could operate in Persia as early as October.

By way of stating the obvious, his response went on: 'It must be recognised, however, that if you do not succeed in defeating and destroying Rommel then there is no possibility of making sufficient transference to the north ... The only way in which a sufficient army can be gathered is in your defeating or destroying Rommel and driving him at least to a safe distance.'

Now, there's a thing! How far is a safe distance? And how could the Eighth Army release substantial forces so long as Rommel remained in the Desert, with reinforcements still flowing to him? And even if he was destroyed, who would fill the vast vacuum of North Africa in the absence of adequate British forces?

Still, Auchinleck could take only one step at a time, and on 15 July, the day on which *Bacon* was sliding into disaster, he replied that he understood the implication of the London message to be that 'unless we can destroy the German forces here and so be enabled to transfer troops to Persia, we stand to lose Iraq and the oil should the Russian front break ... I understand I am to continue to apply all my available resources to destroying the German forces opposing me as soon as possible.'

At this stage, Auchinleck was not too displeased with the way the battle was going, despite the heavy losses on Ruweisat Ridge. For his part, Dorman Smith considered, after 16 July at least, that as the Germans had now lost their capacity to attack, it was time to pause. He was to say later that it was the message from Churchill that led Auchinleck to plan yet another attack, though he conceded that Auchinleck had no intention of giving Rommel any respite. He wanted to destroy Rommel and was perhaps happy to move on to London the responsibility for continued action. Certainly this can be inferred from the careful wording of his reply.

As Dorman Smith saw it, what now followed was a separate battle from what had gone before, just as the subsequent Battle of Alam Halfa was. It was being fought on orders from London not to protect Egypt but to create a situation that would permit troops to be sent north. In his view, the battle was premature and could well have been postponed until the first week of August when it would have had a better chance of success. Logically he is right; but it is impossible not to despair of the Eighth Army carrying through anything to a successful conclusion.

While the generals planned, the two armies bickered at one another through the period 17 to 20 July, fighting limited battles and sending out recces to capture and kill - the usual sort of quiet time slaughter. There was also housekeeping to attend to, like cleaning up the battlefield by removing debris and bodies - the bodies for the sake of decency and hygiene, the debris because derelict vehicles can conceal enemy, and some may be repairable. The changed shape of the front line also called for some rearrangement of the minefields. Always careful to conserve resources, the army liked to lift mines from old fields, which were dangerous to leave around, anyway, and recycle them in new fields. The sappers knew how to do it, but it was a high risk operation. A number were killed when mines exploded, and one group disappeared entirely when a truck loaded with mines hit one still in the ground.

The heat did not improve, and neither did the flies, whose breeding grounds had multiplied in the carnage of recent days.

'It was bad enough for us at headquarters, where we could at least walk about, get into some shade, and rig up fairly fly-proof trucks for officers and messes,' Kippenberger wrote. 'For the troops in the line, who all day had to remain in their narrow slits, it was purgatory.'[1]

Up on Ruweisat, the Indians carried out a coup that restored possession of the ridge to the Eighth Army - too late, of course, for the armour to exploit, but there was some satisfaction in wresting back the territory that the New Zealanders had won and lost. It began on 17 July when one company of the 4/5th Rajputana Rifles of the 5th Indian Brigade, which had withstood the German counter-attack on 16 July, edged forward and took post about a kilometre west of Point 64. Next day a depleted 2nd West Yorkshire Regiment, all that was left of the 9th Indian Brigade, was brought up to leapfrog ahead to the western Point 63, where the 4th NZ Brigade had been overrun on 15 July. The regiment was reinforced for the task by a troop from 1st Light Anti-Aircraft Regiment, a battery of six-pounders from the 149th Anti-Tank Regiment, and a machine-gun company from the 6th Rajputana Rifles. All but one platoon of the machine-gunners were posted in scrub about 2,000 metres south west of Point 64 to support the attack from the flank.

As the West Yorks assembled in broad daylight around 4.30pm there was no sign of interest from the enemy, and even when they moved forward to the start line nothing stirred to the west. But the opening barrage at 5.30pm stung the enemy into action, and shells came hurtling back. The West Yorks moved forward in classic 1914-18 style, following a creeping barrage that moved forward 100 yards in two minutes. Their supporting arms trundled along behind. As the troops and barrage approached, the Axis infantry broke and ran, with the enthusiastic West Yorks overshooting their objective in hot pursuit. It took some time to bring them back to Point 63 and restore order, but they were ready when the Axis counter-attacked with ten tanks in support. The attack was repulsed and the Yorks continued to hold the inhospitable ridge under constant shelling and dive bombing.

How could one weak battalion take a position from which only a few days before two New Zealand brigades had been ejected? The answer lies in the north.

In the north the 24th Australian Brigade, with the support of 15 tanks, secured Tell el Makh Khad on the morning of 17 July, losing six tanks on an uncharted minefield. With the remaining tanks they went on to take a ruin on Miteiriya Ridge, a location with which they were to become familiar before the month ended. They were pushed off both features by a combined German-Italian force, aided by bombers. The Australians claimed 800 prisoners, the enemy 500.

Another Australian thrust westwards from an area south of Alamein was, so Rommel reported, driven back by Trento Division 'with heavy loss to the enemy'.

Limited though the Australian operation was, it kept Rommel skipping. Panzerarmee's diary reported that early on the morning of 17 July 'two strong battle groups ... of 9th Australian Division attacked south-west along the Qattara Track from the area Mahk Khad ... overran the right wing of Trieste Division and the Bergsaglieri strong point of XXI Corps and pushed forward quickly to area north of Sanyet el Miteiriya. A strong force had to be brought up from the central sector to seal off this penetration ... Panzerarmee was thus forced to abandon its attempt to win back X Corps' old positions in the central sector ...'

The attack thus drew more enemy troops to the north, in addition to those moved up the previous day to counter the Australian thrust to the Tell el Eisa mounds, and at the same time the Afrika Korps commander, Nehring, was ordered to go on the defensive. On 18 July, 15th Panzer had only nine battleworthy tanks, and 21st Panzer 19.

The knocked-about New Zealand Division, meanwhile, sent what was left of 4th Brigade back to base and brought up its 6th Brigade, which had not yet seen battle in the defence of Alamein.

Ruweisat was a serious blow to the New Zealanders and a significant contribution to Rommel's determination to eliminate the division. Because of the entry of Japan into the war, there had been no reinforcements from New Zealand since September 1941, and some battalions had been almost destroyed in the Crusader campaign in November-December 1941 and had to be rebuilt - and this on top of the enormous losses in Greece and Crete.

For the rest of the African campaign the New Zealand Division fielded only two brigades, the 5th and 6th. The 4th was rebuilt as an armoured brigade, with the remnants of the 22nd Battalion from 5th Brigade forming the basis of the lorried infantry. Ironically, all this was completed and the division readied as a true desert formation as the Germans were finally thrown out of Africa. But at least the New Zealanders reached Italy with their own tank support, a solution to the bitterness of July that satisfied everyone.

Rommel, besides conducting his shooting war, was engaged at this time in a paper war with Rome, pleading for reinforcements and supplies, and receiving in reply gratuitous advice from the Italians on how to run his campaign.

He told his Lu that things were 'going downright badly for me at the moment'. The enemy, he said, was destroying the Italian formations one by one, and the Germans were too weak to stand alone.

'It's enough to make one weep,' he wrote.

To repel the Ruweisat attack on 14-15 July, Rommel said in his journal, he had thrown in 'every last German reserve', and he was not amused to receive a visit from his Rome-based German and Italian superiors, Field Marshal Kesselring and Count Cavallero, particularly when Cavallero 'typically set about belittling our supply difficulties when I had just been stressing how serious they were. A long wrangle followed ...'[2]

In another letter to Lu on 18 July he said 17 July had been a critical day. 'But it can't go on like it for long, otherwise the front will crack,' he wrote.

That's the background against which he sent off to Rome on the afternoon of 15 July a warning that the situation had become critical and that the main bodies of Brescia and Pavia Divisions had been wiped out, 'i.e. were captured or left their positions'.

'Recently,' he complained, 'it has happened on many occasions that Italian troops have abandoned their positions on coming under shell fire, and even their officers cannot persuade them to oppose the enemy. This serious position makes it urgently necessary to request the sending over of more German troops to Panzerarmee immediately. This applies to infantry and anti-tank troops.'

GHQ Rome replied on 17 July with advice that 'to hasten the reinforcement of the Panzerarmee Afrika, which is now a matter of urgency', various forces identified in the message would be sent from Crete 'by the quickest means', and replaced there by Italians. On 18 July a further message came from Rome, not this time from German GHQ but from the nit-picking Cavallero, who listed supplies that were being sent across the Mediterranean by lighter. These included tanks ('some of them German'), assault guns, locomotives for the railway from Tobruk, each with the capacity to draw up to 180 tonnes at 35 k.p.h. In addition the immediate transfer of the Italian parachute division had been arranged, and if necessary another Italian division could be sent from Greece.

Coming as it did from Cavallero, this message was probably received with scepticism by Rommel, who that very afternoon had signalled that

British air and naval forces were playing havoc with his coastal shipping, making the army's supply situation 'precarious'. Two ships had been sunk and the petrol dump at Tobruk destroyed by a direct hit. The loss amounted to 2,200 tonnes of ammunition and 2,400 cubic metres of petrol, and temporary relief could not be expected until ships then en route to Tobruk with 3,000 tonnes of ammunition and 2,200 cubic metres of petrol had been unloaded.

'Supplies will not be finally assured until the arrival of cargo lighters,' he said.

Perhaps as he wrote he leafed back to a message that came from Rome on 14 July, on the eve of Ruweisat, advising that the Fuhrer had ordered that units of Panzerarmee were to be replenished to their full strength in men and material, and kept permanently at this level. Some hope! There are limits even to the powers of dictators or Rommel would have been through to Cairo within the month.

What must really have made his day, though, were two messages on 17 July from Bastico, one passing on operational policy from the Duce and another from himself telling Rommel how to whip up a fighting spirit among Italian troops.

If London had no clear idea of what was happening in Africa, neither, surely, did Rome. And yet the news came through loud and clear.

'Our situation is critical, and the crisis is not yet over, as our front is very thin and we have no reserves behind it,' Panzerarmee reported on 20 July. 'Continual day and night enemy air attacks on Mersa Matruh, and night bombardments by light enemy naval forces are at present making the port usable by large ships only with great difficulty.'

By contrast, German air reconnaissance had shown over 200,000 tonnes of British shipping at Suez, among these 'the large troop transport Queen Elizabeth (85,000 tonnes) was recognised'.

While Rommel was enduring the counselling attentions of his superiors, his enemy was again planning his downfall. Word of this filtered through to the air force units, who were to have a significant part to play.

'Rumours of "today is the decisive (or significant) day, and we shall probably move pdq" still persist,' wrote a scribe in one squadron of 223 Wing. 'It would seem that some initiative has been lost somewhere in the vicinity of El Alamein and that both sides are seeking it. If found, the finder will use it as an infallible lever for the discomforture and displacement of the other side. The finder's side will then commence a rapid advance and the loser's side will be ordered off the field. In the meantime the existing state of super-mobility and sleeping in the open, having existed since the early days of the withdrawal, has lost its novelty.'

The rumours were true. At Auchinleck's headquarters, battle plans had been drawn up under the lofty code name of *Splendour*. The intention was given, again, "To destroy the enemy's army in its present location, with an attack provisionally set down for 30 July', by which time the newly arrived 23rd Armoured Brigade, fresh from England, would be ready for action.

13th Corps was to deliver the main blow in the centre, with only subsidiary attacks in the north and south. The Australians in their salient were given the job of seizing the Tell el Eisa mounds and a whole series of high points, and then exploiting west 'as opportunity offers', and every-one was to be ready to pursue and surround the defeated and fleeing enemy.

Splendour was planned in splendid detail. Nothing was left to chance. This was to be the definitive break-through, the end of Rommel for all time, an ambition that even at the time sounded excessively optimistic. Operation Order No.102 on 20 July gave a lead to expectations with an opening general statement, 'Our ability to pursue the enemy relentlessly and inflict the maximum destruction will depend largely on our operating on a hard scale ...' 13th and 30th Corps (less 1st South African Division) were both to 'pursue immediately and without waiting for further orders with all available mobile and armoured forces. Divisions will pursue with battle groups ...'

Perhaps given until 30 July the Eighth Army might have been able to put together the ultimate master stroke. As it happened, Splendour came forward with a rush, the 23rd Armoured Brigade was hastened up to the Desert, and on 21 July the wheels were set in motion. Even as the troops made preparations on that day, the orders kept coming.

The battle that was ever after to be known simply as Mreir, after its first objective, though by some as Second Ruweisat, was the closest the Eighth Army came in July to a full-scale set piece attack. It was magnificent in its planning, devastating in its failure.

CHAPTER FIFTEEN

21-22 JULY - MREIR, 'ANOTHER BLOODY DISASTER'

S uch portents of catastrophe! The New Zealanders were nervous, the Australians hostile. Poor innocent tanks crews, recent arrivals from Britain and children in the ways of war and the Desert, scented danger but were ordered on to a massacre. Before the battle began, Kippenberger had his opinion put on record: '... there will be another bloody disaster'.[1]

He was not alone in his concern. Gott and some others were unhappy, and Dorman Smith was later to admit that *Splendour* was 'a gamble that bloody near came off'. But it *was* a bloody disaster.

Splendour had some resemblance to *Bacon*, but it was more complex and promised greater rewards.

In the first phase, the Indians were to descend from Ruweisat Ridge, where they had established themselves during the preceding week, penetrate the enemy minefields and seize Deir el Shein of proud but unhappy memory.

The New Zealanders were to secure the eastern end of Mreir Depression, just south west of the tip of the ridge. The Indians were to be followed through on the morning of 22 July by two regiments of the 23rd Armoured Brigade, which would charge on to Point 59, just north of the mid-point of Mreir Depression. The New Zealanders were to be joined at first light by tanks of the 2nd Armoured Brigade, which would secure against counter-attack and exploit as possible - a repeat of what was intended at Ruweisat a week previously.

While this was going on, there would be diversionary attacks in the south by 69th Brigade of 50th Division, and 7th Armoured Division, and the Australians would stir things along in their Tell el Eisa salient.

Forty eight hours after Mreir had been seized, the tanks were to side-step deftly to join the Australians in the north and support them in the final stroke while most of the enemy were busy dealing with the New Zealanders and Indians.

Fundamental to this plan was the belief that Rommel, having been stretched this way and that, now had his forces dispersed, and the infantry attacks would ensure that he could not concentrate to oppose the 23rd Armoured Brigade. However, although there were German forces interspersed among the Italians, Rommel had now concentrated his cohesive German units, and the Eighth Army was about to do just what Rommel did on 1 July - put its head in the lion's mouth. Mreir on the night of 21 July was the heartland of panzer country. But then the tanks of 2nd Armoured Brigade were due to arrive at dawn.

The New Zealanders would commit the three battalions of their 6th Brigade to the attack. The Indians on the ridge would send in 161st Motor Brigade, another newcomer to the Desert. As the Indians moved forward to reclaim Deir el Shein, New Zealand and Indian sappers would come in close behind them and clear a way through the enemy minefields for the Valentines of the 40th and 46th RTR of the 23rd Armoured Brigade. All going well they should be able to motor through to their objective.

The South Africans (2nd Botha) were to seize a small depression just to the north, and at the time the 23rd put in its attack on the morning of 22 July, the 24th and 26th Australian Brigades would make scattershot attacks west, south-west and south and be ready to chase the foe as he fled west.

The New Zealanders, Indians and South Africans were to attack under cover of darkness on the night of 21-22 July. The 23rd and Australians were to attack on the morning of 22 July. The plan in its detail had a number of phases and included a complex bombing operation, but everything depended on those night attacks on Mreir and Deir el Shein.

The arithematic heavily favoured Auchinleck. He had about 400 tanks at his disposal, compared with Rommel's 45 German and 59 Italian. The raw figures, it's true, are misleading, because 150 of the Eighth Army tanks were Valentines and a few Matildas of the 23rd Brigade, which had been in the country only a fortnight after a two-month voyage from Britain; one of its three regiments had been sent to help the Australians in an infantry tank role, the other two had been retained to form a grand cavalry charge. The enthusiasm of these newcomers and their readiness to fight greatly impressed the New Zealand infantry when officers came up in advance to see what a war looked like, but this elan would have to be weighed against the long experience of Panzerarmee. Still, even without the 23rd,

Auchinleck would have had a comfortable majority, against which Rommel could place only a considerable improvement in his manpower - men against steel.

There was, though, a concealed weakness in the British armour. A few days earlier both the divisional commander, Lumsden, and 2nd Armoured Brigade commander, Briggs, had been wounded by the same shell, and two key figures who were only too painfully aware of what had gone wrong on Ruweisat the previous week were absent. Moreover, the new divisional commander, Gatehouse, who had been hastened up from the Delta, where he had commanded 10th Armoured Division, then in training, had no opportunity to participate in the planning of *Splendour* and was briefed only on the part to be played by 23rd Brigade. Briggs' successor was Brigadier J.C. Currie.

Unlike Ruweisat, which had begun without a preliminary barrage, the Mreir attack was to be clearly signalled to the enemy. The enemy, in fact, was able to deduce several days in advance that something was brewing by the increase in air activity and ground patrolling. If any doubt remained, it was dispelled by the barrage put down, as zero hour approached, by bombers, artillery and Vickers guns. It wasn't a creeping barrage in the 1914-18 pattern, but rather a wholesale dumping of high explosive to kill as many enemy as possible before the infantry arrived and rattle the rest out of their wits. It was an operation conducted in style, right through to the final catastrophes - the loss of two more New Zealand battalions and their brigade headquarters and most of 23rd Armoured Brigade.

The 6th NZ Brigade was to attack with all three battalions, the 24th, 25th and 26th. The Indians would attack with two, the 3/7th Rajputana and the 1/1 Punjab.

From the New Zealanders' point of view it was an awkward round-about approach to their objective, though it was square on to their line of attack. The 6th could have assembled behind 5th NZ Brigade, who were due east of Mreir and more or less a stone's throw from the eastern tongue, but it was considered this would cause dangerous overcrowding, and it was decided that the 6th would attack from its own lines further south, swinging out into no-man's-land in a wide arc to face north-north-west, with its left wing practically touching the enemy's forward defence positions. The axis of advance would then be a diagonal line across no-man's-land. This extended the approach march to the objective by up to eight kilometres, increasing the danger of formations losing coherence and submitting troops to the cross-fire of enemy machine-guns firing on fixed lines.

The New Zealanders were to attack with their 24th Battalion in the centre, the 26th Battalion on the right and the 25th Battalion on the left

On the night of 21-22 July, the New Zealanders and Indians again attacked as the first phase of a general break-through, but the operation ended when German units clustered in and around El Mreir Depression converged on the 6th New Zealand Brigade, which did not receive the expected support of 2nd Armoured Brigade. 26th Battalion, on the right, found itself mixed up with 8th Panzer Regiment during the night, and being unable to find the rest of the brigade, turned for home, dividing into two parts as it went. The two Indian battalions that were to have cleared a path for 23rd Armoured Brigade were turned back by the enemy, and the armour charged on to its destruction. See detailed map on page 199.

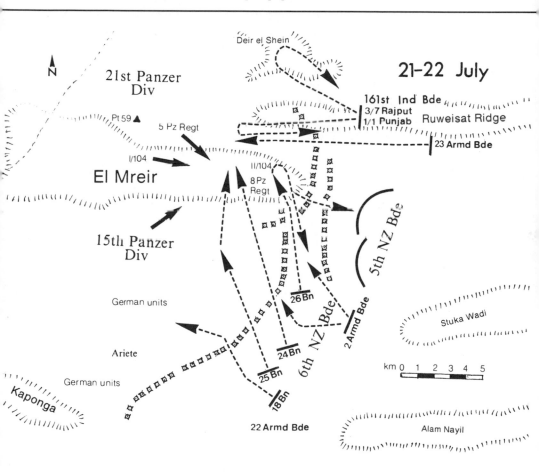

and slightly to the rear of the 24th, halting short of Mreir to form a reserve. 18th NZ Battalion, New Zealand Divisional Cavalry and 22nd Armoured Brigade were to form a screen to the south, and in the far south 69th Brigade was to make a diversionary attack.

The enemy armoured forces were in their usual low state. On the evening of 21 July 15th Panzer had 20 tanks - four Mark IIs, 14 IIIs, one IV and a command vehicle. 21st Panzer had 25, but two of these were Mark IV Specials for which there was no ammunition. Apart from those two there were three Mark IIs, six III Specials and two command vehicles. If Rommel needed more he could call on his headquarters battle group, as he had done in the past.

The great question mark over the whole operation was what 2nd Armoured Brigade would do, and there was a sense of *déjà vu* as the New Zealand divisional conference was convened on 21 July. The armour was represented by the commander of 22nd Brigade, Fisher, who 'swore' that the tanks would be up. 6th NZ Brigade commander, Clifton, pressed him either to have the tanks move up at night or place a regiment under his command. Both requests were refused, but anyway, Fisher could hardly have so committed 2nd Brigade tanks though he could have agreed to ask.

As tanks can't be at two places at the same time, both on the start line and on the objective, and if the tanks were not to move until it was light, this necessarily meant that at best it would be some time after first light before British armour reached the infantry, even assuming they had a clear run without being delayed by the normal hazards of a battlefield, such as unexpected opposition, an uncleared minefield, or getting lost.

The fact that it was Fisher and not Currie who attended the conference was also a cause of mild concern, but the liaison problem came right when Clifton received the services of no fewer than three liaison officers, one each from 2nd and 22nd Armoured Brigades and one from 6th RTR, a 2nd Brigade regiment, which was assigned as the first 'for immediate counter-attack'. They all turned up just before the attack in a Crusader, a Honey and an armoured car. A bemused Clifton noted that the Crusader's commander was Captain the Earl Haig. All this was reassurance indeed of the armour's determination this time to play its part, though none of the three had any more than a vague idea of what was happening, and they had to be briefed as the battle was about to begin.

For all the seeming eagerness of the armour to be in at the kill, buried in the orders was a statement that 6th RTR 'will not be committed without the consent of the commander of 2nd Armoured Brigade unless communications fail, when the decision will rest with the commander of the regiment'.

All these decisions were sequels to that divisional conference, from which an uneasy Inglis had departed leaving instructions for all details of armour/infantry co-ordination to be securely tied up. Kippenberger says that after Inglis had gone, he and Clifton became involved in an unprofitable argument with Fisher before the conference broke up. Kippenberger went back to his 5th Brigade headquarters, ordered out everyone but his brigade major, Fairbrother, and his IO, McPhail, and said to Fairbrother: 'Take this down: The brigadier has returned from the divisional conference and says there will be another bloody disaster.'

First timers don't feel fear. Well, I don't, but then I've got a lot to think about. Maybe next time will be different. I get clear orders: Wait at A Company headquarters until B Company comes around: guide them out on a bearing of 261 degrees to the left flank of the start line. Then the axis of advance will be 351 degrees.

I should be tired, whacked, even, but I'm not. Not a trace of fatigue. Adrenalin, I suppose. Black puff balls of enemy shelling show up as I trudge back to A Company lines. I pass a Grant tank, the crew of which are brewing up on one of those sand and petrol fires that are their speciality. They look up with some surprise as I march past. Well, I'm a sight, I suppose - the complete infantryman, hung about with bandoliers, web gear, haversack, pick, rifle and all the rest, a solitary soldier off to war.

I reach A Company with time to spare, but already about 300 metres out in front there's a line of men moving across to the north, with shells spattering among them. They plod stolidly on as though the smoke balls are nothing more harmful than special effects for a movie.

'Yeah, that's B Company,' the A Company CO says.

But they're going the wrong way! I give chase, jogging as fast as army boots and battle clobber will allow. I overtake the last platoon, the very last. The company commander is ahead somewhere, the platoon commander tells me. I'm off again. There is no evening cool yet, or none that I notice. Though the sun's low it's still broad daylight and warm. Sweat streams. I catch up with B Company HQ. The CO is somewhere ahead. 'Well, send a runner after him. You're too far forward and going the wrong way.' Finally we find him on the rim of a depression. Yes, he knows there was a change in start line, but the commander of the first platoon out, who did not, got away early. Nerves, I suppose; a need to do something. Bloody chaos! In the shadow of the depression, men swarm, ant-like. Shell bursts are smoke splodges, like ink flicked on to a dark photograph. Close by are a few open trucks that have brought up the Vickers. A jeep whirls past, the occupants' faces set and preoccupied. The sun is a blood-red ball low over the western ridge.

Our own shells sigh mournfully overhead and plunge into the great cloud of smoke and dust rising from the banging and roaring over the enemy lines. Our bombers home in with unswerving menace, and their bombs whistle in dimuendo as they seemingly float down to join the explosive violence.

I leave B Company CO to sort out the problem, and he gives me half a dozen men while I go in search of the correct start line. Of course, I have no bearing now because I have lost my starting point. I just know that somewhere 'over there' there's an old iron artillery wheel and two flimsies sitting out in the Desert marking our start line.

My little band attracts enemy interest as we tramp west, and the shells start to arrive. We fall flat as they moan in and explode around us. But half a dozen men lying on their bellies four or five kilometres away are an unrewarding target, and when we hear the shells passing over us to reach further back, we get up and continue on our way. We're probably an irritant to that Jerry OP, because the guns keep coming back to us and we keep falling flat, then reappearing as the guns lift their range.

Eventually the CO turns up with battalion headquarters, his men in his wake. I explain to him what has happened, and without a word he nods, does a right turn, indicates direction with his hands, palms in, and we're off. Just like that. There's no sign of the start line.

Diary note: The artillery was in full cry, and silver-bellied Bostons floated overhead, shifting formation as they approached their target. A battery of Vickers started up, stuttering out a flow of invisible bullets in the general direction of the enemy, shooting at nothing more precise than a map reference, because there was nothing to see except billowing smoke against the last red segment of sun.

Away we go, counting. Bill has come up with the battalion, and he and I count paces while Jackie, the IO, does the steering. Bill has had a few drinks, and he's garrulous and protective. Still, he's brought a beer can filled with brandy in his haversack, and that's an asset on a night like this.

There's a low ridge ahead, and on the forward face a minefield. We pause and challenge a couple of figures coming in from the right. It's dark, now, and anyone who approaches could have malicious intent. They turn out to be sappers with the news that the field is still partly alive, which may be something of an understatement because the area beyond the wire is studded with mines. Since they've been sewn, the wind has swept away most of the sand around them, and they quilt the ground with obvious danger. But then if you can see them you can walk among them, and we mess about a bit, crossing and recrossing the field, and at one point we settle down for a bit among the mines while someone sorts something out. Bill suggests we should have a drink. And why not? What could be more acceptable in the middle of a minefield than a sip of brandy?

Finally, we're on our way again, counting. The usual trick is to have a pocketful of beans or stones, and every time you reach a hundred you move a bean or whatever from one pocket to the other. That way you always know to the last hundred paces how far you've come, whatever the distractions. But I'm bound to say I haven't given a thought to beans, and neither has Bill, so we're relying on memory.

The battlefield has gone uncannily quiet, now. The bombers have packed it in, and the crews are presumably drinking Stella beer in the mess. The artillery has closed down for the night, too, but the Vickers are still going strong, and though we can't hear the guns, the bullets are hissing invisibly overhead ... whispering death, as the Jerries say. Up ahead we see cross tracer from a Spandau hosing from left to right in undulating waves. A white flare goes up on our left, hangs briefly, and goes out. Then there's a wild crackling sound and lights tear past at speed, and we're flat on the ground, tracer streaming low in front, above and behind. We find we've forgotten the count and guess a figure.

The firing stops. No one moves. Cunning bastards, these Jerries. They're waiting for us to stand up. Or maybe they're putting in a new belt. Suddenly the tracer comes again, crackling like fire crackers. And then it stops. We get up and run.

Signs of where the enemy has been - a rifle on the ground, shallow slit trenches. We keep counting. More cross fire. We go down again. This time I shout the last number as we fall. I feel a shock go through my left arm, like a jolt of high powered electricity. In through the elbow and up the arm. Hell, I'm hit ... I think. But it's over in a flash. I've hit my funny bone as I crashed.

We wait for the second burst, then get up and go. Counting. Tracer again, then on our left a primeval yell and the gun stops firing. We move on, secure in the knowledge that the gun crew has been bayoneted.

At last, 2,500 paces, half way. Or it should be, if we've got it right.

And so it goes on to five thousand paces, 4½ kilometres more or less. This is the objective? This! Hard rock, as flat as a billiard table. Come daylight and we'll be like ducks in a shooting gallery. Find a patch of soft sand and start digging. But it's the old story - a great rock slab 20 centimetres down.

Still, we're here, wherever here is, all in one piece.

The 24th and 26th had the hard part that night, bombing and bayoneting their way through strong points on their way to Mreir. For the 25th, being slightly back in reserve, it was something of a stroll across the desert, with a few uncomfortable interruptions. The 25th's main problem was that its left flank practically brushed against the forward enemy posts.

The 24th and 26th, though advancing side by side, had no contact with each other, and with the shorter distance to go, the 26th reached the eastern end of Mreir Depression first. Ominous shapes took form from the dark - panzers. In fact, the New Zealanders' 'old friends' 8th Panzer regiment. Enemy infantry on the north rim showered down grenades and small arms fire. The panzers, restless in the presence of infantry, shuffled around, criss-crossing the depression with red tracer. 26th's most urgent need was to make contact with the 24th, but patrols that went searching to the west could find only enemy. A profound unease set in.

24th Battalion found a more receptive part of the depression awaiting them, but they arrived with only 70 to 80 riflemen, the rest having been killed, wounded or lost in the night. To meet the dangers of the dawn, they had with them four six-pounders, seven two-pounders, ten Bren gun carriers, two machine-guns on carriers, and four mortars - not a lot. A patrol sent east to find 26th Battalion was swallowed up in the darkness and not seen again. It was a small band that set about preparing a defence system among the panzers.

There remained the reserve battalion, the 25th, which was settling in as best it could on the rocky plain several kilometres to the rear.

Coming up behind were the long columns of vehicles - the brigade column, with the brigadier, Clifton, and the battalions' support groups, all of which were to follow a line of green lights that defined the brigade axis. But the brigade column, following the green lights from the start line, found they disappeared into the minefield, and there was a halt while the brigade major scouted around for a way through. He found a gap, at that time being used by the nose to tail column of the 24th's fighting vehicles, and the brigade column looped around to follow them through. Beyond the minefield, Clifton turned his column to follow along the inside of the wire hoping to discover a continuation of the lights, but he found none. He led his vehicles along the line of a wire fence that followed a generally northerly direction, 'hoping for the best'.

Message from Afrika Korps to panzer divisions (timed at 2.15am Eighth Army time):

'21st Panzer will restore situation in the 15th Panzer sector. It will advance at 0415 hours (5.15 am Eighth Army time) and attack the flank of the penetration ... 15th Panzer with Baade Group will attack the same objective as 21st Panzer (advancing to the NE). XX Corps has been asked to send Ariete tanks forward in support of the attack from right rear.'

'Bates, go and find the brigade axis and bring in the portees and carriers.'

The theory is that our fighting vehicles - the Bren carriers and portees - with trucks carrying other gear, should feel their way along the axis until they and I bump into each other. They give me a provost for a companion, and I set a course due east.

The moon is just starting to rise. Five hundred metres or so out we come to a north-south track with a grave beside it - humped up sand with a wooden cross. Then we see two figures lying on the ground, and we approach with caution. They turn out to be two wounded New Zealanders, who warn us that there's a pocket of Italians right in our path.

'They challenged us and then shot us with a machine-gun,' they say.

We consider this complication and decide we'd better take the wounded back to the battalion and report the difficulty.

'Keep going till you find the axis,' is the unsympathetic response, and they reinforce my support team with the provost sergeant, two more provosts, two batmen and, for good measure, the two wounded and a Jerry prisoner, who seems to have been spirited out of the night. The latter three were to be sent back by the first available transport.

We come to the road again at the same point, and I set a new course slightly to the north to avoid the Italians; I'm in no mood for a private war. Some distance on we see shapes of a line of vehicles. Cautious again, we approach to find a column of carriers, portees and tanks, but not the ones we're looking for. Tanks would indicate that this is the brigade column. We exchange hushed inquiries and answers. We're aware of being treated with suspicion. We're directed to the brigade IO, who should be 'up front somewhere', and the provost sergeant and I leave our little band and go searching. But no IO can be found and no one has seen any green lights.

Then a provost comes up and says the 25th's RTO (regimental transport officer) has turned up at the tail of the column in a carrier looking for a guide. And there I find him, just a single carrier with not so much as a portee to bless himself with. He hasn't found any green lights, either, nor has he found a gap in the minefield. His solution to that problem was to drive straight through, a gesture of impetuosity that gave him safe passage but which blew up the truck that followed. A way is now being cleared.

'You'd better come back, Bates, and we'll collect the rest.'

It's been a long day and my legs have gone rubbery, and they have to help me on to the carrier like an old man.

And the bearing back to the support column? The RTO has no idea. As he had plunged through the minefield, so he had driven heedlessly into the night. We slew around. No bearing! I look back at the sky behind us and try to commit the pattern of stars to memory, but I'm no good at that sort of thing. Anyway, it's all totally futile because the RTO doesn't know where he is, where his column is or where he is going, and we circle around the desert aimlessly until, astonishingly, we come across the scene of inaction. On the far side of the wire are the shadowy forms of waiting vehicles. Right in the middle of the minefield there's a damaged truck, and there's a man probing the ground with a bayonet. Just one man. We wait... wait. Hours pass. The moon goes, and aircraft drop parachute flares that hang in the sky and light up the whole world. A few shells come over. A lucky shot hits a truck and sets it on fire. The horn starts sounding and drones on for about quarter of an hour, then dies away as the battery gives out. Fortunately the enemy gunners must be in indolent mood because they make no attempt to use the burning truck as a marker.

At long last, the column begins to file through the minefield, and the RTO swings the carrier around. Now Bates has to find the way home. Remember the drill: Walk out in front and look infinitely wise and completely confident, and say, 'This way.' Pitch dark now. I've guessed a bearing, but one way or another, we grope our way back to the battalion. Seems the battalion had a skirmish with the Italians while we were away, and even now the two groups can't be more than a few hundred metres apart. It could be an unneighbourly daybreak. We haven't been back long before the colonel gets into conversation with the brigadier on the No. 18. He says we're to join him in the 24th Battalion box, whatever that is. The brig puts up two green Verys as a guide, but with flares in all sorts of colours going up everywhere, it's a bit confusing. We ask for two whites as confirmation. The battalion moves off again.

Clifton had reached 24th Battalion in Mreir Depression with his brigade support group (the one we had encountered) at 3.30 am to find it thin on the ground and out of touch with the 26th. He promptly 'whistled up' the 25th, then about three kilometres away and now complete with all its support weapons. He also asked Division to ensure that tanks were there promptly at first light. For good measure, he climbed on to the Honey and had the 6th RTR liaison officer also request tanks at first light.

The desert has gone quiet, except for us. Our carriers clank and roar across the rock like motorised old iron. They must be able to hear us in Berlin. But apart from the odd squirt of tracer in the distance and the interminable flares of the enemy, it could almost be an exercise.

As the 25th converged on the 24th, shedding one company lost in the dark as it advanced, enemy tanks of three divisions awaited them.

The danger was well understood, if not defined in detail, by concerned senior officers of the New Zealand Division. Kippenberger, who had been able to observe some of the earlier part of the advance from his forward positions, told Division that there were panzers in Mreir, adding the warning, 'Our tanks are urgently required before daylight.' The division's GS01, Gentry, unable to contact 1st Armoured Division, called 13th Corps tactical HQ with a report, and closed with a similar warning. A little over an hour later, at 1.25am to be exact, Inglis himself called 13th Corps to express his concern, and at 2.15am, following receipt of reports from Clifton, Gentry telephoned the brigade major of 2nd Armoured Brigade to give him an appreciation of the situation. He concluded, 'It is essential that our tanks are at the depression at first light.' And as a cover he then called 1st Armoured Division, recalled the experiences of Ruweisat, and asked that order be given for the tanks to be on the objective by first light.

At 2.50am Inglis called Gott to ensure that orders for armoured support went through the right channels from corps HQ to 2nd Armoured Brigade. And then he called 1st Armoured Division again and was assured, so the New Zealand official history says, 'that the armour, without fail, would be at Mreir at first light'.[2]

Soft sand underfoot as we go down into the depression. This looks cosier. At least we can dig in here. Just a touch of light in the sky, now.

'The time is just on five o'clock. The first signs of dawn are in the sky but it's still dark in the Mreir Depression. At the rear of 6th Brigade's advance headquarters the riflemen of 25th Battalion move up to take position on the 24th's right preparatory to cleaning up the gap to the 26th. Officers of the 24th Battalion in command of anti-tank and machine-guns are getting their men ready to move into the best defensive positions as soon as it is light enough to choose them. There is little noise. Just the shuffle of feet in the sand and over rocks, an occasional flare and a burst of tracer fire from an enemy machine-gun ....

'Around the lip of the depression and in position on its floor German officers and non-commissioned officers of tank, artillery, machine-gun and infantry units were intent on the time. Their watches showed four o'clock, an hour behind British Army time, a quarter of an hour to zero. They knew approximately where the British forces lay in the depression and they had their guns laid roughly on the area ... Now they watched the minutes. At the quarter, signal and illumination flares burst in the air and down to the depression poured machine-gun and anti-tank tracer, solid and high explosive shells and mortar bombs, into the congested mass of men and vehicles, anti-tank guns, machine-guns and carriers.'[3]

'An Auckland carrier came dashing across the depression, yelling, "Stand to! Tanks! Lots of the bastards!" but that was obvious. A deluge of "golden rain" fell on us from the northern edge of the depression about 400 yards away.'[4]

Tracer coming over the rim of the depression in a long, high arc. Then more. Everyone starts digging. Now it's shells, mortars, the lot. A fire tempest sweeps the area. Motor transport is everywhere in a tight clutter. And that Honey we saw earlier. A shell bams into it, and a man jumps onto the tank to free a jammed hatch cover. There's another almighty bang, and he falls, making a kind of surprised crying, whimpering noise. The tank begins to burn.

There's a pause as though someone has turned off the tap, and then it all comes down again, more furious than before. I flatten myself in my slit trench. There's another bang, like the end of the world. Everything goes red before my eyes and I decide with calm logic that I must be hit. I look up and find the Honey a twisted steel wreck from which a mushroom column of red-tinged smoke is rising. The stuff keeps coming, and there's another monstrous bang nearby that sends up a smoke ring fully ten metres across, rising like some carefully calculated trick into the sky. A motor truck has disappeared completely. A load of mines, of course.

A white-faced officer, crouching in the lee of a carrier, says we're surrounded. A few men are making a dash for it. Several more of us think this might be a good idea, and we get up and run. Hostile fire engulfs us, and we turn and throw ourselves into the nearest slit trench. The one I land in is too short and my feet stick out - ridiculous but not funny. I choose my time to perform an acrobatic act to return to my own.

Within an hour it ends. There are men walking forward with their hands up, and a Mark III rolls down into the depression, the commander standing in the hatch opening. We stand up, shed our gear, and join the mob, refusing to raise our hands, though more in disgust than from bravado. There's not even a feeling of relief that it's over - just a numb sense of disappointment. Black smoke rises from burning vehicles. The wounded lie about. One pleads not to be left here in the desert. 'They'll pick you up,' we assure him. 'Don't leave me, Dig,' he implores. What can we do? The blood-soaked uniform indicates a wound requiring treatment beyond our skills, and anyway, our despair matches his panic. We feel some compassion but we are not moved to offer more than reassurance. Are we being callous? Perhaps. But 1942 is a time when a wounded man in the sand is a commonplace. He's lucky to be alive.

We move on. And that's the end of the great attack. I haven't even fired a shot.

Diary note by Clifton: 'Tanks came up and passed on. They were only interested in meeting our armoured attack and not worrying about us. Put up my hands in my first battle.'

Back in the New Zealand lines, reports began to filter in. A few survivors from 6th Brigade appeared with the customary stories of doom, but such reports are always treated with scepticism, and no one knew what was happening.

However, it was known that there were panzers about. Apart from Clifton's nocturnal reports, 26th Battalion had sent back word during the night that it was being attacked by tanks.

Separated from the rest of the brigade, the 26th had fought its own small battle. Caught among hostile infantry and armour, it had withdrawn from the eastern end of the depression at dawn, pursued only by small arms fire. The main enemy force at this time was busy saturating the area held by 24th and 25th Battalions.

Most of the battalion retraced its steps, but B Company veered to the east and took a short cut to the New Zealand positions, where it found tanks warming themselves in the morning sun in 21st Battalion lines, two or three kilometres from the depression.

At 6.50am, Inglis called 1st Armoured Division and spoke to an officer he believed to be Gatehouse, though Gatehouse said later it was not him, and asked why the promised support had not been given and what it was proposed to do.

'He replied that we had not requested support,' Inglis' diary says. 'I informed him of our conversation with his staff during the night and that I had a record of them. He then said we had not requested support through the correct channels which, he alleged, were his LOs. He said he was ready to attack then.'

Ready to attack? A figure of speech, perhaps. No one could have been less ready to cross a battlefield and engage the enemy. Put bluntly, the armour had no idea how it could reach Mreir, and 1st Armoured Division was about to launch brave men into muddle and disaster, just as it had left the infantry to fall into German hands. Whatever other faults the armour displayed that day, lack of courage was not one of them. The tank crews were also victims. The story of 6th RTR can be briefly told. They were ordered out at first light to support the New Zealanders. C Squadron advanced to deal with tanks believed to be attacking the New Zealanders, and ran into heavy anti-tank fire from the depression, thought to have been cleared. Three Grants were lost, and the squadron withdrew. The squadron tried again at 11.30am, met panzers, and claimed to have knocked out two Mark IVs.

For the 9th Lancers it was not so simple. Told by an unidentified New Zealand brigade, presumably 6th Brigade rear HQ, that it was cut off from 'one of their battalions' by German tanks, as the war diary has it, the Lancers rolled out 'to see what we could do'. But they soon encountered an enemy minefield and halted. And there they sat, baking in the sun, plastered by shells and a Stuka attack, waiting … waiting for sappers to come and clear a way. They waited all morning. They waited until 1.30pm, at which time the sappers turned up and began to clear a lane 20 yards wide. They waited until 4.00pm, when at last they were ordered through the gap and told to clear the enemy from the depression.

Now, consider the situation. British tanks have been sitting in front of the minefield for hours, in plain view of the enemy. The sappers have at last cleared a gap, also in plain view of the enemy, and indeed, according to the Lancers' war diary, it was learned later that a German signal had been intercepted by 1st Armoured Division reporting what was going on, but this information was not passed on to 2nd Armoured Brigade. At 5.00pm, with the light from the evening sun directly in their faces, the Lancers began moving through a gap said to be wide enough to accommodate only one tank at a time, though events were to show that two could squeeze through. B Squadron led, followed by the 2nd Bays, then regimental HQ, and at the rear, A Squadron in cruisers. As B Squadron Grants began filing through the gap, shells from 105mm guns came howling in, and the lead tank, hit by two shells at one, dissolved in a ball of fire. Anti-tank fire, some from 88 mm guns, converged on the gap from both flanks, and nine enemy tanks at the front and another eight on the right joined in. The place was a shooting gallery. Always the front tank was the target, and there was nothing the following tanks could do to help. Grants, of course, can fire only straight ahead, and their 75mm guns were masked by the tank in front. Two more tanks erupted in flame, and in short order one troop leader, the Hon R.E. Lloyd Mostyn, found he had none left. Yet under orders from their CO, the tanks pushed on, and by some miracle enough of them got through to create congestion, and a consequential bunched target for the enemy guns, on the far side of the minefield. For tanks crews it was like presenting themselves for execution. As the war diary has it, 'Every minute was costing a tank', and under that weight of enemy fire, even that might be an understatement. Clearly there was no way forward.

Inevitably, Brigade ordered them back, and one by one they reversed through that slender gap, which was partly blocked by two burning tanks. Help came at last in the form of smoke laid down by E Battery of 1st RHA.

The outcome of what the war diary calls 'this ill-prepared, ill-advised operation' was five Grants destroyed outright and seven so badly damaged as to be useless. In addition, three cruisers had been hit and had to be pulled out for repairs.

Even at that, the tank crews were lucky. The Luftwaffe, scenting blood, came on the scene with 18 Stukas and 10 Ju 88s, and finding the tanks gone, used some New Zealanders as a secondary target, killing some and setting fire to an ammunition truck.

The whole sorry episode was so futile. When the Lancers began to advance on their rescue mission, the New Zealanders in Mreir had long since gone, though of course, the armour did not know this. While the tanks stood under the burning sun, awaiting the arrival of the sappers, the New Zealand infantry had been assembled by their captors some kilometres away, and also left to cook on a barren plain of rock. Like the tanks, they too suffered through the heat of that high summer day with neither food nor water until trucks collected them in the late afternoon, and when the British tanks at last advanced into the fire of the enemy guns, the captured infantry were on their way west towards the first prison camp of a long series. Twelve tanks had been lost, and with them their crews, who had faced up to certain death on a pointless mission.

Of course, no one knew at the time that the infantry had gone and the armour was right to try to reach them. But if this exercise was to be undertaken, the elementary precaution of determining an axis of advance and clearing a path through the minefield under cover of darkness would seem a reasonable course of action. And if a daylight penetration was necessary, the armour might have emulated the Germans and had sappers on the spot. And these were Desert veterans, not naive newcomers. It's a story of incompetence that beggars belief.

There were some few New Zealand survivors from that debacle, among them an angry Clifton, who, by removing his badges of rank and working all day among the wounded as a medical orderly, was able to escape that night and come storming back to tell his general that the armour brigadier was 'either a cold-footed bastard or not competent to command a sanitary fatigue'. He went across to 2nd Armoured Brigade HQ to tell him personally, but, perhaps fortunately for future relations, the brigadier was not there.

The failure of the armour to provide the promised support to the infantry has never been explained.

In fact, however, there are some answers. And bitter though the infantry were, they have to accept a share of the blame.

The problem began with a permissive order that infantry and armour would set their own start lines. In other words, the various formations were given their objectives, and it was up to them to decide how to get there.

The expectations of the New Zealanders on this occasion appeared to be that the armour would follow them along their brigade axis, but this would have been fatal. The infantry advanced obliquely across no-man's-land, and even in darkness was subject to flanking fire. Tanks attempting the same route in daylight would have exposed their vulnerable side armour to every anti-tank gun along the eight kilometre route, and assuming they even found their way through the minefield, would have been shot off the Desert. The alternative would have been to move up under the cover of darkness, then they, like the infantry, would have met the dawn unprepared for whatever the day would bring. In all the circumstances, Dorman Smith, no admirer of the armour, thought the tanks could be exonerated from blame. But it's not that simple.

The infantry had the assurance of the armour that the tanks would be there. And no one apparently told the infantry that the plan for the night attack wouldn't work for the armour. Dorman Smith says the New Zealanders were left to make their own plans because of their cussed independence, but what folly it was not to challenge that plan.

Dorman Smith's view is that the New Zealanders should have given the attack to the 5th NZ Brigade, reinforced with fresh battalions. As the 5th brigade was near the eastern end of the depression, the attack could then have been made due west.

If the New Zealanders had attacked this way they could have maintained better cohesion and would have had short lines of communication back to 5th NZ Brigade which could easily have been kept open for the tanks. The tanks could then have advanced along the same axis as the infantry and not had to muddle through on their own.

The curious thing is, though, that not only did the armour allow the infantry to go their own way, without demur, but they also seemed to have no idea how they were to follow.

In correspondence with Liddell Hart after the war, Gatehouse, who, of course, arrived to command 1st Armoured Division too late to play any part in the planning and who was himself wounded in short order, wrote: 'I do not know what arrangements were made by Fisher with the New Zealanders but I am prepared to believe they are as stated in the New Zealand official history - and this appears quite certain, that the 2nd Armoured Brigade should have made arrangements to be in position at first light so that they could intervene if the New Zealanders were attacked at first light. This was apparently not done and 2nd Armoured Brigade was, apparently, motionless when NZ Brigade was overrun.'[5]

The armour commanders seem to have been frozen by the uncertainties of the battlefield. If this is so, the fate of the 23rd Armoured Brigade was soon to vindicate their fears.

CHAPTER SIXTEEN
22 JULY - BACK TO BALACLAVA

The charge of the 23rd Armoured Brigade on the morning of 22 July was the crowning irony of Mreir, the ultimate in futile heroism, and, so tank crews thought, the blackest day for infantry tanks in the whole North African campaign. Fresh, alert and ready to go, the 23rd was flung like a spear at the enemy shield and was shattered.

The name of Balaclava is invoked many times in Desert histories, but this episode above all others calls for comparison, and a latter-day Tennyson would find a rich vein of gore on which to hone his poetic skills. Not that there are any latter-day Tennysons. That sort of thing has gone out of fashion, and the tragedy of the 23rd is lost in the pedestrian prose of historians. Yet like the 18th Indian Brigade, who stopped the panzers at Deir el Shein on the first day of battle, the 23rd merits special mention. Like the 18th, they were newcomers, ill-prepared for the Desert. Alas, unlike the 18th, they achieved nothing and lost a great deal, and the irony of their case is that they charged when they should have held back, while the veteran armour, which should have been active, allowed the infantry yet again to succumb to counter-attack.

The 23rd should be introduced. It was a territorial brigade drawing men from Liverpool and Bootle for two of its regiments, the 40th and 46th, and from Bristol for the other, the 50th, and it was the first half of the 8th Armoured Division to arrive from Britain. The other brigade, the 24th ran into all sorts of difficulties on the voyage out. The ship carrying the headquarters of its two regiments was held at Durban for repairs. The ship carrying the support group was sent to Bombay by mistake and a third ship was sunk by Japanese raiders. The 23rd reached Egypt in early July after a voyage of two months, complete with its support group consisting of 5th Regiment RHA, 73rd Anti-Tank Regiment RA, 37th Light Anti-Aircraft Battery and the 7th Rifle Brigade. Though equipped with infantry tanks, the trusty Valentine, the brigade was part of a division that had also trained as an armoured division - cavalry - and in their debut in the Desert they performed both roles. 50th Regiment, the men from Bristol, was peeled off to provide infantry support for the Australians in their Tell el Eisa salient, and this, as things turned out, was their good fortune. The 40th and 46th, the men from Liverpool and Bootle were attached to 1st Armoured Division and acted as cavalry.

Tanks are temperamental beasts and cannot simply be unloaded from a ship and driven into battle, especially after so long a voyage as two months, and special adaptations were necessary for the Desert. As Auchinleck's earlier order indicates, it was not at first thought that the 23rd would be out of the workshops and ready for action before the end of the month. But then there was a change of mind, and on 7 July the 23rd was ordered to be ready by 15 July, no doubt in expectation that a breakthrough on that day would require armour to round up the disorganized Axis army.

There followed what the 23rd's war diary calls 'considerable anxiety caused by shortage of tanks and equipment'. No wonder. Though the tanks had been twice overhauled in England in the six months before their departure, to the brigadier's dismay they had, on arrival, been taken directly to No. 4 Base Ordnance Workshop at Geneifa for desert overhaul, and deliveries from here were slow. Moreover, although the brigade had left England fully equipped, losses, breakages and pilfering in transit had created serious shortages, and the de-kitting of the tanks in the workshops, where they were being stripped down, caused unbounded confusion and even more shortages. And the brigade was expected to be on the battlefield in little more than a week's time!

In the end, on orders from General Headquarters, MEF, 164 tanks were released by the workshops labelled 'unexamined'. One result was that their communications systems had not been adapted for tropical conditions. With such equipment the 23rd was about to face the enemy for the first time, not, as it happened, on 15 July but on 22 July.

But then one disaster is as good as another.

The men themselves had hardly had time to get their knees brown, far less become acclimatised, knowledgeable in the ways of the Desert and skilled in navigation. But they were keen, and this was the army's only homogeneous armoured brigade, and from London an impatient and ignorant Churchill kept asking why fresh units could not be thrown into battle as they arrived. Beyond this, there were, so it was said, many resemblances between the situation into which they were about to be thrown and those in which they had trained in Britain, namely that they would attack on the same axis as the infantry with strong artillery support and from a stable line. It has also been suggested, though with what authority it is hard to say, that the Desert veterans wouldn't have accepted the assignment. It was, after all, another head-on-charge, a classic sword-and-shield encounter of the type that had destroyed so many British armoured units in the past.

The 23rd, it will be recalled, was to attack west, just north of Mreir Depression, along a line cleared by Indian infantry and Indian and New Zealand sappers. Their objective was Point 59, just north of the central point of the depression, at which stage they would have broken through the enemy gun lines. The 2nd Armoured Brigade, which, all going to plan, would be up with the New Zealanders in Mreir Depression, would then pass through and exploit. As the New Zealanders began their approach march on Mreir on the evening of 21 July and the South Africans on their more northerly objective, the 161st Indian Motor Brigade struck west along the well-trodden ground of Ruweisat Ridge, where the West Yorks had held grimly against continuous shelling and dive-bombing. Behind the infantry came the engineers to clear a way through the enemy minefields for the tanks in the morning. But though the Indian infantry made progress, things went badly for them, and the sappers found themselves under fierce enemy fire, and had to withdraw, their task incomplete.

In the early hours of the morning 13th Corps commander, Gott, had to consider whether the attack of the 23rd should go ahead. Though reports indicated that the Indians had been unable to clear a passage, the 6th NZ Brigade was known to be on its objective, and there was a clear understanding that it would be joined there at first light by the 2nd Armoured Brigade. That part of the plan, at least, seemed to be working, and this appeared to offer a new opportunity. Because of the concentration of enemy forces around Mreir to contain 6th NZ Brigade, it seemed a good idea now to redirect the 23rd on a course south of the depression, instead of north of it. This, it was reasoned, would give a clear run across territory covered by New Zealand artillery, with both flanks protected - to the north by the forces in Mreir, to the south by 22nd Armoured Brigade, the NZ Divisional Cavalry and 18th NZ Battalion. All that was necessary was to tell the 23rd not to attack along grid line 278, which would take it north of Mreir, but along grid line 276, which would take it south of Mreir. Gott, who had received a radio intercept indicating some state of disarray on the German side, felt the enemy confusion should be exploited.

1st Armoured Division's commander, who was still then Gatehouse, was against it. He was later to say that Gott, when briefing him about the 21-22 July plan earlier, had said he didn't much care for it, and 'when I heard it I didn't think much of it either, and said so'. Gott promised that if the Indians did not capture Point 63* and if the minefield was not lifted, the 23rd's attack would be called off. In the event neither condition was met, but Gott felt he must press on, despite a strong protest from Gatehouse, who noted that Gott gave the impression of being 'a very tired man' and in two minds whether to carry out the attack or not.[1]

It was while watching the attack from the 9th Lancer positions that Gatehouse was wounded later that morning, and Fisher called up to command.

*The Indians claimed to have retained Point 63 after the 2nd West Yorks took it on 18 July, but this agreement suggests this cannot be so.

This diagramatic representation shows generally how the 23rd Armoured Brigade made its disastrous attack on the morning of 22 July. It had to break through an uncleared minefield and charge into the face of anti-tank guns and hull-down panzers. 46th RTR swung its C Squadron to the south to try to sweep around the defences. A few tanks did reach the objective, Point 59, to the left of the area shown on this map, but like the Light Brigade's futile charge in 1854 it was all to no avail.

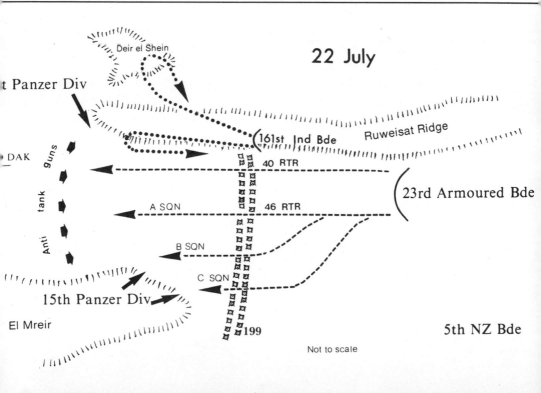

Soldiers like to talk about the devils that intervene in the affairs of battle, and at this point they arrived in force. The order to attack went through to the 23rd, but radio contact was lost before the critical change of axis was given. The 23rd was told to go, and go it did. Engines stirred to life, and the sound of 110 exhaust pipes rumbled across the Desert as the massed Valentines and the half dozen Matildas rolled up to the start line and drew themselves up in impressive array, pennons aflutter on flexing aerials, machine age cavalrymen about to fling themselves at the foe. What they lacked, however, was cavalry speed, and on the stony ground ahead it was not thought the Valentines would reach even their maximum of 24 k.p.h. The best expected was 16 k.p.h., an uncomfortable dawdle when you're trying to close on an enemy who out-ranges you.

There was another cause for concern. Word had filtered through that all had not gone well with the Indians during the night, and even as the tanks stood at the start line stragglers and wounded from the infantry came limping in to report that they had been counter-attacked at dawn. Shocked and confused, they had no idea what the situation was up ahead, and neither could they say if the minefields had been gapped.

Alarmed, the colonels of the two regiments suggested to the Brigadier, Misa, that the attack should be postponed. One writer[2] says staff officers' memories on what happened then 'are curiously vague and non-committal...' Gott was killed soon afterwards, so his memory is not available, but bearing in mind that the brigade was out of radio contact with Corps, it is unlikely that the colonel's concern went past the brigadier. If Misa had been able to communicate with either Gott or Gatehouse it is inconceivable that they would not have taken the opportunity to tell him of the change of axis of advance. The decision to press on in the face of such obvious danger looks more like the thinking of a new commander shrinking from seeming to be reluctant to face the enemy in his unit's first confrontation. Whoever made the decision, it was naturally Misa who gave the final instruction, and in the shake-out after it was all over, it was Misa who suffered demotion to his substantive rank of colonel and transfer to a base job.

As zero hour approached, hatches clanged shut, and as the time came up to 8.00am the whole array moved forward. Ahead lay no friendly troops at all; the New Zealanders were prisoners and the Indians shattered. Nearly ten kilometres separated the tanks from their objective, and even if they could reach it, the possibility of exploitation no longer existed. The advance was without purpose, and panzers and enemy gun lines awaited them.

Men of the 5th NZ Brigade saw them 'thundering past' their northern flank, and soon the Germans saw them, also, and were suitably alarmed. They had only just finished dealing with the incursion by the New Zealanders and Indians, and now found a great armada of steel advancing towards them. It was a magnificent sight.

Guns were alerted, ranges given, and then the enemy waited.

Fire from panzers, anti-tank guns and artillery soon engulfed the two regiments, and the 46th, on the left, even found shells hurtling in from their left. They swung to meet this threat, setting a Mark III on fire, and for good measure scooping up some enemy infantry and anti-tank gunners, who they delivered to following Indian infantry. It was a propitious start.

Heedless of danger, the 23rd ploughed on, right into a minefield. Implacably obedient, 20 tanks in battle formation crashed on to mines and halted, immobilised, still in battle formation, 'a completely unreal sight', as Major Parry, the critical anti-tank gunner, remembered it.[3]

The tank casualties included that of the 40th's CO, Lieutenant-Colonel Dunbar, and he switched to another. But shortly after, that tank was also hit and Dunbar mortally wounded. There were, however, some 30-yard wide gaps, the number not specified, and 40th RTR found its way through these and pushed on. On the left, the 46th split into three prongs. Converging fire poured in on them - from 21st Panzer, 15th Panzer, and anti-tank guns. There could hardly be a closer modern-day replication of Balaclava.

Brigadier Clifton, tending the wounded in Mreir as a supposed private, saw the battle from the German side.

'Shortly after 8.00am much heavier shelling north of the depression opened the next round with the barrage for 23rd Armoured Brigade's attack. Simultaneously, 42 panzers followed by 12 eighty eights roared back through our area to meet this new threat. It was too easy. Most of them snugged down under the rim of the depression and shot fast into the close-packed mass of British tanks hurtling past, headed westwards. Poor gallant devils. The 23rd had been informed that the New Zealanders had captured Mreir, and here were masses of Boche smashing them from the flank at point blank range. Within ten minutes I counted 30 brewed up, burning wrecks and as many knocked out Valentines scattered along the gently sloping rock of Ruweisat Ridge, among the debris of our earlier tragedy. Dust and thick black smoke obscured the arena sufficiently to save surviving crews, who trudged home along their all too-clearly marked route.'[4]

By some miracle four tanks of C Squadron 40th RTR reached the objective at 9.35am, followed ten minutes later by five from B Squadron, and at last another six after a further 20 minutes from A Squadron. Anti-tank fire was sizzling in from north and south, and Mark IIIs were firing from the west and south-west, joined soon by Mark IVs. Doggedly the 15 Valentines stayed there observing A Company of the 7th Rifle Brigade approaching some 1,500 metres back. By 10.30am only five of the original group of 15 tanks could still fight, and they withdrew under heavy fire.

The account of the 46th's advance is confused, but one squadron 'disappeared', and it appears that this was C Squadron, which was ordered to circle round to the south to try to find a way through. Before it was lost to sight, five tanks were seen to be hit and stopped. C Squadron is credited with shooting down an aircraft with a Besa machine-gun. B Squadron, moving up on A Squadron's right, encountered 15 panzers, believed to be Mark IIIs, and, so it is claimed, set six on fire at a range of 900 yards, which if true says something about that two-pounder pop gun.

In the 46th's version of the battle, four of A Squadron's tanks joined six from 40th RTR and part of A Company of the 7th Rifle Brigade and 'decided to hold ridge at selected position'. It is impossible to say whether this was another tiny group tenaciously battling it out against all odds or a variant account of what happened on the objective, but the fact is that the 23rd Armoured Brigade did reach the objective and tried to hold it with the surviving tanks. It did what was asked of it.

Only A Squadron of the 46th brought any tanks home. C Squadron disappeared and B Squadron ceased to exist.

A Squadron's commander, Major Boyd-Moss, had the starboard bogey shot from his tank, and he climbed out to direct operations from its exterior, though if the war diary is to be believed he could not have stood there long.

'The tank received 20 direct hits,' it says, 'and fought for three hours ... and finally withdrew from action without casualties to crew.' Its commander was Second-Lieutenant Beckett. Boyd-Moss himself walked back to the Indian Bridge HQ. How the tank withdrew with a bogey shot away is not explained.

The 46th's CO, Lieutenant-Colonel Clarke, also had a rough time, changing tanks three times as each was successively disabled.

While this was going on, the Indian infantry put in another attack along Ruweisat at 11.00am. Kippenberger, a spectator barely two kilometres away, observed an advance that reminded him of a battle of

1916, with waves of infantry following one another in good alignment. Soon they came against heavy fire and tried to dig in, but on that stony ground it was hopeless.

'The men stood about helplessly for a few minutes and then the whole mass ran back, all the way to their starting positions,' Kippenberger wrote. 'Some stubborn individuals refused to run and followed at a walk but the retirement could not be called anything but a rout.'[5] And the few survivors of the 23rd began hobbling in. Perrett reports an eyewitness seeing an unidentifiable tank emerge from the noon haze to reveal itself as a Valentine stripped of every external fitting so that all that remained was a 'bare hull and turret, a skeleton of our prized Valentines, a ghost'.[6]

How many tanks of the 110 actually came home is not clear, but there were only six from each regiment fit for battle, and these were formed into a composite squadron. An unspecified number of damaged tanks was recovered for repair. Many were beyond reach in enemy-held territory.

The 40th's casualties, recorded at the time, were six killed, 11 wounded and 40 missing; the 46th's were four killed, 14 wounded and 60 missing. Some of the missing would be killed or wounded, but considering the slaughter of the tanks, the number of known killed or wounded was remarkably small. And the reason for that might well lie in the note appended to the 46th's war diary: 'The Valentine tanks performed excellently, stopping all anti-tank shells of less than 88mm, and proving very reliable in spite of very stony ground.' That at least is a comforting footnote to the dismal story of two tank regiments wiped out within a few hours of their first meeting with the enemy.

As Afrika Korps reported its kills the excitement must have mounted at Panzerarmee headquarters. After a preliminary count on 22 July, updated figures came in from individual units ... 8th Panzer Regiment, 31 tanks; 5th Panzer Regiment, 29 tanks; 104 Panzer Grenadier Regiment, 14 tanks; 155th Artillery Regiment, six tanks; 39th Anti-Tank Unit, 17 tanks; 1/18th Anti-Aircraft Regiment, eight tanks; 617th Anti-Tank Battalion, five tanks; 612nd Battalion, three tanks.

And then there was the count of trucks, armoured cars, Bren gun carriers, guns, even a fighter aircraft, not to mention the long lines of prisoners of war.

Despite these huge losses, the Eighth Army still had more tanks than the Axis. German tank strength on 23 July was 40, and four of these were Mark IIs. But weight of numbers seemed to mean little to the stumbling Eighth Army.

One reason no one was able to stop the outbreak of war in 1914 was that the railway mobilisation timetables had to grind their way to their inevitable conclusion. There is the same kind of unstoppable horror about 22 July. Two disasters that morning did not prevent a third from unfolding in the north as the Australians took up their tasks. But with the total collapse of the offensive in and around Mreir, the battle in the north assumed its own identity, and as the few tanks and tank crews, not to mention the survivors of the infantry attacks, straggled back, *Splendour* could be considered over.

Its sole accomplishment was to frighten the Germans, particularly when the 23rd Armoured Brigade came rolling towards them, though it's true that Afrika Korps lost heavily in infantry it could ill afford to lose, and for a time Rommel was not sure his line would hold. And he had a concern for the future. 'It is to be expected the enemy will continue his attack in the night of 22-23 July and on the 23rd,' he signalled Rome on the 22nd. 'The situation is still extremely critical.'

The Indians did have another try for Deir el Shein in the early hours of 23 July, but they got lost on their way and came under heavy fire at day break.

Angry waves were now lapping at the door of army command. Inglis, according to Kippenberger, was 'angry almost beyond words and swore he would never again place faith in British armour'. The tank men themselves were angry, and a regimental commander from 2nd Brigade stopped his tank to apologise to Kippenberger.

'He said he felt bitterly humiliated but I'm afraid I did not answer very graciously,' Kippenberger says.[7]

Clifton, in 'observations' accompanying his official report, says: 'The failure of 2nd Armoured Brigade to carry out their orders was in my opinion, criminally negligent.' Harsh words, and in the circumstances understandable. He had just lost his brigade, and was left with only the LOBs and 26th Battalion.

Did Auchinleck comprehend all this? Reporting to the CIGS in London on 25 July, he said in part: 'I was disappointed when our big effort of 21-22 July came to nothing, as I had great hopes of it. I still do not know the full story of the battle in the centre, but it does seem as if the 23rd Armoured Brigade, though gallant enough, lost control and missed direction. The infantry, too, seem to have made some avoidable mistakes. Perhaps I ask too much of them. Well, there it is; we undoubtedly gave the enemy a rude shock, judging from the many intercepted messages from various enemy units, but we failed to get our objective, which was to break through.'

Mistakes? Yes. But the blame, it seems, lay everywhere but with army and corps command. As Kippenberger saw 21-22 July, two infantry and two armoured brigades made three unrelated attacks from different directions at different times.

'A single small panzer division of some 20 or 30 tanks and a fifth rate Italian division easily dealt with all three attacks in succession and inflicted crippling losses,' he wrote.[8]

By the evening of 22 July the Eighth Army was really a spent force. Auchinleck, however, did not yet recognise this, and there was to be still one more flutter of activity before the Battle of Egypt finally sputtered out. Oddly enough, it was this last push that almost toppled Rommel.

CHAPTER SEVENTEEN

22-31 JULY - THE LAST GASP

N
ow it was the Australians' turn. The Australians had been fighting in their own private battleground in the salient they had carved out during their bid to secure the Tell el Eisa mounds. No formation fought longer or more constantly in the Battle of Egypt than the Australian 9th Division, and they alone had taken territory and held it. From that first westward strike on 10 July they were continuously engaged, their deeds obscured to some degree by their removal from the grand sweep of events further south. Yet their very presence in the north, not to speak of their torrid battles, drew enemy strength from the south, and it was the Australians who fought the Battle of Egypt through to its last desperate gasp. They were attacking as their part of *Splendour* as the New Zealanders were marching west from Mreir as prisoners of war and as the two regiments of 23rd Armoured Brigade were dying under German guns, and they were still fighting in partnership with the 69th Brigade of the 50th Division when finally the shooting stopped five days later, and both armies collapsed in exhaustion.

The plan in the north fell into two parts: an Australian attack on 22 July as part of *Splendour* which, it must be said, was more like a shot gun discharge than a coherent offensive, requiring two brigades to make three divergent simultaneous attacks, which meant they would be fighting their way into an ever widening front; and the supposed coup de grace 48 hours later to break through on the Miteiriya Ridge.

This led to a crisis in command right on the eve of battle.

And here we find ourselves faced again with a division between the memory and written record. The two accounts agree that Morshead was unhappy with the part planned for the Australians and that a compromise plan was worked out with Auchinleck in a most civilised manner over tea. Dorman Smith was to complain ever after that the Australians' reluctance to attack on 24 July had caused a 48-hour delay that compromised the plan's success. He repeatedly blamed the Australians for this final failure, though he tempered this by saying that because of Pienaar's touchy disposition, the South Africans had not been called on as much as they might have been, and a greater burden was therefore placed on the Australians. But perhaps this merely reflects the personality tensions between the generals rather than a true reluctance among the South Africans to fight .

Putting all the evidence together the sequence of events look like this. During the morning of 21 July, Morshead confronts Ramsden, saying he doesn't like the plan for 22 July. More than this, his troops are being asked to attack again within 48 hours, and Morshead says he feels he should consult his Government.

Ramsden, alarmed, passes this information on to Auchinleck, who, according to Barnett, exploded 'in sudden, terrible anger,'[1] an unusual reaction for a man usually so controlled but understandable after the stresses of July and on the eve of a carefully planned and complex battle. Ramsden gives his view that the Australians have been listening to New Zealanders' stories about tanks.

Morshead's diary entry for 21 July explains what happened:

'Two hours conference with Ramsden, during which I objected strongly to scope of my attack to take place tomorrow and several changes in timings. As a result Commander-in-Chief sent for me and conference was held at 30th Corps. Present, Commander-in-Chief, Ramsden, DCGS (Dorman Smith) who took notes! Commander-in-Chief explained plan of 13th Corps attack. I did not like our plan because of wide dispersion and difficulty to support and pointed out that our immediate objectives were much more difficult than realised by Army and Corps. Commander-in-Chief, according to Ramsden, was very annoyed and perturbed but he did not show it. He stressed that he realised he must have a willing commander. I stressed that my concern was a task which was reasonably certain of success and could be held and supported, and that my job was to minimise casualties. Altogether it turned out to be rather like a family party.'[2]

The compromise agreed was that for the 24 July attack Auchinleck would call up 69th Brigade from the south, where it was attached to 7th Armoured Division. The 69th itself was not in particularly good shape, and when it arrived 24 hours after the original attack date, a further 24-hour delay was requested to provide time for rest and replacement of one regiment. The Germans used this time to sort themselves out and sew more mines, and as Dorman Smith saw it, this frustrated Eighth Army's last throw, and he urged that the operation should be replanned. This was not done.

The plan for 22 July was highly complex. The 26th Brigade, at the western extremity of the Tell el Eisa salient, was to reach west along the coast road towards the enemy's headquarters as well as south west to seize the twin heights of Tell el Eisa, East and West Points 24.

The 24th Brigade was to attack south west and take the high ground of the Makh Khad Ridge to the south of Tell el Eisa, and south to Miteiriya Ridge to take the area identified by the ruin the Australians had taken and lost during a previous engagement.

The whole operation involved various companies going various ways into heavily defended enemy territory. There were six objectives to be attacked from six different directions. No wonder Morshead was alarmed.

Pre-dawn, dark and cool. Restless movement. The Australian troops hitch on their web gear and drape their bandoliers about them. In the faint glimmer, domed helmets form nodding patterns. By cautiously shielded light, the intelligence officer checks his map. Baillieu's Bluff is the goal - well, that's what the Australians call it. More properly it's Ring Contour 25, a contour line on the map that encircles a low feature not quite 3,000 metres away to the west ... not far for a walk, if it could be just a walk.

Conversation is muted, whispered. No one trusts the dark. The dark cloaks the unknown. Beyond this point, anywhere beyond this point, lies only hostility and danger, and eyes must be watchful, ears alert, tongues silent. The men move carefully, led forward to prepared start lines, the tread of heavy army boots muffled into a subdued unco-ordinated shuffle.

A flare goes up and arcs in the general direction of the enemy. Christ! What's that? *That* is a Very pistol accidentally discharged by an officer of the 2/24th Battalion. Captain Baillieu has just remarked that he hopes the success signal will fire considering that the cartridge is swollen with sweat. A fellow officer takes the pistol to inspect it, inadvertently pulling the trigger. The flare streaks past Baillieu's head and out into the night. It falls and dies, and darkness closes in again. Stealth seems silly now. Every bloody Jerry between here and Benghasi will be awake and waiting.

All lined up; watches show zero hour. Forward.

Lined across, men carefully spaced, rifles at the high port, bayonets

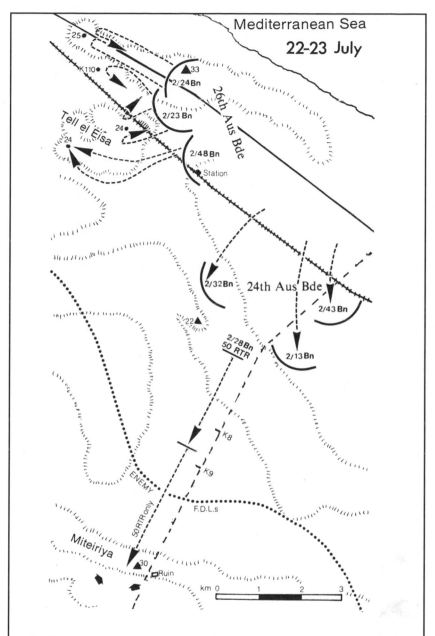

Unable to make progress to the west, Morshead, the Australian commander, decided to drive south. But 2/28th Battalion stopped short of the objective, and the tanks which went on, had to be called back.

fixed, they move towards the enemy. Daylight is coming. And shells. The soft moan of incoming shells, the eruption of their arrival. The crackle of machine-guns, streams of tracer race into the ranks. Two companies of the 2/24th Battalion advanced through that fire, gradually losing coherence as men and officers fell and platoons and sections took evasive action. Somehow they covered that 3,000 metres and found themselves on rocky ground too hard for digging, swept by machine-gun fire from the flank and rear. Hardly surprising. They had driven a corridor through the enemy's defences, and there was no protection on the flanks and no support troops to follow and mop up. But they were there, on the objective, before the sluggards of Cairo were out of bed, and they fired the success signal.

A few kilometres to the south the panzers were closing in on the New Zealanders in Mreir.

Hanging on was a tenuous matter of guts. Sergeant W.T. Hughes, observing that one of his sections was in trouble with two Spandaus, crawled forward and with his rifle shot the No. One of each gun, and when the No. Twos took over, he shot them, too, and then tried to carry out the section leader. He was awarded the DCM.

Courage like this was of little avail, however, to troops who had fought their way into a salient and who could expect no reinforcement. By 6.45am on a day that had hardly begun it was decided the companies would have to pull back. The message did not reach some outlying sections, which fought through to the afternoon until they were overrun.

Next to the 2/24th was the 2/23rd, one of whose companies, so the 2/24th thought, was to advance on the 2/24th's left flank to a point called Kilo 109 at the same time as their attack. But the commander understood he was not to advance until he saw the success signal fired from Ring Contour 25, and as this went up he led his men forward into 'terrible enemy fire'. The men then still on Ring Contour 25 were able, amidst their own turmoil, to observe them struggling forward.

But the 2/23rd's main attack that morning was south with two companies to East Point 24. They advanced behind a heavy artillery concentration, and after fierce fighting reached their objective and fired the success signal at 6.20am. The battle continued around the point in dense dust that made it impossible to see more than a few metres.

On the left of the 2/23rd was the 2/48th awaiting the outcome of the assault on East Point 24 before they struck at West Point 24. As word came through, the companies moved off in a generally south-westerly direction, one company heading directly for the objective, the other making a slight leftward sweep to approach from the south.

'Before dawn ... the silence of the night was shattered by the wicked bark of 25 pounders, and pin points of flame danced across the desert as B and D Companies made their way down the coastal ridge,' says the battalion's history.[3] 'This was to be a daylight show, and the troops did not like it.'

Both companies advanced through shell and mortar fire 'leaving a trail of fallen men in the desert.'[4] The right company lost all its officers, and the left all but one, and he was out of touch. A hundred metres from the enemy positions, the right company was pinned down by accurate artillery and machine-gun fire. Private A.S. Gurney jumped to his feet and charged across open ground through machine-gun fire. He hurled a blast grenade into the first machine-gun post and bayonetted a German who leapt out. He was joined by Ivan Hanel, and together they charged into the post and bayonetted two more Germans. Gurney dashed 30 metres to a second post, where he bayonetted two more Germans and sent a third back as prisoner. As he was charging a third post, a grenade blew him off his feet. He got up, grabbed his rifle, and charged on. He was last seen using his bayonet. His body was later found in an enemy post. Gurney was awarded a posthumous VC.

As reports came back of the problems at the front, tanks were called for, and 11 turned up at 2/48th headquarters at 11.00 am. The tank commander asked for half an hour before moving, but in fact nothing happened for $4^1/_2$ hours.

'On crossing the (railway) line they found a small enemy minefield, withdrew, held a conference, and moved forward to attack again. Two tanks moved forward gingerly and were knocked out by an enemy anti-tank gun, the only one seen in the area. The tanks then withdrew completely[5].'

Meanwhile, at East Point 24, the companies of the 2/23rd were fighting off a counter-attack, and the other company trying to reach Kilo 109 was pinned down, with the commanding officer dead and half the company casualties. Now out on a limb, it was withdrawn.

The outcome of the day's fighting was that the enemy withdrew from both East and West Points 24, but the two thrusts to ring Contour 25 and Kilo 109 had failed.

While the 26th Brigade was so engaged, the 24th Brigade had sent forward its 2/32nd Battalion to take Trig 22 on the Makh Khad Ridge.

Following a 15-minute barrage, the battalion began a 1,500-metre advance at 5.30am into heavy enemy fire. As the left company was pinned down on an escarpment below Point 22, one officer went forward armed only with a pistol, overcame a machine-gun nest that had been causing many casualties, and turned the Spandau on the German defenders until it jammed. The 2/32nd fought off counter-attacks throughout the day, and by mid-afternoon was able to report that it was secure.

It was now clear to Morshead that the way west was blocked and that there was no point in trying to exploit in that direction, and after consultation with Ramsden in the late afternoon, he decided instead to attack south to take the ruin feature on Miteriya Ridge, also referred to in the Australian history as Ruin Ridge, by last light, using the 2/28th Battalion, assisted by 52 Valentines of 50th RTR, the third regiment of the ill-fated 23rd Armoured Brigade. The 2/28th was to consolidate on the reverse slope - that's the slope facing away from the enemy.

Some time after 6.00pm, as the Australian troops were assembling, a report came in that a reconnaissance aircraft had seen 500 enemy vehicles and at least 20 gun positions along the Miteiriya Ridge, with infantry digging in. Disturbing news, but the Australians were now committed.

The tanks, some carrying infantry and engineers, were to spearhead this evening attack, followed by six-pounders and machine-guns, then the main body of the infantry of foot, and finally the rest of 50th RTR.

It was all done in a rush and in some confusion, and only the infantry rode on tanks. The engineers said the tank men had ordered them off. The leading tanks moved off, and despite a warning from the offended sappers, travelled east of the north-south track instead of west, and 28 carrying a platoon of B Company were disabled on a known minefield. The rest pushed on into heavy fire that soon forced the tank-borne infantry to drop off.

The tanks, with accompanying Bren carriers, rolled on to the ruin, where they hotly engaged the enemy while they waited for the infantry to catch up. Their guns winkled out 60 Germans, who were marshalled and marched to the rear under the guard of carriers.

As in all battles, the sequence of events becomes obscure, but according to the history of the 2/28th Battalion the infantry had been about 800 metres from the start line when the tanks set off and had only just crossed the start line when the tanks were shuffling around uncomfortably on the objective, awaiting the 2/28th's arrival.

'At that critical moment,' says the history, 'the intelligence officer drove up in a Jeep and claimed that the tanks and carriers had come one ridge too far. There was a ridge about 1,000 yards to the rear, he said, with ruins on one side of the track.'[6]

The tank crews knew from their odometers that they had travelled the correct distance, but they were in no mood to hang about and be shot up if the infantry weren't going to join them, and the armour fell back.

The infantry meanwhile, was wading through enemy fire. A description by Jack Costello in the unit history tells the story:

'From a Jeep closely following the infantry I had a first-class view of the long lines of men moving forward into the setting sun - a sight so stirring that one almost forgot personal danger and longed for a movie camera to record it. With the light behind them the Germans had excellent shooting conditions and threw everything they had against us. The Australians must have escaped fearful casualties only by keeping their text-book formation and moving so fast that the gunners failed to lower their sights. It was noticeable that a great many shells of all sizes landed well behind the infantry, while the wide spacing and steady movement of the men, the dust from exploding shells and churning tank tracks, and occasional pieces of dead ground all reduced the danger from aimed machine gun fire. Such a storm of fire was the severest test of battle discipline, especially when the men were so imperfectly briefed about what they were supposed to be doing. I saw only two men check during the whole advance. Each of them did so only to stick a rifle and bayonet with a tin hat on it into the ground alongside a fallen mate, and then doubled up to fall in again with the advance.'

The battalion reached the first ruins as daylight was fading and the decision was made that this was the objective. At 10.45pm the first signal went back to Brigade: 'We struck the ridge with what appeared to be a ruin on left, and we were all up by 2040 hours. There seemed to be a large flat on top of the ridge and we were half way across when it began to become dark and we withdrew to reverse slope. At moment we are sorting out and getting into position. At moment five Italian tanks are on ridge on our left and five on our left front - two fairly close and three further back. Our tanks withdrew from ridge at dusk.'

By midnight the night's work had been done, or so it was thought. The infantry were digging in, about 50 prisoners, many of them from 90th Light, had been sent back, and the tanks had fallen back to laager. But to the 1st Tank Brigade commander, Richards, who was armoured adviser to the Australians, they seemed too far back, and at 1.30am he went forward to see where the infantry were. He returned with the news that the 2/28th Battalion was more than 2,000 metres short of the objective.

The official Australian history says the error could only have resulted from 'extreme fatigue, accentuated by constant air-burst shelling of the battalion over the preceding days.' But when the brigadier, Godfrey, came up at first light to see for himself he laid the blame on Cox, the temporary battalion commander. He fired him and brought in a Tobruk veteran, Major L. McCarter MC from 2/32nd Battalion, promoting him to temporary lieutenant-colonel. But the 2/28th Battalion history argues that the haste with which the operation was mounted was really to blame for the error.

The attack towards the ruin was the last in *Splendour*, an operation that was to have sent Rommel fleeing west. It had begun at dusk on 21 July when the New Zealanders attacked Mreir Depression. It ended, just over 24 hours later in this nameless part of the wilderness which hardly mattered to anyone. True, the Australians were holding their own, despite the failure of the westward drive, and the Germans had taken a bad knock. The official historian noted that the 9th Division alone 'had achieved valuable gains in the Eighth Army's costly and abortive offensive ...' Valuable gains? The Australians were certainly the only troops to achieve any gains at all, and these included the Tell el Eisa mounds that had haunted the South Africans in the Alamein Box from the beginning, but the exploitation phase had secured only more empty desert.

As the divisional report saw it, though the day's fighting had been disappointing, the enemy had had to move up 90th Light, together with the elements of three Italian divisions, to hold his left flank. Panzerarmee's daily report said the position was extremely critical. But this was a situation that was endemic during July on the Axis side of the line.

'It is questionable whether the whole front will be able to be held any longer against such heavy pressure,' it said.

Heavy pressure is just what Auchinleck had in mind. And whatever the outcome might have been, his instinct was right. All Rommel needed was a hefty push and he would fall over. Alas, as things turned out it was the Eighth Army that fell, flat on its face.

Auchinleck planned to develop from the Australian position reached by the 2/28th Battalion - at that false ruin - on the night of 25-26 July, 24 hours later than the original plan, and he summoned the 69th Brigade north to replace some of the recalcitrant Australians. The 69th had been in constant action since the night of 21-22 July, when it had captured the Taqa Plateau at the southern-most extremity of the Alamein positions, but having no protective Government to whom it could appeal, it obediently dragged itself north in a difficult night move, reporting to 30th Corps on the morning of 25 July to learn that it was expected to attack that night. The brigadier, E.C. Cooke-Collis, protested that his command had been in direct contact with the enemy for 60 hours, during which it had dealt with a night attack by the enemy and carried out a night withdrawal. Moreover, while he considered the 5th East Yorks and 6th Green Howards would be fit to fight again after a 24-hour spell, his composite Guards battalion was not battleworthy.

And so the 24-hour delay was extended yet another day while the troops rested and a Durham Light Infantry regiment was pieced together from battalions of the 151st Brigade. 9th Battalion provided an A Company, 8th Battalion a B Company and 6th Battalion provided a C Company. The commander was Lieutenant-Colonel A.B.S. Clarke.

Dorman Smith, alarmed by these setbacks, considered the attack should be called off, but Auchinleck was all for pressing on, and on 25 July issued a Special Order of the Day.

'You have done well,' he said. 'You have turned a retreat into a firm stand and stopped the enemy on the threshold of Egypt. You have wrenched the initiative from him by sheer guts and hard fighting and put him on the defensive in these last weeks.

'He has lost heavily and is short of men, ammunition, petrol and other things. He is trying desperately to bring these things over to Africa but the Navy and Air Force are after his ships.

'You have done much but I ask you for more. We must not slacken. If we stick to it we will break him.

'STICK TO IT.'

Morshead issued his own message in the form of a more mundane instruction warning that the division's battle cunning, developed so well in Tobruk, had gone 'a bit rusty'.

And so the Eighth Army, with admonitions and words of cheer, faced up to its last strike.

Manhood - now there's a name to conjure with. Chosen to symbolise maturity? Or as a compromise between the earthiness of *Bacon* and the ethereal heights of *Splendour*? Or just a stab in the dark? Whatever,

Manhood, the operation that began on 26 July, did not bring the Eighth Army consummation of its hopes.

Manhood was launched with the knowledge that the enemy was strongest at the point of attack, but also with the knowledge that he had no reserves. If he could be beaten here, where he was strong, that would be the end of the matter.

Operation Order No 105, dated 25 July said the intention was to disrupt and disorganise the enemy's army with a view to its destruction'.

13th Corps tasks were to give maximum fire support, to hold its positions on Ruweisat, and to keep the enemy busy. If he withdrew, 13th Corps was to pursue.

All this was accompanied by devices to deceive the enemy, set out in Operation Order No 106 the same day. 13th Corps was to generate traffic movement and begin artillery registration 'as if hurriedly'. New Zealand patrols were to leave 69th Brigade identification as near as possible to the enemy to conceal the fact that it had moved to the north to attack, and there was to be radio traffic to simulate 1st Armoured Division and 3rd Armoured Brigade in the 13th Corps area, and - the crowning touch - the sonic unit (which appears for the first time) was to simulate tank movements in 13th Corps area on the night D1/D2. It was all very ingenious, and certainly deceived 90th Light, but with only an hour and a half between the start of the feint attack in the south and the real attack in the north there was hardly time for the enemy to react and weaken his northern positions. 90th Light's war diary reports a 'strong artillery attack on Qattara work' (Kaponga) just before 7.00pm, and half an hour later an observation post reported vehicles approaching, and also tanks, using a smoke screen. When fired on, the tanks dispersed and stood in a glowering semi-circle to the north of Kaponga. And then from the observation post came a report of 'strong motor noises' from behind the tanks. Alas for the deception, the OP thought they were, not tanks, but motor trucks.

'No infantry is observed debussing,' wrote an apparently puzzled war diarist.

However, the outcome of all this was, as hoped, a German expectation that the Eighth Army, having failed to break through on 22 July, was now about to make a similar attack in the south, and German and Italian units were placed on stand-by. But then at 8.30pm ' a very heavy artillery drumfire begins ... in the northern sector'.

If 30th Corps could carry the day, the course of history would take a new direction.

The curiosity of *Manhood* is that the course of history was to turn on something as mundane as a gap in a minefield - its size, its location, its suitability for the passage of tanks. We know now that of all the crises the Axis faced during July, this attack came nearest to collapsing the line, and might at the bitter end have brought success to the Eighth Army, but like the previous offensives, it was to stop short for want of tank support, and disaster for the infantry would ensue. It was like a repetitive bad dream.

This last stab at the enemy reveals yet another facet of the Eighth Army's incompetence, and provides a kind of mournful finale to the old

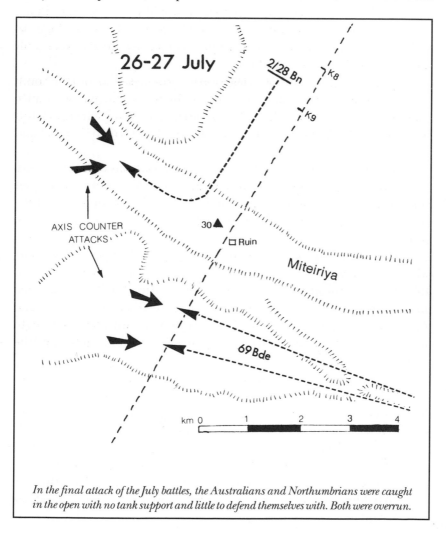

In the final attack of the July battles, the Australians and Northumbrians were caught in the open with no tank support and little to defend themselves with. Both were overrun.

army before its rebirth in August. It was Auchinleck's final frustration, and we might wonder what he felt and thought as the reports came in and the tattered remnants of yet more good infantry units fell back while their comrades lay either dead or wounded, and many more tramped that now well-established path to Benghasi.

The plan of attack was a most novel one.

The 2/28th Australian Battalion, dug in at its false ruin several thousand metres short of the true ruin, was to continue its *southerly* thrust, then on reaching its objective, the true ruin, execute a right-hand turn and face *west*. The 2/43rd Australian Battalion would follow through in the morning and continue the attack west along the Miteiriya Ridge. In committing one battalion of his division at a time, Morshead was certainly aiming to minimize his casualties.

The 69th Brigade of the 50th Division was to attack *west* from the South African positions - that is, at right angles to the Australian axis of advance - and secure Deir el Dibh, where they would then be to the left and slightly to the rear of the 2/28th when that battalion had performed its right hand turn.

In other words, two formations were to attack from two widely separated start lines and on two different axes, unable to offer each other support until they reached their objectives, so that the outcome of the operation hung on both achieving initial success and arriving at the right place.

The principal armour component was again 2nd Armoured Brigade, which had moved north under cover of night to be on hand. It was to follow the 69th through the minefields and move to El Wishka, a plan that this time gave it the same axis of advance as the infantry. After the 2nd Armoured would come the 4th Light Armoured Brigade, whose light tanks, armoured cars and motorised infantry were to rampage around the enemy rear.

For the Australians, the major problem was that in the two days since they had halted in error short of the ruin, the enemy had been working like beavers to prepare a reception. More than this, on the southward leg of their attack the Australians would have the enemy on their right flank, as the New Zealanders had experienced them on their left during their advance on Mreir. 2/28th's new commander, McCarter, felt it necessary to warn his officers that the men must reply by shooting from the hip, without halting or changing direction. It was just this that had caused loss of cohesion in earlier attacks.

For the Tynesiders of the 69th Brigade the attack was more straightforward. What was critical from their point of view, and for that matter from the Australians', was that 2nd Armoured Brigade should come through in good time to give protection against counter-attack at dawn. And that depended on a gap that was being made in the enemy minefield by South African engineers.

So much has been written about the tanks being unable to find this gap or about the gap being too narrow that an understanding of what took place is critical.

After clearing two gaps in their own minefield, two parties of sappers, one from the 1st South African Brigade, the other from the 2nd South African Brigade, were jointly to make one 550-metre wide gap in the enemy minefield south west of the Alamein Box during the night 26-27 July. Infantry were to protect them while they carried out this hazardous task, which was to be completed an hour before the Australians reached the ruin in the early hours of 27 July. The 69th would then pass through the gap and advance.

For reasons that remain obscure, the two groups were instructed to begin their work from opposite ends of the proposed gap, which meant that if they were unable to finish there would be not one but two gaps, and these might well be two gaps that were too small rather than one that might be adequate had they worked out from the centre, and it was this that led to confusion.

1st SA Brigade was responsible for the northern section, 2nd SA Brigade for the southern. When the Australians crossed their start line in the north at midnight, South African sappers were at work in the south clearing the way for the attack from that direction.

The air was cool and bracing as the Australian infantry moved forward, and bright moonlight illuminated the wrecks of tanks brewed up in the attack of 22 July. Predictably, tracer came racing towards them from their right, but they filtered through the minefield, leaving their wireless van and hence their means of communications with Brigade, burning, and took the objective with a bayonet charge. At 2.00am, McCarter, using a short-range No 18 radio, reached 2/43rd Battalion with a cryptic, 'We are here, Mac', the agreed success signal. The 2/43rd passed it back to Brigade.

Five minutes later another message crackled through: 'Ammunition immediately'. A convoy of trucks with ammunition and stores, awaiting just this message, immediately began rolling. At 2,500 metres from the start line they blundered into the minefield. Several vehicles were hit by shells or blew up on mines, but others, including two Bren carriers and some six-pounder Portees, sped through a gap. The next two trucks were hit by a gun located somewhere to the right, and burst into flames. Burning vehicles now lit the scene, but the convoy commander, Major Brian Simpson, charged through. The next truck, carrying engineering stores, was hit, and there were now 13 vehicles blazing, blocking the minefield gap and illuminating it with daylight brightness. The cause was identified as being a single 50 mm PAK gun.

Up on the ridge all was quiet, except for the clang and scrape of picks and shovels. McCarter, aware of what was happening at the minefield, ordered a pioneer officer to 'get that bloody gun', and he took off with four men to search for it. But it was too well protected, and it kept the fires going by periodically firing into the ammunition truck.

So by the early hours of the morning the first piece of the plan was in place, if not very comfortably. Though the Australian battalion was alone in a perilous salient, the 69th Brigade was due to come up, followed by 2nd Armoured Brigade. And if the need should arise, 50th RTR, the Australian's old friends in the north, were on stand-by to help.

Meanwhile, the South African sappers were at work to enable the 69th and 2nd Armoured to play their part.

The group from 2nd SA Brigade in the south understood they were to start at midnight and have a preliminary gap clear within the first half hour, with their whole 275-metre stretch finished by first light. Working under shell fire, they had this preliminary gap, 27 metres wide, clear some time after 1.00am.

In the north, the group from 1st SA Brigade had, curiously, been unable to find any mines, but around 1.40am word came back to 1st SA Division tactical HQ that two 27-metre wide gaps were available.

Down in his part of the desert, the 69th Brigade commander was already deeply troubled. At 30th Corps HQ he had been given a marked map showing enemy gun positions and minefields, but Ramsden told him the gun positions were wrong, and everyone to whom the distracted brigadier showed the map told him the minefield was also inaccurately marked. No one could tell him where the enemy infantry were or how strong they were, except for a vague statement from 1st SA Division that the enemy was digging and blasting on a track that ran roughly parallel with the minefield and about 800 metres behind it.

And that was just the beginning. The artillery plan didn't reach him until 7.30pm, and the officer commanding 104th RHA said he didn't like it. Some parts, he said, were dangerous to covering South African troops, and these he cancelled.

For all this discouraging beginning, the East Yorks and DLI were on the start line by 1.30am and moving forward at 2.00 am, supposedly towards the south gap in the minefield.

The experience of an anti-tank formation from the 6th Green Howards, which was supposed to follow the 5th East Yorks through the south gap and then form a screen facing south, is an indication that muddle was already beginning. In fact, for this group, led by Lieutenant-Colonel G.W. Evans, nothing went according to plan. The route to the minefield gap was supposed to be marked and manned, and at the entrance there were to be more men with black-out torches. Evans found neither. As the gunners followed the East Yorks, the infantry appeared to drift north and strike the minefield at a point where there was no gap. The DLI had apparently gone that way, too, but South Africans said it was not the prepared gap.

Evans turned his column south and followed the wire, encountering several South Africans who could provide no information.

And then, at 4.30am he came to a marked gap, although several South Africans nearby couldn't say if it was the north or south gap. Some said there was only one gap. With time running out and an enemy machine-gun chattering just to the south, Evans decided he had better use what was offering, and he sent the first of his vehicles through. Alas, they soon found that South African sappers were still at work.

In this precarious situation, Evans arranged his forces as best he could, and when daylight came and the day advanced, there was some uncertainty over who was who, and where everyone was. The guns stayed to engage the enemy all day, and withdrew with the British armour in the evening. But they got nowhere near the infantry they were supposed to protect.

The infantry, meanwhile, were having troubles of their own. In all the confusion it seems they did use a gap, presumably the north one, but long before they got there they ran into heavy shelling and machine-gun fire. DLI troops went to ground in some old slit trenches, and the men of the East Yorks, drifting to the north as the Green Howards had observed, overtook and overlapped the DLI, and chaos abounded.

'From this time onwards the advance became disorganised ...' according to a report by Lieutenant E.D. Rule, who led a ten man Australian liaison squad. 'I completely lost touch with battalion HQ.'

This is probably a fair description of the situation. Leading elements of the DLI were moving through the gap, cleaning out machine-gun posts at the point of the bayonet as they went, and then moving on to deal with more enemy positions in bayonet charges. The DLI war diary says rather ambiguously, 'In the heat of the attack a few prisoners were being taken.'

Back behind the wire, meanwhile, it took some little time to unscramble the confusion between the DLI and the East Yorks, a task made no easier by enemy fire.

The Australian liaison patrol, having lost the CO, attached itself to the battalion wireless van, which had been sent back to shelter in a hollow because it had been attracting too much enemy fire. With the advance now under way, a runner was sent back to bring the van forward, and it moved through the gap and headed in the direction of the attacking infantry, guided by the battalion intelligence sergeant.

'It was soon found without doubt that the enemy still maintained machine-gun posts on both flanks as my patrol was continuously fired on by them,' Rule reported 'After advancing about 1,000 yards the intelligence sergeant admitted he was lost. I pushed my patrol forward taking the wireless van with me in an endeavour to locate 6 DLI Battalion HQ and made a thorough and systematic search all the way ...

'From the time the patrol started out behind the wireless van up to this time I could see many small groups of DLI personnel lost and without any knowledge of battalion whereabouts ...' As daylight was approaching and Rule reckoned he had no hope of contacting the 2/28th Battalion, which was his reason for being there, he took his patrol back to the start line.

Just what was happening up front those at the start line could not tell. Fighting could be heard going on in the distance in the direction of the objective, and as it was not heavy, it was assumed the objective had been taken. At daybreak the support vehicles began to move up through a slight mist but soon ran into enemy fire that drove them back.

And so the day began with the Australians precariously in place and the 69th also presumably so. Neither had support weapons, or precious few.

But of course there were the tanks of 2nd Armoured Brigade, lined up on their start line and ready to go.

The operation now has to be seen from two perspectives: that of the Australians, who knew only what they heard; and that of the South Africans, who were on the spot and knew what was happening.

On the Australian side, Morshead heard at 7.00am that the tanks would move at 7.30am, and at 7.40am he heard that it would be 8.15. At 24th

Australian Brigade HQ various moves were put in hand to reach the 2/28th, which was now out of touch following the breakdown of its solitary No 18 just after 3.00am. A brigade liaison officer, Lieutenant John Cook, was sent out to discover what was happening, but his Bantam was shot up by mortars, and he had to walk home after being forced to take cover in scrub. Then just after 9.00am a terse four-word message came through to the listening 2/43rd: 'We are in trouble.'

The 2/28th had had a night of anxiety, and just before dawn, with no way of calling for help, they observed 18 truck loads of German infantry arriving on their right flank. Around 9.00am tanks and armoured cars hove in view, thought at first to be friendly but soon identified as hostile when the officer who went out to meet them was shot. Miraculously, inspired improvisation at that point brought the No 18 back on air, and at 9.05am that first call of alarm went through, followed nine minutes later by another: 'We need help now. We need armour.'

There followed a crisp exchange.

Message out from Brigade: Where is the trouble coming from?

Message in: On our front and right flank. Rock it in.

Message out: You are getting what you asked for in arty support. Send map refs in clear of arty and bombing targets.

Because the artillery liaison officer and been killed, the 2/28th was struggling with artillery directions without expert knowledge, and the situation was further confounded when observers at the rear saw what appeared to be tanks mixed up with the Australian infantry and firing west. Thinking they must be British, the artillery called a pause, and it was ten minutes before shelling resumed.

Message in 9.43am: Are there any of our tanks helping us? There are tanks all around us.

Message out: Whose are they?

Message in: They are Jerries. You had better hurry up. Rock arty in.

There followed an exchange on targets, and then at 9.49am a message went to the 2/28th: Our witchcraft* with you soon. Stick it out, Mac.

The witchcraft referred to were not 2nd Armoured Brigade but the Valentines of 50th RTR, which had been standing by in case of an emergency, but they ran into a ring of anti-tank guns as they breasted a ridge just to the north of the Australians. Twenty two tanks were knocked out and the rest pulled back.

* The code word for tanks.

As 10.00am approached, 2/28th sent back a map reference where there were tanks, adding: If not ours, lay barrage. We are one third strength. Is that barrage for tanks now?

Message out 9.52am: Enclosing you in arty box.

Message in 10.03: We have got to give in.

A desperate call to the battalion brought no reply.

A ray of hope at 10.00am was news received by Morshead that 2nd Armoured Brigade was dealing with an enemy pocket behind the 69th Brigade and was preparing for a full-scale attack, probably north through the 2/28th, but the report was false, and in any case now irrelevant. Tanks were closing in on the 2/28th from three directions, and as they approached battalion HQ a Bren gunner ran forward and sprayed them ineffectually with .303 bullets. Seeing the position was hopeless, McCarter radioed his Brigade: 'We have got to give in', and standing up in his weapon pit he signalled his men to cease firing.

It was getting on towards midday when Morshead heard that the armour 'was not playing until the infantry guaranteed the mines clear', and it was nearly 1.00pm when, as Morshead later wrote, 'We heard that they had discovered the gap but what they did with it we never heard.'

That gap! Such a saga! By 4.20am the southern group of sappers, it is claimed, had finished their task and signposted the 275 metre area clear of mines, though the Green Howards found sappers still working there at 4.30am. The northern group had still found no mines, which is very strange, and the South Africans reported this to 30th Corps. Already the Royal Engineers officer commanding the 2nd Armoured Field Squadron was on the spot making a reconnaissance of what now, in theory at least, was one large gap 550 metres across. For some reason he was interested only in the northern part, where no mines had been found, and the South African sappers history says with a touch of pique, 'Both British infantry and armour completely ignored the southern part of the gap, though it was clearly marked with lanterns.'[8]

At this point Murphy's Law came into play; a single mine was unearthed, and then more. They were soon lifted, and it was then that the vehicles of the 69th Brigade went through in pursuit of the infantry, which were still making their troubled way towards Deir el Dhib.

At this stage the engineer officer told the dismayed South Africans he considered it unsafe to bring tanks forward until there had been a thorough investigation of the gap in daylight. And to compound his caution, his scout car ran over a mine, though the sappers' history says it was outside the area marked as clear. Still, considering the armour's reputation for coyness, it was not calculated to promote confidence, and memories of the fate of the 23rd Armoured Brigade were fresh.

As shells rained down, sappers in the southern sector moved back to safer ground, but in the north they worked on till after 9.00am. Around 11.00am the 6th RTR, the leading elements of 2nd Armoured, passed through the northern part of the gap and were immediately halted by heavy enemy fire.

Like the Australians (and the New Zealanders on 15 July), the Tynesiders at Deir el Dhib were now out in front with no help in sight, cut off by strong enemy forces behind them. By midday it was all over. First 90th Light attacked, and then tanks and armoured cars came forward against nothing more menacing than small arms fire.

During that morning more than 1,000 officers and men of the Australian and Northumbrian units were either killed or taken prisoner.

And the British armour? While it was still held back by strong anti-tank fire, 11 panzers came steaming up from the south and for the rest of the day a static battle ensued. At 3.00pm, long after the infantry had succumbed, the British tanks were ordered to retire at dusk, and at 7.30pm, as darkness was falling, 11 enemy tanks attacked. Though they were halted, the British tanks withdrew, and Liddell Hart says, 'The 6th RTR were fortunate in having lost only three Grants out of its 41 during the day's fighting.'[9]

And that was that.

'Perceiving that the situation had become hopelessly confused and out of control,' Auchinleck said in his subsequent despatch, 'General Ramsden decided with my approval to discontinue the operation and rally the 69th Brigade east of the enemy minefields. The brigade had suffered so heavily that it had to be taken out of the line.'

The time to weep is now. In *Rommel*, Desmond Young quotes Bayerlein as follows:

'We were very impressed and very much disturbed by the way you attacked us all through July. You very nearly succeeded in breaking through our positions several times between the 10th and 26th. If you could have continued to attack for only a couple of days more you would have done so. We then had no ammunition at all for our heavy artillery, and Rommel had determined to withdraw to the Frontier if the attack was resumed.'[10]

Rommel himself was able to write that the British 'again suffered heavy casualties - a thousand prisoners and 32 tanks ... I was now certain that we could continue to hold our front, and that, after the crises we had been through, was at least something'.[11]

As the last battle flickered out, Rommel, indeed, had some small comforts for his soul. Reckoning up, he could record 60,000 British, South African, Indian, New Zealand, Australian and French prisoners taken between 26 May and 20 July, and he took more after that. He claimed to have destroyed 'well over' 2,000 British tanks and armoured vehicles, and the equipment of an entire army lay destroyed in the desert. His own German losses had been heavy - 2,300 officers and men killed, 7,500 wounded and 2,700 taken prisoner. The Italians had lost 1,000 killed, more than 10,000 wounded and 5,000 taken prisoner.

After the crises of July, Rommel's main comfort was that he and his army lived to fight another day. But he regarded the lull that now followed as 'dangerous'. In his judgement, the build-up that would now take place on both sides would not favour him.

'The future did not look very bright,' he wrote.[12]

Auchinleck was thinking ahead even before the battle ended, or rather Dorman Smith was. On the afternoon of 27 July, as the army muddled through the last disaster, Dorman Smith put before Auchinleck a proposal to reorganise the Desert army to ensure that infantry and armour would always work under one commander. Without complete reorganisation, he told Auchinleck, there was little hope of doing better than had already been achieved. Auchinleck approved it.

As the two sides counted their losses, Auchinleck, with his customary care for detail, issued another cautionary withdrawal plan on 28 July. The defences of Alexandria were being strengthened, he said, and the Wadi Natrun position was being constructed.

With what dismay these orders must have been received! So much hard fighting, and Egypt was still in danger; that was the only interpretation that could be placed on this new information. Auchinleck seemed convinced that Rommel had the upper hand, and certainly what had been his own fully-equipped fighting units when the month began were now little more than shells.

It is a sad document, designated for officers only, an operation instruction rather than an order, No 108, signed by him personally instead of by his Chief-of-Staff, Whitely, whose elegant script normally certified the orders. After the high hopes of *Exalted, Bacon, Splendour* and *Manhood*, it comes as an anti-climax, describing a future of uncertainty and the possibility of yet another defensive battle. After all the exertions of those first three days of July and the attacks that had been launched since with such optimism, the Eighth Army was grounded, unable to do anything more than face its enemy through the heat haze of no-man's-land.

On the German side, preparations were being made for the long haul. By 31 July, having received the tanks Hitler had sent him, Rommel had built up his panzer strength to 123, including 39 Mark III Specials, and plans were being put in hand to establish petrol and ammunition dumps.

And so as July ended, Rommel was planning to attack, Auchinleck to defend. Rommel's expectations were that, in the long term at least, the British could out-bid him in re-equipping. Auchinleck's expectations, in the short term at least, were that the Germans could stage a come-back faster than he could.

For the moment the fighting was over. The silence of stupefaction settled on the battlefield.

CHAPTER EIGHTEEN

'OUR TANKS ARE FIGHTING LIKE HELL!'

The silent Desert shimmered in the heat as a lone army staff jolted down a desert track, trailing a cloud of choking dust. It halted at the collection of tents and vehicles that were Eighth Army Tactical Headquarters, only a few kilometres from where the two opposing armies now pointedly ignored each other as they reached back into their supply lines for new strength.

Colonel Ian Jacob, a member of Churchill's staff, alighted to be greeted by Auchinleck's personal assistant, Angus Mackinnon, and together they went into Auchinleck's caravan, where the general sat behind his desk. Jacob saluted and expressed Churchill's condolence on the death of Gott, who had been killed a few days earlier when the aircraft carrying him back from the Desert was shot down, and then handed Auchinleck a plain white envelope, its flap sealed with red wax. It was addressed to Auchinleck and marked 'Most secret and personal', and written on the back in Churchill's hand were the words 'To be opened by General Auchinleck'.

'For you, sir, from the Prime Minister,' Jacob said.

Jacob knew the contents, and as he watched Auchinleck break the seal and take out the letter, he felt, he was to say later, 'as if I were just going to murder an unsuspecting friend'.

The letter, bearing that day's date, 8 August, was brief and to the point. After some opening flim flam, it said bluntly, 'The War Cabinet have now decided ... that the moment has come for a change.' Alexander would command Middle East, Montgomery the Eighth Army. Auchinleck was offered a newly-created command in Iraq and Persia, which was being peeled off from the Middle East command. Auchinleck's short time as army commander was over, and so too was his appointment as

Commander-in-Chief. After careful thought he declined the step down to the lesser command offered him in the north.

With Auchinleck went his confidant, Dorman Smith. Though he did not yet know it, the whole weight of the July failures was to descend on him, and according to Jacob everyone regarded him 'as a menace of the first order'. By a grotesque twist of circumstance, only three days before his firing Auchinleck had sent Dorman Smith to Cairo to tell Brooke how he believed the army should be reorganised to make it responsive to the needs of Desert warfare. Dorman Smith later recalled, 'I plodded through it all one sweaty Cairo August day in a hot office.' Brooke listened impassively, and Dorman Smith, already unknowingly discredited, might well have been talking to stone. Even when he and Auchinleck shook hands on Auchinleck's departure for India he was unaware of what awaited him. Their parting marked more than a leaving for different destinations.

Auchinleck experienced rebirth of a kind. Though he fought no more battles he went on to new appointments, a knighthood and promotion to field marshall, and in the years after the war he was offered the directorships that come the way of famous men who give prestige to a company prospectus. As the years went by and revisionists studied more closely the foibles and failings of Montgomery, Auchinleck attracted historians who began to portray him as an ill-used hero who had been the victim of the wily Churchill. He died an honoured soldier.

Dorman Smith, who had toiled beside him, went home to Britain to disgrace, demotion and obscurity, and he lived the rest of his life as a rightfully resentful scapegoat, writing long letters often of some thousands of words, and willingly explaining to anyone who would listen the 'truth' about July. For many years he had no contact even with old friends, and he believed people to be deliberately avoiding him. Eventually chance put him in touch with Lieutenant-General Sir Oliver Leese, who had been his pupil and who had gone on to higher things. He also struck up a correspondence with Auchinleck, awkwardly adjusting to addressing his old chief by his Christian name. The army ethos stayed with him to the end. He died without honour, known to few.

Such was the fate of the two men who saved Egypt.*

Under them the major achievement of the Eighth Army had been

*Corbett was also dismissed though he had not played a direct part in the events of July.

to stop the Axis forces and to hold them at Alamein until a new and stronger army could strike back. To that extent the victory belongs to them - but not entirely. In the end it was the resilience and tenacity of the troops who stuck to their task in the face of what looked like impending doom that truly won the day.

If a memorial is ever erected to the defenders of Egypt (an unlikely occurrence) the name of the 18th Indian Brigade should stand at the top. It gave the Eighth Army time to turn and fight and even to destroy an enemy on the point of exhaustion. So why did we fail?

Those who have read the dedication of this book will recall that the simple answer offered is that we were an old army fighting an old war. We were beaten not by superior enemy strength but by our own muddle. So how was it possible for intelligent men holding senior rank to launch three attacks that did not proceed beyond the first phase and each time end in disaster?

What was wrong with the old army?

One explanation for the armour's failure comes from Perrett, who writes:

'The root of the problem lay in the way the two arms viewed their casualties. When an infantryman was killed or wounded it was by a bullet, bayonet or high explosive shell, all things which he understood. But the tankman fought in a travelling bomb, packed with high explosives and high octane fuel. All tankmen have a horror of being burned to death in a blazing vehicle while they are trapped because of jammed hatches or personal injury, and the tankmen of the earlier desert battles had heard the screams and smelled the stench too often not to pay the greatest respect to the crack of an 88 shot. As a result their actions were now governed by supreme caution and staleness, not that this in any way excuses them from failing to protect their infantry; and especially not as the same performance was to be repeated a week later.'[1]

Kippenberger gives some substance to this when he describes how, when he went out to watch a tank battle on 2 July, he was 'distressed to find several slightly damaged Crusaders making no attempt to get back into the battle. One officer asked me if he should and was disappointed with my emphatic reply'.[2]

These two comments suggest that tank crews had lost their nerve, yet we know that they faced up to the enemy as steadfastly as the infantry. Though there may have been occasions when tired men shrank from battle, they also displayed a suicidal obedience to orders and suffered the consequences.

But at the time the infantry were not so understanding, and Kippenberger recalls that 'there was throughout the Eighth Army, not only in the New Zealand Division, a most intense distrust, almost a hatred, of our armour. Everywhere one heard stories of other arms being let down; it was regarded as axiomatic that the tanks would not be where they were wanted on time'.[3]

Now the odd thing about all this is the studied silence from the armour commanders. Even Liddell Hart in his massive two-volume work *The Tanks* brushes lightly over the problem, and no one seems to have taken up the task of answering the trenchant criticism that continued into the peace. For instance Briggs, the brigadier to whom Kippenberger appealed on 15 July and who later commanded the 1st Armoured Division, was given an explicit opportunity to reply when Brigadier Harry Latham, of the Historical Section of the Cabinet Office, on 21 October 1953, sent him a copy of what was to appear in the New Zealand official history with the casual comment, 'There can be little doubt that they are very sore with the armour's failure, in their eyes, to support them ...' If Briggs replied, his papers at the Imperial War Museum contain no copy, and no answer appears in the New Zealand history. Was the issue beneath their contempt, or did the tank men simply not understand what it was all about?

There are some things that can be said in defence both of the armour in general and the tank crews in particular.

To begin with, fighting in a tank in the Desert was murderously uncomfortable. True, the Desert was hard on everyone. The front line infantryman, for instance, lay all day in the inhospitable surface of the Desert, beset by flies and broiled by the tropical sun. But in the cool of the night, if not on patrol, he could relax, and field kitchens brought him hot food. For tank crews things were different.

In July 1942 the Medical Research Section at General Headquarters, Middle East Forces, produced a report that identified fatigue a major problem among tank crews at that time. As the battles were being fought in the summer, there was more daylight for fighting, or for watchfulness when there was no fighting, and fewer night hours to do all the things required of tank crews when darkness sent opposing tank formations into laager to refuel, rearm and carry out maintenance. Three hours' sleep a night is given as the average attainable. Some officers reported going without sleep for 48 and 72 hours.

Throughout the day crews were confined within their tanks, with engine noise and fumes, gun fumes and the wearing of head-phones adding to their fatigue.

The opinion of British regimental officers was that in these conditions men could not fight with any degree of efficiency for more than a week; some thought a shorter time. The suggested solution was to have alternative tank crews.

All this provides some background to the arrival of the distraught Lumsden at 30th Corps HQ on 2 July. The tanks, then, had been in and out of battle for weeks without pause. However, during July men were sent on leave, and the hardships suffered by British tank crews were hardly greater than those endured by the men of the panzers considering the pressure they were under. And so the question remains: Why were commitments accepted by the armour not carried out? If the armour had a problem, why didn't someone say so? Why did the tanks wait until the protection the infantry gave them had evaporated, and the guns of the panzers and anti-tank units awaited them?

While the armour had every reason to treat with caution infantry assurances that adequate gaps had been made in the minefields, they appeared to make no attempt to make their own plans for reaching the objective and did not even have their own sappers on hand when they bumped into mines. They simply did not seem to know what to do.

If there's a simple explanation of why this was so, it might lie in two words: mind set. The Dominions' infantry had no experience with armour, and thought in infantry terms. To the infantry, tanks were tanks, and there was an assumption that they would follow through. The armour, raised in the United Kingdom, had been trained only in armoured warfare and knew nothing of infantry, and we might suspect did not want to know anything. A service in which a colonel can think of regiments in terms of being cosy clubs is clearly in no mind to establish a relationship with common foot soldiers - trade unionists.

This was the weak point of the old army. The Eighth Army in July was not a cohesive force with all its parts working in unison. The left hand hardly seemed to know what the right was doing, yet plans were made that required the two to co-operate, and to co-operate to the most precise timetables. Not even a football coach, where the only disaster could be a lost match, would attempt such an exercise. Those who made the army's plans were expecting a water-to-wine miracle from men too tired to do anything but follow the well-trodden paths of custom. Of course, it's fair to ask whether after three years of war such inefficiency should have been permitted, but that's another story.

In later battles, the army fought not just with better tanks but also closer co-ordination. Yet even then all was not sweetness and light. There continued to be inexcusable glitches, and anyone who reads a report by the German Lehr Division dated 27 July, 1944 - an uncannily coincidental date - must surely have a feeling *déjà vu.*

'A successful break-in by the enemy,' it said, 'is never exploited to pursuit. If our troops are ready near the front for a local counter-attack, the ground is immediately regained.'

So Auchinleck the infantryman had cavalrymen under him, and this may explain why he was unable to bend the armour to his will or to impel his subordinates, the corps commanders, to see that the job was done.

To be scrupulously fair, Dorman Smith's view that Auchinleck had to exercise great caution in dealing with the Dominions' divisions has to be borne in mind. And it is true that in July the frustration engendered by the succession of disasters experienced during 1940 and 1941 boiled to the surface, and the divisional commanders were determined at this critical hour that they would fight as infantry and as complete formations. It was Auchinleck's misfortune to inherit bitterness from the past.

Indeed, Dorman Smith might have better understood his own fate if he had recognised that in an army made up of a number of little national armies, as was the Eighth Army, army command could not play the numbers game. The Dominions' divisions had wills of their own and could not be thrown into battle, Haig style, and neither could their losses be shrugged off as just one of those things. What Auchinleck and Dorman Smith saw as limited successes, the Dominions' divisions saw as unmitigated disasters, and when Churchill, all pink and white from the cooler English summer, arrived with his entourage in August, he could hardly ignore the cries of outrage to be heard on every side, not to mention the newspaper headlines at home following the Gazala debacle. It was Dorman Smith's misfortune to have all the blame heaped on him. And it might be asked whether this was so because of some logical analysis or whether Dorman Smith's personality made him the odd man out, the one on whom the pack turns when there's a lust for blood.

And so, the crunch question: Was Churchill right to sack Auchinleck? The answer must be yes, but for the wrong reasons. Auchinleck was sacked not because of July's disasters - Dorman Smith was the sacrifice for those - but because he resisted Churchill's demands that he should attack again without delay. It was something so trivial as denial of an ignorant man's impatience.

But in truth, as the commanding general, he ought to have borne the responsibility for what happened in July. Though he saved Egypt, Auchinleck also needlessly almost destroyed the army he had vowed to preserve. In this manic dance of war, while the Eighth Army had called the tune, Rommel had dealt resounding blows with a mailed fist as he jigged back and forth, and when the music stopped at the end of July, the piper was as bloody as the dancer. And quite as bad as the physical damage done to the army was the destruction of its unity and morale. The New Zealanders, in embittered arrogance, had become quite insufferable, and Clifton and Kippenberger, two brigadiers whose units had been heavily clobbered, found it necessary to call on their men to desist. Kippenberger reminded them that 'we are fighting the Germans and Italians and not the South Africans, British and Indians ...'

If one wants to make a plea in mitigation of Auchinleck's performance it can only be said that in picking up an army on the run and turning it around he achieved a minor miracle, and he truly had little time to introduce reforms. But the reforms were long overdue, and as commander-in-chief and army commander he had to carry the can.

Another inescapable question is: What would have happened if the Eighth Army had toppled Rommel in July? It has to be said that trying to answer this involves a great deal of guesswork, and yet it is fascinating, and not without some historical interest to wonder whether Auchinleck's failure was not a providential postponement of the final showdown. It is unlikely that a July victory would have ended the North African war.

If the Eighth Army had collapsed the Axis line, it would have sent columns racing across the Desert to cut off the survivors at Daba and Fuka, and pounded the stragglers from the air. Without a doubt Rommel's army would have been annihilated. But could the Eighth Army have filled the vast vacuum that would then have existed between Cairo and Tripoli, particularly as there was so much concern that the Germans might break through in the north?

At this time reinforcements and Sherman tanks were arriving but these would have taken time to integrate into the field army. Even if success had come early in the month or even no later than 15 July, when the army was still in reasonable shape, the Eighth Army was desperately in need of new blood, and by 27 July, when the final attack failed, there was little left from which to assemble a force capable of taking possession so vast an area.

German and Italian reinforcements were also coming forward, and while they too, were inadequate, the reaction of the Germans when the

British and Americans closed in on Tripoli the following year suggests that British success in July 1942 would have brought greater reinforcements running, with a new commander if necessary, and at this time the Eighth Army, its sins of faulty planning and organisation all unredeemed, would have had to deal with this new Axis army alone. The whole dreary business of attack and counter-attack could well have started all over again.

The final irony of Alamein in July may have been that in its failure to overthrow the Axis forces the Eighth Army escaped from the trap into which Rommel fell - of winning an indigestible victory. In war, fortune often does favour the brave, but not always. Rommel learned that lesson.

Auchinleck's admirers feel he was dismissed unjustly and to the extent that he was the victim of his army's ineptness, perhaps he was. But he had to go because in human affairs symbols are needed as well as substance, and Auchinleck was compromised by the disasters that occurred under his generalship. As things turned out, Montgomery offered the Eighth Army exactly what it needed - a new start and an iron determination that in future everyone would do as they were told. In Montgomery the Eighth Army got a touch, just a touch, of Rommel.

CHAPTER REFERENCES

Chapter 1
1. W. Churchill, The Hinge of Fate, pp. 338-9
2. R. Parkinson, The Auk, p.216
3. W. Tute, The North African War, p.75
4. J. Connell, Auchinleck p.638
5. B Maughn, Tobruk and Alamein, p.599
6. J.L. Scoullar, Battle for Egypt, p.154
7. Ibid, p.385
8. D.F. Parry, Eighth Army - Defeat and Disgrace, p.145 (unpublished)
9. Letter to John Connell, 3 February 1959. John Rylands Library, University of Manchester.

Chapter 2
1. D. Young, Rommel, p.141
2. The Hinge of Fate, p.359 (quoted but not named).
3. I. Playfair, History of the Second World War, Vol III p.360
4. T. Dupuy, A Genius for War, pp. 4 and 302
5. Rommel, p.147
6. B Pitt, Crucible of War, Western Desert, 1941, pp. 129-130
7. D. Young, Rommel, p.147
8. B. Liddell Hart (ed.), Rommel Papers, p.244

Chapter 3
1. Document at Imperial War Museum
2. Michael Carver, Tobruk, pp.253-4
3. F. Hinsley, British Intelligence in the Second World War, Vol 2 p.402

Chapter 4
1. Rommel Papers, p.140
2. P. Lewellyn, Journey Towards Christmas, p.247

Chapter 5
1. G. Clifton, The Happy Hunted p.177
2. J. Agar-Hamilton and L. Turner, Crisis in the Desert, p.277
3. A. Pollock, Pienaar of Alamein
4. Battle for Egypt, p.142
5. Ibid, p.143

6. Ibid, p.144
7. Ibid, p.144
8. H. Kippenberger, Infantry Brigadier, p.139
9. R. Parkinson, The Auk, p.198
10. C. Semmler (ed.), The War Diaries of Kenneth Slessor, p.423
11. W. Heckman, Rommel's War in Africa, p.290

Chapter 6
1. Battle for Egypt, p.125
2. Rommel Papers, p.23
3. Hinge of Fate, p.383

Chapter 7
1. Rommel Papers, p.246
2. F. von Mellenthin, Panzer Battles 1939-45, p.128
3. Rommel Papers, p.248
4. Auchinleck, p.634

Chapter 8
1. R. Waller & A Howell, The Royal Artillery Commemoration Book, p.224

Chapter 9
1. Rommel Papers, p.249
2. Ibid, p.249
3. Battle for Egypt, p.177

Chapter 10
1. F. Tuker, Approach to Battle, p.159
2. Rommel Papers, p.250
3. Auchinleck, p. 656
4. Crisis in the Desert, p.318
5. Panzer Battles, 1939-1945, p.129
6. Rommel Papers, p.248
7. Ibid, p.249

Chapter 11
1. Infantry Brigadier, p.150
2. F.Tuker, Approach to Battle, p.160
3. Rommel Papers, pp.250-1
4. E. Axelson, The SAAF in North Africa, Vol II: The Battle for Egypt, 26 May to 3 November 1942, p. 164 (unpublished papers)

Chapter 12
1. Rommel Papers, p.252
2. Ibid, p.252
3. Crisis in the Desert, p.328
4. D Goodhart, We of the Turning Tide, p.30
5. Rommel Papers, p.253
6. We of the Turning Tide, p.19

Chapter 13
1. Infantry Brigadier, p.157
2. Ibid, p.165
3. Ibid, p.167
4. Ibid, pp 169-70
5. Approach to Battle, p.161
6. Ibid, p.162
7. Ibid, p.168
8. Battle for Egypt, p.303

Chapter 14
1. Infantry Brigadier, p.179
2. Rommel Papers, p.257

Chapter 15
1. Infantry Brigadier, p.184
2. Battle for Egypt, p.349
3. Ibid, p.352
4. The Happy Hunted, p.192
5. Gatehouse Papers, Kings College, London

Chapter 16
1. Gatehouse Papers, Kings College, London

2. B. Perrett, The Valentines in North Africa, p.16
3. Document at Imperial War Museum
4. The Happy Hunted, p.194
5. Infantry Brigadier, p.189
6. The Valentines in North Africa, p.23
7. Infantry Brigadier, p.189
8. Ibid, p.190

Chapter 17
1. C. Barnett, The Desert Generals, pp.222
2. Tobruk and Alamein, p.579
3. J. Glenn, Tobruk to Tarakau, p.119
4. Tobruk and Alamein, p. 582
5. Ibid, pp. 582-3
6. P. Masel, The Second 28th, p.78
7. Ibid, p.79
8. N. Orpen & H. Martin, Salute the Sappers, p.395
9. B. Liddell Hart, The Tanks, p.208
10. Rommel, p.156
11. Rommel Papers, p.260
12. Ibid, p.262

Chapter 18
1. The Valentines in North Africa, p.11
2. Infantry Brigadier, p.141
3. Ibid, p.180

BIBLIOGRAPHY

Agar Hamilton, J.A.I. and Turner L.C.F., Crisis in the Desert, May-July 1942, Oxford 1952

Baillieu, Everard, Both Sides of the Hill, Second/24th Battalion Association, 1985

Barker, A.J., Panzers at War, Ian Allan, 1978

Barnett, Correlli, The Desert Generals, Pan, 1983

Behrendt, Hans-Otto, Rommel's Intelligence in the Desert Campaign, William Kimber (English translation), 1985

Bharucha P.C., India and Pakistan, North Africa Campaign, 1940-43, India & Pakistan Combined Inter-Services Historical Section, 1956

Braddock D.W., The Campaigns of Egypt and Libya, 1940-42, Gale and Polden, 1964

Brownlow, Donald Grey, Checkmate at Ruweisat, Auchinleck's Finest Hour, The Christopher Publishing House, 1977

Bryant, Arthur, The Turn of the Tide, Collins, 1957

Burdon, R.M., 24th Battalion, NZ Government, 1953

Carver, Michael, The Seven Ages of the British Army, Weidenfeld and Nicolson, 1984

Carver, Michael, Tobruk, Batsford, 1964

Churchill, Winston, The Hinge of Fate, Cassell, 1951

Clifton, George, The Happy Hunted, Cassell, 1952

Connell, John, Auchinleck, a Critical Biography, Cassell, 1959

Crow, Duncan, and Icks, Robert J., Encyclopaedia of Tanks, Barrie and Jenkins, 1975

Douglas-Home, Charles, Rommel, Weidenfeld and Nicholson, 1977

Dupuy, T., A Genius for War, MacDonald and Janes, 1977

Forty, George, Desert Rats at War, North Africa, Ian Allan, 1975

Forty, George (ed), The Diary of Jake Waldrop, William Kimber, 1981

Glenn, John G., Tobruk to Tarakau, the History of the 2/48th Battalion, AIF, Rigby, 1960

Goodhart, David, We of the Turning Tide, F.W. Preece, 1947

Gregory F.H., Rommel, Wayland, 1974

Heckman, Wolf, Rommel's War in Africa, Granada, 1981

Hinsley F.H., British Intelligence in the Second World War, Volume 2, HMSO, 1981

Hogg, Ian V., Armour in Conflict, Janes, 1980

Irving, David, The Trail of the Fox, The Life of Field Marshal Erwin Rommel, Weidenfeld and Nicolson, 1977

Jackson W.G.E., The Battle for North Africa, 1940-43, Mason/Charten, 1975

Kippenberger, Howard, Infantry Brigadier, Oxford, 1949

Lewellyn, Peter, Journey Towards Christmas (The official history of 1st Ammunition Company), NZ Government, 1949

Liddell Hart, Basil (ed), The Rommel Papers, Collins, 1953

Liddell Hart, Basil, The Tanks (two vols), Cassell, 1959

Lucas, James, Panzer Army Africa, MacDonald and Janes, 1977

Macksey, Kenneth, Tank Tactics 1939-45, Almark Publishing, 1976

Macksey, Kenneth, A History of the Royal Armoured Corps, 1914-1975, Newton Publications, 1983

Masel, Philip, The second/28th, the 2/28th and 24th Anti-Tank Assocation, 1961

Maughn, Barton, Tobruk and Alamein, Australian War Memorial, 1966

Messenger, Charles, The Unknown Alamein, Ian Allan, 1982

Messenger, Charles, The Art of Blitzkrieg, Ian Allan, 1976

McLeod, John, Myth and Reality, The New Zealand Soldier in World War II, Reed Methuen, 1986

Mitchie, Allan A., Retreat to Victory, George Allen and Unwin, 1942

Montgomery, Bernard, A Concise History of Warfare, Collins, 1968

Norton, Fraser, 26th Battalion, NZ Government, 1952

Orpen Neil, and Martin H.J., Salute the Sappers, Sapper Association, Johannesburg, 1981

Orpen, Neil, War in the Desert, Purnell, 1971

Overy, R.J., Goering, the 'Iron Man', Routledge and Kegan Paul, 1984

Parkinson, Roger, The Auk (Auchinleck of Alamein), Granada, 1977

Parkinson, Roger, The War in the Desert, Granada, 1976

Perrett, Bryan, Through Mud and Blood, Robert Hale, 1975

Perrett, Bryan, British Tanks in North Africa, Osprey, 1981

Perrett, Bryan, The Valentine in North Africa 1942-3, Ian Allan, 1972

Pitt, Barry, The Crucible of War, Western Desert 1941, Jonathan Cape, 1980

Pitt, Barry, The Crucible of War, The Year of Alamein 1942, Jonathan Cape, 1982

Playfair I.S.O., History of the Second World War Vol III; The Mediterranean and the Middle East, HMSO, 1960

Pollock A.M., Pienaar of Alamein, Cape Times, 1943

Puttick, Edward, 25th Battalion, NZ Government, 1960

Scoullar J.L., The Battle for Egypt, NZ Government, 1955

Searle R.P. (ed), 2/24th, A History of the 2/24th Australian Infantry Battalion, Jacaranda Press, 1963

Semmler, Clement (ed.), The War Diaries of Kenneth Slessor, University of Queensland, 1985

Terraine, John, The Right of the Line, Hodder and Stoughton, 1985

Thompson H L, New Zealanders with the Royal Air Force, Vol III, NZ Government, 1959

Tuker, Francis, Approach to Battle, Cassell, 1963

Tute, Warren, The North African War, Sidgwick and Jackson, 1976

Von Mellenthin F.W., Panzer Battles 1939-1945, Cassell, 1955

Waller R.P. and Howell A.H.E., article in The Royal Artillery Commemoration Book 1939-1945, G.Bell and Sons, 1950

Warner, Philip, Auchinleck, The Lonely Soldier, Buchan and Enright, 1981

Warner, Philip, Alamein, William Kimber, 1979

Wright, John, Libya, Ernest Benn, 1969

Young, Desmond, Rommel, Collins, 1950

INDEX